PILGRIM

FINDING A NEW WAY ON THE
CAMINO DE SANTIAGO

By

Carolyn Gillespie

ISBN-13: 978-1-7398189-2-0
STURDY GIRL BOOKS

To Ann,
From

Tom & Lorraine

Happy Christmas ———— 2022.

For Ali, who was with me every step of the Way.

To Chris,

From

Tom's pennies

Happy Christmas ————— 2022.

PROLOGUE

Edinburgh: 24ᵗʰ May

'What's that hideous smell?' I asked, looking around the fitting room in search of a culprit. I knew that odour, and usually a dead mouse was at the bottom of it.

'I'm not sure,' said the personal shopper, forcing a smile as she handed me another completely unsuitable dress. 'Why don't you get yourself into this, and I'll go and get some heels. They'll complete the look.'

It had been six days since I arrived home from Spain. I had lived out of a rucksack for 40 days and as I stood in front of the long mirror in my faded sports bra and navy-blue granny pants I felt out of place amongst the fancy clothes. I was a different person to the one who had stood in the same changing room a year ago, three stone overweight, and reluctant to catch sight of herself in the mirror. Now my legs were strong, and I couldn't help being impressed by the muscle definition in my calves and my thighs. My belly was still a bit squishy, but my shoulders and arms were toned and I was happy with what I saw. I looked healthy and happy.

That smell, though, was truly dreadful. I screwed up my nose, making a face at my reflection in the mirror. It was Friday and my nephew's wedding was the following day. All of my clothes were hanging off me and I needed an outfit suitable for the occasion. Knowing I wasn't much of a shopper, a friend suggested a personal stylist, and I had booked a one-hour slot, reckoning that would be plenty of time to kit myself out. Perhaps I should have worn better underwear but I was reluctant to return to the real world and had grown fond of my stretchy bra and big knickers. I was quite a sight. My legs were tanned from high ankle to mid thigh, but my white feet gave the impression that I was still wearing socks and a wound stretched down the front of my right shin – I'd have to wear tights to the wedding. All around me dresses hung from hooks and on the floor to one side were the lightweight trainers that I had bought in Burgos.

I loved those trainers. Every day for the last four weeks, they had hugged my bare, battered feet when the walking boots and sweaty socks came off at the end of the day's walk. Four weeks of daily wear. I peered at them. 'Surely not,' I said to myself. I picked one up and took a whiff: it nearly knocked me off my feet. That smell, it was all mine.

Pulling on the floral dress with a sticky out skirt, I tiptoed across the corridor and stashed the offending footwear in a room full of empty garment rails. Shamefaced, I returned to the stylist.

'I'm so sorry, the terrible smell, it's me. I mean, it's my trainers. I've just come back from walking the Camino de Santiago and I think I must have become immune to the pong.'

She laughed. 'I didn't like to say. I haven't heard of that. What is it?'

'It's a pilgrimage to Santiago de Compostela, in the North West corner of Spain. There are lots of routes that all converge on the city – you can start from Madrid, or Portugal, even London – but I started in Saint Jean Pied-de-Port in the South West of France, and crossed the top of Spain in a big smile.' I drew out the curve with my hand, pleased to be talking about it. 'People used to believe that the remains of Saint James the Apostle were buried in the cathedral in Santiago and they walked there to pray for miracles or to ask forgiveness for their sins. The stories are just legends, fairy tales really, but pilgrims have been making the journey to Santiago for a thousand years and there's definitely something special about the walk.'

In the days since I had returned my legs had been jerking constantly, as if they were itching to keep walking.

'How far was it?' she asked, zipping me into a yellow dress that I knew I was never going to buy.

'We walked 900km,' I said.

'Wow. That's a long way. No wonder your trainers smell bad.'

CHAPTER 1

'We should have sloped off quietly,' whispered Ali, not one for a fuss.

It was an early start but families and friends had turned out to wave us off at Edinburgh Airport. They were a noisy, enthusiastic bunch and a hum of excitement vibrated around us, but Ali looked like she wanted to get going, and I shared her discomfort. I have never been the sporty, outdoors sort. In fact, until recently, I would have taken the car to the corner shop. But here I was, thinking I could walk more than 900km across an entire country. Their excitement was tinged with expectation, and that was the bit that was making me nervous.

I hoisted my rucksack onto my back. My scallop shell, tied on with string, swung for a moment and I tucked it into a side pocket. Ali had one too. The shells marked our status as pilgrims, but only to those in the know.

David, my husband, was quieter than the rest. He smiled reassuringly, his dark brown eyes fixed on mine, but I could sense his anxiety and all of a sudden I knew I needed to say goodbye quickly. One last kiss, holding back the tears, and we were off.

I left school at seventeen, too young to head straight to university, and spent a 'year off' working in a shoe shop, long before the 'gap yaar' became a thing. It never occurred to me that I could backpack round South East Asia, or round up livestock on a cattle ranch in Australia as my children and their friends did these days. But now, thirty years later, on a dreich Edinburgh morning, I was in my walking boots and ready for the off, in some existential turning of the tables.

For the past year, I had planned and trained for this journey, this walk, this pilgrimage. I wasn't yet sure what to call it, but whatever it was, it had been a dream for much longer than that. I was about twenty and reading English at Oxford, when I first heard about the Camino de Santiago. Two friends had walked a section of the route, sleeping under the stars and visiting some of the historical sites. Julian and Anthony had tacked the trek onto the end of a holiday in the South of France. They wanted to follow the route that Wellington had taken over the Pyrenees and had found themselves on the Camino by accident.

Twenty years later, I had my first taste of slow travel when thanks to a volcanic eruption in Iceland, my sister and I found ourselves taking the long way back to Scotland from Madrid. Waiting for the ferry we met a woman who was homewardbound after walking the Camino. She talked about the mysticism of the walk, which she referred to as 'the Way'. As she spoke, the route that I had understood to be historically significant became something live and powerful, and I was hooked.

And now I was at the airport, ready to go. Just a year before I had been working 80 hours a week in a boarding school in rural Scotland. I loved my work. Loved teaching receptive, interested kids and running a house full of bright, creative girls who piled into my kitchen to eat hot dogs and make me laugh with their banter and their lust for life. My door was always open and usually there was someone walking through it.

My colleagues were a wholehearted, eccentric bunch who kept squirrels in their freezers for art classes and thought nothing of digging ice holes up a mountain for an overnight camp. But bracing as the lifestyle was, somewhere along the line I had been swallowed whole.

Maybe it was some kind of middle-aged survival instinct that urged me to run knock-kneed while I still had the chance? To jump, like an overweight Lara Croft, off the platform I had been on for so long? To roll into the long, cool grass? The only thing I knew for certain was that I wanted to walk the Camino de Santiago. And so, with no clear plan, I took a deep breath and handed in my resignation. And now, nine months later, I was on my way.

Once through security we spotted Jenny, the third member of our party. She had dodged the send-off and had arranged to meet us airside. A friend and colleague from school, late at night, over too many glasses of Rioja, she had helped me turn a dream into a plan. She had maps. She spoke Spanish. She was our most valuable asset.

At first I had planned to walk alone, but caught up in the excitement of the preparation, Jenny offered to join me for the first few days. The Camino is sticky, she said. Once you've heard about it, it's hard to shake it off.

More friends became similarly stuck, and before long I had a list of people who'd signed up to join me for part of the Way. The walk was going to take me around 40 days: 36 days of walking and four days of rest. Ali, a dear friend, and physiotherapist, signed up early on, originally committing to just one week. We were well matched in terms of fitness and temperament and I was delighted when she decided she was in for the long haul to Santiago. At Burgos, Tinker and Lynne, old friends of ours, would be joining us for a week. Marguerite, a pal of mine from university, was hoping to come over at some stage and Ali's husband Guy and my husband David were planning to tagalong for a few days. If what I needed from the walk was solitude and time for reflection, I was hoping I hadn't scuppered my chances.

'Repacking already?' I asked Jenny, who had dry bags in every colour of the rainbow spread out on the floor around her.

'Only so that I can make room for all the shortbread I've bought for our hosts in Saint Jean,' she explained.

At Stansted we hit our first hurdle.

'I'm afraid walking poles are considered potentially dangerous weapons, and as such are not permitted in the cabin,' the security woman said, confiscating the three pairs.

Our deflated faces must have softened her a little as she suggested we package them up and went off to get us some tape while Jenny produced a carrier bag from her 'sac magique'.

Poles wrapped up, Security Woman escorted me back to check-in where the poles were deposited and returned me to the gate where the girls were waiting. 'Good luck on your big walk,' she called as we queued to board the plane to Biarritz. 'I hope the poles come in handy.'

'Are you guys heading to Saint Jean?' asked an Australian in the queue behind us. He rhymed Jean with keen.

'No, we're going to Saint Jean Pied-de-Port,' I replied, trying to impress Jenny, the modern languages teacher, with my pronunciation of 'San Shon'.

'When I saw your shells I guessed you were fellow pilgrims. I was pretty sure the Camino started in Saint Jean. I hope we're heading to the right place. Lynette, check the guidebook would you?'

His travelling companion pulled a book from the side pocket of his rucksack and opened it at the first page, pointing at the name Saint Jean Pied-de-Port. We were going to the same place. I looked at the floor, embarrassed by my rookie error.

'Blessings on your Camino,' said Lynette, putting the book back in the side pocket of the rucksack.

Being 'spotted' like that was strangely unsettling. I had never really considered who else might be walking the Camino. We shifted in the queue, trying to avoid eye contact with any other would-be pilgrims. I'm not a natural 'joiner in' and in my mind this walk was a solitary endeavour. I was happy to be walking alongside friends but I hoped that they would be too focused on their own parallel, solitary endeavours to be bothered about what was going on in mine. I was looking forward to having time and space to sift through the muddle inside my head, to figuring out where the rest of my life was heading. I had looked at the maps and planned the routes but had thought very little about how the walk would unfold. With apprehension it struck me that perhaps the next 40 days were going to involve more of the 'group thing' than I had imagined.

As we waited for our seats to be called I glanced at my friends, trying to gauge their feelings. Was it just me?

'Kari, if this is going to get all Kumbaya, I might have to have another think,' muttered Ali.

Kattaline, Jenny's friend, met us at Biarritz Airport, and while we waited for the dangerous walking poles to appear on the luggage carousel a gangly, befuddled young man approached. 'Are you going to Saint Jean?' he asked in broken English.

Ali raised her eyebrows. 'Again? Is it really that obvious?'

'I booked a blablacar but I can't find it,' the young man continued.

'We're going to Saint Jean. You can come with us,' Kattaline offered.

I looked at Ali and mouthed, 'Blablacar?'

She shrugged. 'Not a clue.'

Out in the car park the sky was overcast. We dumped our rucksacks in the boot of Kattaline's people carrier and piled in, the gangly young man nobly clambering into the third row, or the far, far back as my children used to call it back in the 90s, when they were little, and VW Sharans were all the rage.

But we hadn't even left the car park before the young man yelled, 'Stop the car!' and with a flail of limbs, tumbled over the seats and out of the door.

'I have wrong rucksack! Just go!' he shouted to us as he ran back towards the terminal.

'Eh, bien,' said Kattaline as if this sort of thing happened every day, and we set off once more.

We watched as our erstwhile travel companion was greeted by a group who had clearly been looking for him – whether it was his carshare companions or a group trying to resolve the rucksack mix-up, we were not sure.

'Would you give some random Jimmy a lift if he stopped

you at Edinburgh Airport?' I whispered to Ali.

'Not bloody likely,' she said.

BLOOMIN

Kattaline and Jenny were old friends and while they caught up, in French, Ali tried to get her new phone to work. I had considered the possibility of leaving all technology behind but David reacted almost as badly to that as he did to the suggestion that I should leave my jewellery, wedding ring included, at home. We reached a compromise. I would take my wedding band, the phone, and the charger, but he agreed not to ring unless there was an emergency and I promised to check in every day when we reached our destination.

Perhaps it's my slightly ditsy demeanour, or maybe it's just that I'd never done anything remotely adventurous before, but David wasn't the only one to fear for my survival. People seemed to picture me with my map upside down, like Edina from *Absolutely Fabulous*, staggering around in platforms, clueless and ill prepared. My son had insisted on giving me self-defence lessons and folk who barely knew me felt they had the right to ask me if I had thought this mad plan through. To appease them, and to prove that this was more than just a mad plan, I promised that in addition to my nightly phone call to David, I would write a daily update on Facebook. How difficult could it be? I would type it up on my phone and post it before I went to sleep at night, provided there was Wi-Fi of course. But other than those two commitments, I was looking forward to being free of the phone, to silencing its beck and call.

It was a short drive to *Campsite Narbaitz*, the business run by Kattaline and her husband Xavier, just outside of Saint Jean. Before supper we headed into town to the pilgrim office to collect our *credencial del peregrino* (pilgrim passport). The medieval buildings were painted cream, with pinky stone quoins and wooden lintels. Shutters edged the windows and vines twisted up the sides of doors. From the citadel we looked down over the vineyards and small farms that patched the hillsides. Kattaline explained the lay of the land.

'My uncle has a vineyard over there.' She pointed. 'And down to the left, that's my father's farm where we keep our geese.'

Saint Jean Pied-de-Port was the ancient capital of the Basque Region and the street signs were in both Basque and French. It was a ribbon of a town and the houses and shops all followed the path of the one main street that ran from the Porte Saint Jacques down to the Porte D'Espagne. As the name suggests, the town sat at the foot of the pass, the pass we would be walking the next day, leading us from France into Spain.

On a waymarker we spotted the first of the yellow arrows that would point out our path all the way to Santiago; and set amongst the cobbles, we saw for the first time, the brass scallop shell, the symbol of Saint James, the fisherman. Pilgrims traditionally dangled the shells from their staffs as they made their way to his shrine. Perhaps these had a practical function as they could be used to scoop water out of drinking troughs or to receive gifts of food, but more significantly, they were badges of purpose which enabled pilgrims to spot each other along the Way. Ours had served that role already. As we stood over the shell, three pairs of clean boots forming a triangle around it, my heart surged with excitement and I swallowed back sudden tears. We were *really* there. This was *really* happening.

In the pilgrim office we took pictures of the woman stamping our passports: tangible proof that we were ready to begin. At every stop along the Way, at albergues, cafés, churches and museums, these passports would be stamped as a record of our journey. And when we finally reached Santiago, we would present the passport at the pilgrim office and receive the Compostela – our certificate of completion. As I looked at the little piece of spotless cardboard my sense of anticipation grew. Was it really *when* we reached Santiago, and not *if?*

Once the paperwork was completed, the official gave us

the bad news. Our planned route, Route de Napoléon, which rose steeply through the village of Orisson to the Col de Lepoeder, was closed due to severe weather.

'It is forbidden for pilgrims to walk this way,' she told us sternly. 'Three days ago, a Brazilian man fell in the snow and had to be airlifted off the mountain by helicopter. He had hypothermia and a broken leg. He is lucky to be alive.'

Kattaline nodded, reinforcing her message. Shepherds near her father's farm had reported that a few pilgrims were ignoring the warnings. 'You would be foolish to take this path. The snow's too deep and the temperature's too low.'

We had clothing suitable for wind and rain, but not for snow. We returned to her house, crestfallen. Xavier got out his maps and sitting in front of their huge open fire, we drank good wine and identified the alternative route.

The Napoleon Route, now closed to us, had kept me awake at night these past months. I could see the profile of the climb when I shut my eyes. It was a tough, steep walk through the Pyrenees but I had worked hard to get myself fit enough for the challenge and I was surprised at how disappointed I felt now that it had been snatched from us. As Xavier pointed out, the alternative route still involved some strenuous climbs, but because it ran through woodland most of the way it would be sheltered from the worst of the weather. We would have none of the spectacular mountaintop views of the Route de Napoléon. And none of the risk.

It might have been the sensible course of action, but it felt like a damp squib, the chicken's way out of the chamber of horrors. I had spent the last year persuading myself that I was no coward, but now I wasn't being given the chance to prove it. We were falling at the first hurdle.

But the warmth of the fire and the wine soon soothed me and encouraged by the others I put my disappointment to one side. Kattaline and Xavier's home was welcoming and relaxed. The walls were painted in warm reds and ochres, the colours of the local soil, and as we sat eating home-produced foie gras on crusty bread, it was tempting to accept their kind offer to stay for a couple of days until the forecast ghastly weather blew over. But the snow at the top was likely to stay around for weeks, not days, so even if we did wait for the rain to pass, the Route de Napoléon would remain closed.

'A bit of rain never hurt anyone. We are Scottish, after all,' said Ali.

And the decision was made. We would start on the alternative route in the morning. Rain or no rain.

We ate like kings, feasting on vegetable soup made from their own produce, bacon and onion quiche, Gateau Basque and locally produced cheese. And later, when I headed upstairs to my bedroom, I was so full I was not sure I would ever move again, never mind walk to Santiago.

I found my pyjamas in a dry bag and went through the contents of my rucksack once more so that I had a mental picture of where everything was stored. Red: walking kit; blue: 'non-walking clothes'; yellow: socks and underwear; brown: dirty clothes. For weeks, everything had been laid out on the floor of our spare room, and I had cut and culled until only the bare essentials remained. Despite all my efforts, my pack still weighed in at 7kg and that was without water or food.

Four non-essential items had made the cut: a small, olive-wood cross, a tiny film canister containing oil of chrism that my sister insisted I pack, and two small stones from my garden in Edinburgh stashed in the bottom of the bag. There is no shortage of Camino folklore and over the last few weeks I had been reading up on it in a book that my father-in-law, Big-John, had given me. In accordance with tradition, the pilgrim should bring a stone from their home to lay at the foot of the Iron Cross near Foncebadón. All being well we would reach the Cruz de Ferro in 28 days' time. The other stone would be thrown into the sea at Finisterre, the end of the earth, an ancient place of pilgrimage some 87km west of Santiago. If I ever got that far.

As I repacked, I found a letter and postcards from David hidden in all the zip compartments of my backpack. He must have sneaked them the night before after I had fallen asleep. I put most of them back unread, happy that they were there if I needed them and that I had a little bit of him with me. But one had a picture of a mountain and the words 'And So the Adventure Begins' on the front, so I lay down on the bed and turned it over.

'This is the card for the Pyrenees,' he had written on the top.

'I predict there will be a few of these comments:
Bugger me, they're high
Bloody hell, it's wet
How much bloody further?
Bugger this for a game of soldiers

All very natural. It's bound to feel impossible. Especially at the start. That's what makes it an adventure. And you, my beautiful, are an adventurer. You are a star. And stars shine. So go forth and be our hero.'

I held it for a moment, disappointed all over again that I wasn't going to be anybody's hero.

But this was too early in the game to admit defeat. I picked myself up, finished my repacking and changed into my pyjamas. When packing so little, nightwear had seemed an extravagance to some, but I wasn't looking forward to sharing a dorm with strange men and I was relieved my modesty would be preserved by my flowery jammy bottoms.

I took my micro wash bag to the bathroom and wondered when I had last travelled with so little 'stuff'. I had a stick deodorant, mini toothpaste, a fold-up toothbrush, a mini hairbrush, a tin of body/hair soap and a small bottle of oil for my face that my sister had given me. And that was it. I looked at myself in the mirror. What would I look like in 40 days' time? Those tiny figures carved out of old apple cores came to mind.

I checked my bag and checked it again, and finally got into bed, confident that my wet-weather gear was easily accessible and that the tiny blister kit was in the top pocket of my rucksack. And then I was done. All set.

Day 0
8th April
Edinburgh – Saint Jean Pied-de-Port
Kari, Ali, Jenny

I am typing one fingered on my phone and feel jittery with excitement and nerves. For the last time in a while I am tucked up in a bed with sheets and a duvet. From here on it will be sleeping bags on bunk beds and sharing dorms with dozens of others. I am 46 and I have never spent more than a couple of nights away from my family. I am not really cut out for this. I have never done anything brave, or impressive. I have lived a safe life and taken no chances. I don't know that I can really articulate why I'm here, but I do know that I have felt the tug of the Camino and that it feels right to be here. Maybe my colleagues were right. Maybe I have lost the plot.

CHAPTER 2

The alarm went at 5.30am and I was washed, dressed and fully packed in less than ten minutes. Confining myself to a tiny area at the end of the bed and squashing the life out of my dry bags so that they occupied as little space as possible, I felt ready for whatever the dorms might throw at me. I had this nailed.

Ali, not so much. When I put my head round her door she was pushing waterproofs into her pack, pulling them out again, and shoving them in once more in some kind of manic rucksack hokey-cokey. I smiled smugly. She might be the one married to the ex-soldier, but the military precision brownie badge was all mine. Looming in the doorway didn't appear to be helping so I took myself off downstairs and gave her some space.

Kattaline and Xavier were generous hosts and by the time I appeared in the kitchen, Kattaline had already been to the bread shop.

'It is important that you eat a good breakfast on your first day,' she said, producing fruit, yoghurt, cheese and eggs.

Later, when she was satisfied that the three of us had eaten enough, she piled sandwiches wrapped in greaseproof paper onto the table.

'And you must carry enough food for at least a meal and a half.' She added a bag of prunes soaked in Armagnac, a hefty wodge of last night's Gateau Basque and a slab of locally made chocolate to the pile. Delighted and grateful, we packed the stash into the side pockets of our rucksacks. We would not go hungry that day.

And Kattaline didn't stop there. She insisted that Jenny take a better sleeping bag than the one she had brought, warning us that the albergues would be bitterly cold. And when she was absolutely sure that we would not change our minds and stay a few more days she drove us back to the pilgrim office in the centre of town.

From there, in the lightest of drizzles, we waved goodbye and began our walk.

In silence, we headed through the Porte Saint Jacques, down the narrow cobbled Rue de la Citadelle, and stopped at the brass scallop shell that we had spotted the night before. An arrow beneath the shell pointed out the way, reassuring us we were headed in the right direction, reminding us that we were part of something bigger than ourselves.

Moments later, as we crossed the River Nive, we looked back at the archway. The Virgin on the Bridge was looking down on us just us as she had looked down at every pilgrim who had walked this way over the years. The sun was not fully up and she was still spot lit, the clock above her telling us it was 6.30am. Feeling small and inadequate, I paused to look up, offering a silent prayer, asking for strength, determination and blister-free feet, like millions before me, I supposed. Then buoyed by the history of this pilgrimage and my excitement at being part of it, I strode on.

Plenty of temporary signs warned us that the Route de Napoléon was closed and although the alternative route was marked I was pleased that Jenny was with us. Neither Ali nor I were accomplished map-readers – we had got lost in the Pentland Hills on more than one occasion. One wet Sunday's two-hour walk turned into an all-day expedition when we found ourselves on the wrong side of a deer fence. We had to carry Indie, my big, black Labrador, through acres of bracken and brambles and it was dark when we finally made it back to the car park.

Jenny, on the other hand, was used to adventure and

unfazed by warnings of extreme danger should we take the wrong route. Her idea of a fun holiday was carrying her kayak up a mountain so that she could paddle down the rapids from the top. I was happy for Jenny to take the lead. A few metres ahead of us, she stopped to check her map, which she kept in her hand at all times. 'You have to orient your map to the ground,' she said, swivelling the book. And Ali and I nodded as if we knew what she meant. She looked at the map with assured comprehension and where she led we would follow, with the utter confidence of small children.

We passed under the Porte D'Espagne and before long we were heading through farming country of small fields and full hedgerows. The rain threatened, but stayed off and the route dipped down towards a stream. We walked in single file along the muddy paths, through the woods, watching our feet on the slippy terrain. For the most part we were silent and I began to notice the sounds around me. It was as if the volume in my head was being turned down and the volume outside turned up. For some time, we followed the course of the stream, enjoying the little waterfalls that fed into it and the noise of the fast water, which crackled like static.

Eventually the path rose from the left bank and crossed a rickety wooden bridge, bringing us into a built-up area. This was the border crossing into Spain, marked only by a metal signpost and a cluster of uninspiring shops. I paused, looking for some landmark worthy of a photograph, but there was nothing, just adverts for discount stores. Jenny urged us on, and soon we were down by the stream again, this time on the right bank.

We arrived at Arneguy at 9.30am, having covered about 8.5km. Our pace had been fairly brisk and we were pleased with our progress.

Jenny checked her watch. 'Plenty of time for a coffee if you feel like one.' Ali and I nodded vigorously, relieved that Jenny seemed as eager as we were to sidestep the more abstemious approach to pilgrimage. There would be no sackcloth and ashes for us. I would not be giving up the coffee.

The village had a couple of cafés and we turned to Jenny, who had a nose for these things, to sniff out the best option. As she was only with us for another seven days it was imperative that she trained us up quickly and effectively. We didn't just need to know the lingo, although that would no doubt help, we needed to blend in with the locals, avoid the tourist traps and ensure the biggest bang for our buck.

'Right, ladies. First we survey the scene. Then we narrow down our options. Look for key indicators. What do you see? This place has a Gaggia coffee machine, there are four locals sitting at a table by the window and there are fresh pastries in the cabinet. Three ticks. That's all we need.' And with that she left her rucksack and went in to order.

'Tres cafés con leche grandes.'

She turned back to us, and looked over her sunglasses. 'Never say please; only simpletons and the English say please.'

The coffee was delicious.

We continued on through Valcarlos, a Basque town in the heart of the valley, where the white-painted buildings were topped with orange roofs. A tile mounted on a wall depicted St Anthony of Padua and I stopped to take a photograph. St Anthony had always been my family's go-to saint and he was frequently called upon to intercede when things were lost. Lost in the loosest sense of the word. Sometimes things were obviously lost like the tape-measure or the car keys or the passports the night before a holiday. But at other times the lost things were longed for but elusive, like a pass in a driving test, a new job, or a much-wanted baby. He usually helped. But always at a cost. The price, of course, depended on the size of the job and the debt, St Anthony's bread, was to be paid to the poor and the needy.

My mother was elderly, and my sister, Patsy, who had retired a few years earlier, shouldered the bulk of her care. They lived three miles apart and although my mum still valued her independence, the truth was that she could only live alone because my sister was so close at hand.

Until a few months ago, I had been working full time and the two of them had found a routine that worked for them. Shopping, collecting her pension, all the practical stuff was covered. My sister sometimes said that I was the Mary to her Martha, a comparison that made me feel sad and a little bit feckless. But to be fair, it was probably quite close to the truth. Although I didn't feel I was much use, I visited Mum at least once a week, and I knew my sister appreciated my support. Mum and I had done battle for years and although more recently we had reached a precarious rapprochement, there was much to regret. Six weeks was a long time for my sister to have sole care of our mother, and as I walked that first day, I couldn't seem to silence the critical voice that was muttering to me, reminding me of things best forgotten, pointing out that I was here, on my own, with nothing to think about but myself, while they carried on without me at home.

In the Valcarlos valley, surrounded by the Pyrenees, stories of Charlemagne abound and as we left the town, Jenny distracted me with tales of Roland, his heroic knight. It was he who led the rearguard of Charlemagne's army as they returned to France. Tipped off by Roland's jealous stepfather, the Saracens (or the Basques to be more historically accurate) ambushed Roland and his men at Roncesvalles. In the midst of the massacre brave Roland refused to blow his Olifant horn to call for help, as to do so would have been an act of cowardice, an admission of defeat. But finally, with his dying breath, he blew, summoning the Emperor to mete out vengeance on the enemy. Jenny told the story with great verve, her voice transporting me until I could hear the final horn blast echoing, strong and evocative.

The day continued cold and drizzly and I was glad I had brought my luminous pink bobble hat and my fleecy gloves. Ali suffered from Raynaud's Syndrome and her fingers became bloodless in the cold. While Jenny forged ahead, we kept together, reading each other's faces for signs of fatigue. Ali was a person who kept her emotions in check and I had become adept at reading between the lines. My face, on the other hand, was far less inscrutable, and Ali's skill lay in the timing, regularly distracting me before a storm broke. We would take care of each other on this walk, I was sure of that.

Eventually the path left the river and skirted the side of a road that climbed steadily, snaking round miles and miles of interminable bends. My pack had begun to feel heavy and my legs were starting to grumble when a group of young people in their late teens and early twenties gave me the motivation I needed. Since mid-morning we had been keeping pace with this noisy group. Usually I would say I lack any trace of competitive instinct but there was no way I was going to let them get the better of me on this hill. As the gradient became steeper I overtook them, unable to suppress a smirk of satisfaction. I had worked hard for this and it was all I could do not to punch the air.

'Eat my bubbles!' beamed Ali, as she swished past them. 'Looks like all those expeditions to the Pentlands have paid off.'

In time we turned off the road and into the woods, but the path continued to wind back and forth, just the same. The last 9km were brutal and as we began the final ascent the forecast rain started to come down in stair-rods. We put on our wet-weather gear and rustled through the woods, heads down and silent. I found myself fighting to keep control of my breath. The trees obscured the path and every time I thought we must have reached the top, I realised there was more to go.

'How much bloody further?' I grumbled to Ali who knew how I struggled with hills.

'It's just around this next corner,' she said, encouragingly. But I knew better than to fall for that old trick. She had used it one too many times before. The beeches and hazels gave us some shelter from the worst of the weather and when the rain subsided a little we sat under a tree and ate some of the sandwiches that Kattaline had packed for us for lunch. They were as delicious as I had imagined they would be. Jenny pulled out the bag of prunes soaked in Armagnac and we treated ourselves to just one each.

While we rested the group of young people caught up with us and shouted their greetings as they carried on up the hill. Ahead of us. My spirits plummeted.

'What if there's no room for us in Roncesvalles?' Ali said, voicing my thoughts. There was just one place to stay – the monastery – and if that was full our only option was to carry on for another 7km. Not an appealing prospect at that point of the day. We hadn't booked any of our accommodation in advance. I had persuaded Ali that to be true to the spirit of the pilgrimage we needed to go with the flow and avoid over-planning. But she was not entirely comfortable with this decision, and for a moment I wondered whether she might have a point.

Fear gave us the jump-start we needed to get through the last few kilometres. Footsore, we pushed up and up, through the clouds and into the snow. I counted my steps and worked hard to regulate my breathing, forcing myself to exhale slowly. The pride I had felt earlier on was biting me on the bum as I puffed up the hill, stopping every hundred metres or so, praying that it would level out soon.

And respite did come. At the summit the temperature dropped and the wind picked up but a snow-covered chapel gave us an excuse to stop for a moment and we peered inside through tiny trefoil windows. One whole wall was constructed of stained-glass fragments and the light shone into the darkness like sunlight through leaves, flooding the interior with colour. All four seasons were contained within the window: the lime greens of spring, the yellows of summer, the oranges of autumn, the whites and blacks of winter. From the outside the window was flat and dull, but from the inside it was alive, a moving kaleidoscope of shapes and colours. We were looking into a secret space and it was magical.

At the top of the mountain we looked south towards Navarre and spotted the steep, grey roof of the monastery: Roncesvalles at last. I breathed out as I saw the collection of tall, whitewashed buildings with dozens of tiny windows. There would be room enough for all.

Tiredness forgotten, we took pictures by the road sign, elated that we had made it to the end of the first walk, the one that had been keeping us awake at night. It had been tough, but we had been refreshed by the birdsong and the sounds of the waterfalls.

We slid through the snow down to the huge, white abbey, laughing and smiling broadly, our faces tingling with cold. Once our pilgrim passports had been stamped, we were allocated beds and given tickets for dinner and breakfast. Two men wearing 'hospitalero' badges showed us to a bench where we could take off our rucksacks and boots. The relief was immense. Although my legs were twitching and wobbly I felt as if I was walking on air as I padded down the corridor in my sweaty socks, leaving a trail of damp footprints on the limestone floor.

'Are those men just here to give first aid to people with blisters?' I asked as we stowed our boots in the drying room.

'No, hospitalero is just the name for a volunteer who helps run the albergue. It's a hangover from the Knights of St John. They were the Hospitallers,' Jenny explained.

Upstairs, our modern dorm was divided into cubicles and the three of us were together with one spare bed. Powerful showers went some way to relieve the pain in my shoulders, and back in the cubicle I changed into fresh clothes.

During the planning stage, I hadn't given my hair much thought, and I certainly hadn't road tested any of my equipment. It only took one shower to establish that my travel towel was about as absorbent as a plastic bag and my hair was still dripping wet after I had rubbed it down. My sorry excuse for a brush might have been compact but it struggled to get through my thick thatch of unconditioned hair and I soon gave up trying, opting for the Raquel Welch, *One Million Years BC* look instead. Every day of my adult life I had washed and blow-dried my hair but in that cold dormitory, I would have been lucky if it was dry by morning.

And then there was another problem.

'Aah,' I said, 'there's no way I'm putting my boots back on, but the only other shoes I have are my flip-flops and it's snowing outside.' Ali and I had worked through any number of permutations when we were planning our kit, but we hadn't considered the possibility of snow.

'I know,' she said. 'I didn't think we were coming to Benidorm, but I hadn't expected this.'

Jenny, the more seasoned adventurer, had brought trainers.

Our feet were certainly refreshed by the trip across the courtyard as we headed out for a coffee. It was icy, and worried I might slip in my completely inappropriate, flat-bottomed flip-flops I watched my feet. In between the cobbles I caught sight of an ancient-looking iron nail, about seven inches in length. I picked it up and put it in my pocket, wondering how long it had been nestled between these stones. I would keep it there, a meditation on suffering.

Warmed up by the coffee, I told the girls that I was heading to the pilgrim mass. I knew that I wanted to spend time on my journey in prayer, reconnecting with God and it felt right to start my journey this way. But as I was the only Catholic of our group, I didn't want Jenny or Ali to feel obliged to join me.

'Don't worry. I don't think you're secretly trying to convert me,' said Ali, as all three of us headed into the white stone church. 'I'm just looking forward to sitting still for an hour.'

The ecumenism at the monastery felt welcoming and inclusive. The priest spoke in Spanish but the congregation was international and people from all over the world were assembled here at the start of their pilgrimage. For the first time, the sheer scale of the Camino struck me – I knew that it was a well-known pilgrimage route, but I had had no idea that its reach was so far and so strong. Looking around the church, the weight of its history in the 12th Century walls, I felt a little overwhelmed, trepidatious, but held tight.

In the front row a striking woman with blonde hair and an

orange waterproof jacket knelt, ramrod straight, on the stone floor: her pale face looked up towards the altar, her hands open and out in prayer. Light from a tall, thin, stained-glass window caught her pale face and she looked transfigured. It was hard not to stare.

After mass we made our way to the dining room. By the time we arrived my toes were blue and I was shivering again. All I wanted was my bed and to shut my eyes, and the whole communal dining thing filled me with dread. I was too tired for polite conversation, but once I was seated at the round table with Ali, Jenny and five other pilgrims, it was clear that there was no option.

To our surprise the gangly young man from the airport was at our table – he and his rucksack had been reunited after all. He told us that he was Hungarian and that he worked in London.

A couple from Canada, told us they had been walking with the group of young people we had passed on the hill. 'Yeah, we call them *the kids*,' she said. 'We've left our own grown kids behind in Toronto, but this group seem to have adopted us as their Camino mom and dad. To be honest we could have done with a bit of peace and quiet. They never stopped talking.' She was taking a sabbatical from her work in the sportswear business and he had just retired from a lifetime's service in the navy.

A Frenchman who picked grapes in the summer and worked as a waiter in the winter joined in with the conversation. An old, Spanish man from Barcelona who spoke no English said he was too tired to talk and I wished I had been brave enough to say the same. Despite his reluctance to chat, he told Jenny, in Spanish, that he had walked all of the Spanish Caminos and that this was his second time on the Camino Frances.

As we walked back from supper, we saw the white sun setting, the landscape veiled in a cold, white mist. Ghosts of trees and the mountains were just visible, but the path ahead remained a mystery to us, for tonight at least.

Before I headed upstairs to bed I called David, to let him know that we had made it. It felt good to hear his voice. He knew that I had been worried about today and he sounded relieved that we were safe and sound. When I returned to our cubicle, the bunk that we had hoped would be empty was occupied by the elderly Spaniard. He was already fast asleep.

'The place is half empty. Couldn't they have put him somewhere else? At least with some other men,' Jenny whispered, loudly.

It felt quite strange to be sleeping so close to a man we didn't know and we changed in the bathroom where there was some light and a little privacy.

Day 1
9th April
Saint Jean Pied-de-Port – Roncesvalles
Kari, Ali, Jenny
We have survived the first day. The climb went on forever, but we made it to the top and there were beds for us at the monastery so we are still smiling. I'm now in bed typing on my phone and I can hear a woman in the next cubicle talking, quite loudly. She's from Boston and is travelling with her daughter. I know quite a lot about her now, whether I want to or not. Her daughter is a dancer and they had planned to walk the Camino when she graduated from college. But her daughter quit college.
"When she asked me if we could still go, what could I say? No, that's only something I wanted to do with you if you graduated. Of course not. So here we are. Not quite the way I planned it, but life throws you curveballs."
They are sharing their cubicle with two ridiculously good-looking priests. How awkward would that be – sleeping with two priests?
It is noisy in this dorm and my bunk is narrow. Watching Ali try to wriggle into her silk liner and then into her mummy sleeping bag was entertaining, but I am less amused by being twisted up in my own. These compression socks are going to take some getting used to.

CHAPTER 3

Getting dressed in the dark was a new experience and even though I had sorted out my dry bags before I went to bed, squashing my sleeping bag into the stuff sack and packing my rucksack without waking the old man from Barcelona was quite a challenge. Ali dithered about doing some precautionary blister plastering but, despite the faffing, we were still early for our 7am breakfast slot. I'm a chronically early person and Ali is habitually late. We knew each other well, but 40 days was a long time to spend with another person and I hoped that our differences wouldn't begin to grate. We propped our rucksacks against the wall in the snow and joined the queue for our first *desayunos peregrino* (pilgrim breakfast). Nothing to get excited about, as it turned out: sliced white bread and mediocre coffee. The room was too full of loud Americans and the jabber a bit much at that time of the morning so we didn't linger.

Outside, I heaved on my rucksack and smiled as I saw the sun rise over the foggy, frosty mountains. I relaxed as I breathed in the cold air. This was good.

'Look,' said Ali, a few minutes later. She was pointing her walking pole at a sign that read: Santiago – 790km. 'That can't be right. We walked such a long way yesterday, surely we have made more progress than that.'

The three of us put our collective foot down, and walked fast past the noisy young people from the previous day. Before long I felt strong and my legs powerful; my rucksack was sitting comfortably and the terrain was pleasingly flat. For now.

Soon we found ourselves in 'The Oakwood of Witches' – Sorginaritz. I had been looking forward to this.

In these enchanted forests witches gathered to hold their covens, supposedly practising magic. These women were shamanic, harnessing the healing powers of nature, beyond the controlling eyes of the social order. There was little evidence of the nefarious practices for which they were condemned. It was their non-conformity that got them burned at the stake.

We passed a white cross, erected to ward off the witches, but which, for me, served as a monument to these persecuted women on the margins of society, whose power was such a threat to the church and the patriarchy. I stopped to lay a little flower at the foot of the cross.

'You and your witchy ways, Kari,' said Ali. 'If you had been around in the 16th Century, I bet you would have been out here dancing round your bonfire.'

Maybe she was right. The lifestyle undoubtedly had a certain appeal. If the alternative was a life as a chattel, the moveable property of some man, I would certainly have been tempted to join them. I thought about them as we walked, feeling strengthened by their eccentricity.

Once out of the woods we were climbing again and though the peaks were not as high as yesterday this was an up-and-down sort of walk. As we pushed on I fantasised about constructing a network of sky-walkways that connected the high points. There was surely nothing more dispiriting than walking downhill when the next uphill was already looming ahead, ready for you to climb as soon as you hit the bottom.

At times all three of us walked together, talking, but when the going got tough and chatting required too much breath, we walked at our own pace and focused on the silence. Jenny, the fittest, took the lead. She walked fast, and I liked to keep her purple-jacketed, tall frame in view. In the quiet I thought about my children, and how empty and quiet our home was without them. I loved the noise and the movement that came with a houseful and I missed it now that they had gone. When they were little I used to dream of five minutes' peace, for a sentence that didn't start with, 'Mu'um…' But since they had left, everything was just a bit too orderly. The fridge was too full and the living room too tidy. Now I was the needy one, waiting for their phone calls, looking for their texts. Would this walk help me to break that cycle, give me the space to give them the space to grow?

About 8ish the sun came out and as our wide natural path wiggled through the countryside we saw balls of mistletoe in the bare trees. We passed through Burguete, where Hemingway famously signed the piano, and in a deserted mountain village of honey yellow stone stopped for water and watched five cats, sitting in a line, on top of the woodpile. Three politely looked the other way while the tom forced himself on the fourth, her caterwaul the only sound in the village.

At the brow of the hill we could see our path, like Dorothy's yellow brick road, winding its way down the hillside to Viskarret, a village nestled in the valley, all white walls and orange roofs, striking against the green fields and cloudy blue sky. We reached it at 10am and stopped for coffee in *Café Juan* where two men who must have been in the bar since the night before offered us chewing gum and told us we were beautiful.

And then we trudged through miles and miles of mud – claggy, grey, sticky mud. It clung to our boots, our poles and our trousers, uphill to Alto de Erro and downhill into Zubiri where we crossed the medieval bridge over the Rio Arga into the town. We had covered 22km and it was still only lunchtime.

We got our passports stamped in a small albergue where Jenny got some information from the hospitalero. And then, with the sun on our faces, we sat in the square and ate the last of the sandwiches from Kattaline, while a local walked his guinea pig and others collected their bread.

'Am I hallucinating?' I asked, blinking.

'No. I saw it too,' said Ali, who had taken her boots off and now had her eyes shut, lost to the sunshine and the joy of wiggling her toes.

Taking the weight off our feet and our backs revived us and after consulting the map we decided to push on a bit further to Larrasoaña. I found this place name all but impossible to pronounce so Jenny broke it down into syllables which we repeated after her until we mastered it. La – Ra – So – An – Ya. At least we could now tell people where we were going, should they feel the need to ask.

We had a steep climb out of Zubiri and the last 5km of this 28km walk hurt. At the top of the hill we passed a van selling drinks. A box of unwanted items sat on a chair to one side. A sign read: 'Looking for a husband or wife? Leave your underwear. Magic Works.'

'I could see people might want to lighten their load after all those hills, but I for one will be keeping my pants on,' said Ali.

When we finally saw the second medieval bridge of the day I was ready to drop to my knees, but although Jenny was up ahead, Ali kept me company at the back, assuring me that the end was in sight. As we crossed the bridge an enterprising hospitalero handed us a flier for his private albergue. An albergue, we had discovered, was a hostel and there were three types – municipal (run by the town), parochial (run by some sort of church group), and private (run for profit). They all charged roughly the same – between €8 and €10 per night – but standards seemed to vary. Larrasoaña was not an official stop on the pilgrimage so there was no municipal alternative, and, given the lack of choice we decided to take him up on his offer.

Albergue San Nicolas turned out to be lovely. We showered, put a load of washing in their coin-operated machine, and sat in the sunshine in the little garden with a bottle of red wine, feeling pretty pleased with ourselves. It wasn't long before we were joined by Dan, a laid-back Canadian. He didn't seem fazed by the sight of three women massaging each other's feet and was happy to chat while we groaned. 'Oh yes, that's so good. Do it there. Oh yes.' I was putty in Ali's expert hands.

Dan told us that he had lived in Slovenia for the last 15 years.

'We have two sons who found the Slovenian school system pretty tough. They came to us with the suggestion that they go to boarding school back home in Canada and we went with that.'

I didn't want to talk shop. Just like doctors, who at dinner parties find themselves diagnosing piles, a teacher is invariably regaled with the ups and downs of children's school careers. And usually it is some poor teacher's fault that their little darling didn't make it as a brain surgeon after all. Jenny and I exchanged a look, and kept shtum.

We had finished the bottle of red by 5pm and, perhaps predictably given the amount of walking we had done, it went straight to our heads. In an effort to sober up before dinner we took a turn round the village, admiring the hand-shaped doorknockers on the ancient wooden doors and giggling a little more than we should at nothing in particular. Ali leaned on me and I hooked my arm through hers. She was having fun and I was glad of it.

At dinner the three of us sat at one table while a group of Italians whooped it up on the other. Their leader, a greying man with a Hollywood idol tan and a glint in his eye, chin-chinned us with his glass of red wine. Dan joined our table and we introduced ourselves to a French woman from Saint Jean who only had to step out of her front door to start her pilgrimage. A disappointed American was the sixth pilgrim at our table.

'I hoped the Camino would be full of stimulating conversations with interesting strangers but so far the walk has not met my expectations,' he informed us, stopping short of calling us boring, but only just.

'It is only the second day, perhaps you need to give it a little more time,' I suggested.

He spent the rest of evening boring Jenny to death with his treatise on 'The problem with England.' Jenny put on her best listening face, nodding now and then and occasionally dropping in a 'How interesting,' her go-to response when something is anything but. We should have rescued her really.

Day 2
10th April
Roncesvalles – Larrasoaña
Kari, Ali, Jenny
Today our walk has given us more than we had asked for: Griffon vultures, sparrow hawks and kites flying above spring meadows; a conga of processionary caterpillars wiggling into the blackthorn, cow bells, stepping stones, bubbling rivers, the last of the dates, and an albergue with wonderful showers. The day spent in the fresh air, catching sight of the beautiful, has worked its magic and I am breathing a little more easy, the nagging voice in my head having quietened a little. We are very happy to have a room for four all to ourselves and we won't have to worry about getting dressed in the dark tomorrow.

Since we have pushed on a little further today, we will have a reasonably short walk to Pamplona where the bulls should be waiting for us. My feet are feeling refreshed after that massage from the magic fingers of Dr R and I am ready for an early bed. Here on the Camino, red wine seems to flow like water and I am loving every step of the Way.

CHAPTER 4

The walk to Pamplona was only 15km but by bedtime we had clocked up another 7km walking round the city, most of them spent on a hopeless hunt for churros.

When I stepped out of bed that morning walking any distance at all seemed impossible. I felt like the Little Mermaid. My feet had clearly been cursed by the sea-witch and I was walking on knives. To add to my woes, my hips and my knees had seized up. As I shuffled to the bathroom, wincing with every step, the told-you-so voice was back again, whispering in my head, willing me to quit. But by the time I was dressed the voice was quiet, the joints were oiled, and normal movement had resumed once again.

'All set?' I asked Ali, in an attempt to hurry her along without sounding too bossy.

'Just you go downstairs and I'll be there as quick as I can,' she replied. Clearly my attempt was doomed and she was keen to rid herself of my hovering presence.

The previous evening we had bought some breakfast supplies at a little shop near our albergue. We were planning to eat before we set off but when I got to the kitchen I discovered that our teabags, milk, butter and jam had disappeared. I broke the news to the girls who took it rather well and we made do with a dry breakfast of chorizo washed down with terrible coffee from a vending machine. It would have been easy to feel irritated by this petty theft but the weather was glorious and as we set off at sunrise through the open countryside along the Rio Agra, it was hard to be grumpy. Spring had almost sprung and the colours of the new flowers kept us smiling.

We appeared to be the only people awake when we arrived in the sleepy little town of Zuriáin at about 9am. I was keenly anticipating the coffee and bread that our guidebook had promised – fresh from the 'horno' – but when we peered through the door of the café there was no sign of life. Instead we sat on a wall and had to make do with our massive oranges.

I had been struggling with the weight of my backpack and my shoulders were more painful than my feet. Every hour or so I shifted the weight by adjusting my straps, but couldn't seem find a comfortable position. It was such a relief when I took it off. I seemed to grow taller and my feet felt as if they were hovering above the ground.

'I know this sounds bonkers, but I think this orange was just too heavy for me,' I said, peeling off the skin. My friends laughed, but my backpack felt more manageable when I heaved it back on again and I was happy to have lightened the load. Marginal gains. Marginal gains.

Jenny, map constantly at the ready, suggested we take a detour to Zabaldika to see the 13th Century church of San Esteban. We agreed a little half-heartedly. Without Jenny there would have been no chance of Ali or me taking a diversion. My load may have been lighter without the enormous orange, but I wasn't entirely comfortable. As we climbed the ludicrously steep hill to the church, I muttered to Ali, under my breath, 'This better be bloody worth it.' And she raised her eyebrows, sharing the sentiment.

But when we reached the well-tended garden that surrounded the church, I relaxed a little. A tiny little Sacred Heart nun appeared in the doorway and welcomed us into the nave. She spoke no English but in Spanish she told us to take off our rucksacks so that we would be more comfortable.

Thankful, we shrugged them off and climbed the 52 steps to the ancient belfry. The stone walls were creamy white and massive oak beams cut through them, showing the structure of the ancient tower. Three enormous brass bells hung in rectangular openings and the only light in the darkened tower squeezed through the gaps around their edges, radiating in shafts like sunbeams in a child's drawing. The brass gleamed and I caught flashes of brilliant green from the fields beyond. We took it in turns to ring the bell, sending our prayers out over the valley. Every time a bell rang the tremendous noise reverberated through the bell tower and through us for 24 glorious seconds before silence was restored. The sound was made visible as the sunbeams flickered and the light filled my ears and my heart. I smiled at Jenny. Yes, this had been worth the climb.

Back down in the body of the kirk, the nun had been joined by one of her sisters and they gave us each a copy of a prayer entitled, *The Beatitudes of the Pilgrim.*

'One of the sisters spent a year on the Camino, taking photographs and researching what pilgrimage means to people in this day and age,' Jenny translated. 'She wrote this when she returned. You might like to read it when you reach Santiago.'

We sat quietly in the empty church and I read the prayer, surprised to find that my eyes had filled with tears. In the silence I was moved by the sincerity of the sisters, strengthened with the sense that our walk had begun to feel like a pilgrimage.

Before we left we spoke to the nuns for a little while and I told them that I had been a pupil at a Sacred Heart Convent when I was a child. I didn't tell them that my experience had been an unhappy one and focused instead on the few nuns who had made my time there bearable. The taller of the two nuns went off to fetch a little white book.

'This is our version of Hello Magazine,' she said. 'We like to keep up to date on all the news.' It contained information about all the Sacred Heart sisters around the world and I was astonished to discover that some of the nuns, who had seemed ancient when they taught me 35 years ago, were not only still alive, but amazingly were still working. The little nuns blessed us, kissed us goodbye and wished us *'Buen Camino'* – the first of the countless times we would hear those words on our journey.

As we walked on, in the sunshine and the blossom, I felt different. As if the spirituality of this walk had, unbidden, revealed itself to me. I didn't have to *do* anything at all. It didn't matter if I could not understand or fully rationalise my faith. All I had to do was open myself up to this experience and let it happen.

In Puente de Arre we stopped for a breather and from there on we were in the outskirts of Pamplona, walking on pavements that were punishing on the joints. We passed a red house, decorated with shells in elaborate heraldic motifs, but despite the relative shortness of the day's walk we were longing to reach our destination and I sensed Ali's frustration as I stopped to take a photograph. She just wanted to get there and couldn't care less if I liked the colours of the faded graffiti on the Barrio de la Magdalena. I was as quick as I could be.

And then, all of a sudden, the Portal de Francia was ahead of us and we crossed this famous drawbridge, complete with massive iron chains, into the ancient city of Pamplona, as pilgrims have been doing for more than 1,000 years.

The walled city was very quiet but, anxious about availability, we made our way directly to our chosen albergue – *Jesus y Maria*. We needn't have worried, we were the first to arrive. We picked it because it was centrally located and because we thought sleeping in a 17th Century Jesuit church would be interesting. I say we, but actually I mean me, because Ali would opt for comfort over interest every time.

It was certainly basic. Two long dorms were furnished with metal, prison-style bunk beds, and as we were so early, we were right by the door. Still – for €8 a night we were not complaining. Not out loud anyway.

'I don't know about you, but I think I'm ready for a beer,'

said Ali, and we found a bar where we rewarded our effort with cerveza, bocadillo and a slice of tortilla before hitting the narrow streets where the bulls are run every July.

Hemingway was everywhere, from the eponymous Doner Kebab y Pizzeria to the hulking statue of the bearded writer outside the bullring, all massive shoulders and chunky knitwear. For a period in the 20s he visited the city every year during the festival of San Fermin. This celebration of masculinity, virility and brutality apparently appealed to something atavistic in his nature and his first novel, *The Sun Also Rises*, is based on his time here.

Everywhere we looked we saw the white and red costumes of the corredores. Jenny told us a bit about San Fermin and we walked to the small statue in the wall where the men pray for his blessing before they run with the bulls. We stopped by the shop windows full of brightly coloured, papier-mâché masks – a giant with a black beard and no eyes, a toothless crone and a matador with a cigar sticking out of his mouth – and I found myself thinking that my family would love it here, and planning a return trip. Although perhaps not in the bull-running season.

In striking contrast to the vivid, provoking city, the cathedral was a still place that soothed the senses. We stepped away from all that colour into an inner courtyard where a water fountain bubbled quietly and birds sang. The cloisters were cool, the colours of the frescoes fading gracefully, and we recharged for a while.

I watched Jenny as she stood in the light by the fountain, her face turned up to the sun, enjoying the heat and the quiet. At work she is serious and determined with a razor-sharp intellect and fearlessness which some find disconcerting. She has no time for chitchat or socialising, she always has too much to do. Jenny lives on site with her husband and son, as I did, and she struggles, as I did, to balance the demands of working in a boarding school with family life. I am sure she can't remember the last time she did anything just for herself, and as she stood in the sun, I could see her breathing out, enjoying being herself, just Jenny. Jenny, who is funny and silly and brave and kind, and so much more than the sum of the individual roles she fulfils so brilliantly.

'What we need now is churros con chocolate,' said Ali firmly, waking Jenny from her reverie. We left the cathedral, laughing at the smirking Madonna with the double chin, in search of a sugar fix. But despite trailing the streets the long, sweet doughnut sticks proved elusive. We were in Basque country where they hold their culinary traditions dear and churros, it turned out, are a speciality of Madrid. They should stay there as far as the Basques were concerned.

Just as we were about to give up we spotted a queue of people winding down the road.

'What's that about?' I asked.

Jenny sniffed the air like a beagle. 'This is our place. If there's a queue, it must be worth waiting for.' We followed the line to the front door of a very simple bakery, *Pastas Caseras Beatriz*. 'They don't have to waste any money on promotion, because everyone locally knows it's good.'

And so we joined the line and waited our turn to fill a box with the most divine tiny pastries I have ever eaten: some filled with a praline of chocolate, some dusted with sugar and tasting of lemon, some with almond paste. Why did we not buy more?

Stopping for a coffee in a nearby bar, we nodded a greeting to an American couple that we thought we had seen before. She was a petite, short-haired woman of about fifty, with a bright scarf around her shoulders. He was about the same age, grey and tanned, but frowning as if he was afraid to let down his guard. They were drinking wine with Bernard, a large, sarcophagus-shaped German in a long black coat.

'Where are you guys from?' he asked, his English excellent, twanging American.

'We're from Scotland.'

'Hey, that's really cool. I have done the Camino four times and I have never met anyone from Scotland. *Ock Eye the noo!*'

We headed back to the albergue to put our feet up for an hour or so. The dorm had filled up and an array of garments, on coat hangers, was hanging from hooks opposite our beds.

'Who brings coat hangers on a pilgrimage?' Jenny asked.

A young French woman limped up the dorm, clearly suffering.

'Are you coping with that?' Ali asked her. 'Do you have any tape?'

Ali, who had spent her adult life working as physio, had a highly developed sense of compassion. Her warm heart was twinned with a clinical, diagnostic brain and she loved puzzles of all descriptions. To her the human body was the ultimate conundrum. If there was a problem she tussled with it until she found a solution. Fixing things made her happy. The French woman instantly put her trust in Ali and before long she was strapped up and practising some exercises to help alleviate the pain. It turned out she was a dancer and although fit she was struggling. I smirked, feeling smug that I was holding up. She was also, it transpired, the owner of the clothes lining the walls.

'I've got a tip for you too,' I muttered. 'Ditch the coat hangers and lighten your load.'

Dan, the laid-back Canadian, was horizontal on the bunk beside me and he was fast asleep by the time we left for supper.

On the way, Jenny taught us her two golden rules for eating in towns:

1. Don't eat in a square
2. Don't eat anywhere with pictures of the food

For a foodie like me, the prospect of tapas in Pamplona filled me with excitement and I was an eager pupil. Jenny picked somewhere unassuming but busy and we sat on high stools and ate until we could eat no more. We learned that *Bocatas* were delicious morsels of things like Serrano ham and cheese, served on bread. *Pinchos* (or *pintxos* in Basque country) were smaller plates of food like fried pimentos or garlic prawns and *raciones* were larger plates of dishes such as squid and patatas bravas. Just to be sure we had learned our lessons we tried a bit of everything and washed it all down with plenty of good, red wine. When the bill came, Jenny covered it with her hand, saying, 'Wait. Before we look, how much do you think it will be?' And Ali and I were astonished when the total turned out to be just a third of our best guess.

Day 3
11ᵗʰ April
Larrasoaña – Pamplona
Kari, Ali, Jenny
It has been a day full of contrasts. My body is aching and exhausted but I have spent less time thinking about walking and more time considering why I am here. Something has changed in my outlook today. Perhaps I am hoping for an answer to the question 'What should I do with the rest of my life?' But maybe it should be less about the asking, and more about the thanking? Thank you, God, for my children, who by your grace seem to have turned out all right.
For now though, my thoughts are all about the physical. As I type I am in bed, freezing. The door to the street is ajar: I will be sleeping with my coat on and with one eye open.

CHAPTER 5

We left Pamplona at dawn through quiet streets lit by street lamps on a path that took us through the Universidad de Navarre. The handsome campus impressed us, old and new happily coexisting around wide, green spaces.

'Maybe Finlay could study here,' Jenny suggested, knowing Ali's youngest was keen to read Spanish.

'I hope not,' said Ali. 'I just know that if some crazy friend suggested running with the bulls, he would be the first to join in. Let's just keep this option to ourselves.'

In no time at all the noise of the busy roads had faded and the countryside opened up in front of us. The soil turned from grey to red and we passed fields of yellow rape and new-green barley. We seemed to walk pretty briskly on the first leg of the morning and passed a young couple early on. The girl muttered something to her partner as we passed, thinking we couldn't understand them. Little did they know that Jenny has a babel fish in her ear and she sniggered as we overtook them.

'She just told her boyfriend that they were being overtaken by old-age pensioners, and that if he didn't hurry up she was leaving him behind.'

Mid-morning, we saw two figures on the road ahead of us. Ali's sensors tingled. They looked like Piglet and Pooh, one sprightly and loose limbed, the other large and voluptuous, bent under the weight of an enormous backpack, hobbling slowly. As we got closer even Jenny and I could see that she was in a good deal of pain. She was a curvy girl and I was struck by her slow, steady determination, in the face of quite staggering odds, and of the gentle support of her smaller companion. We caught up and walked alongside them for a few minutes. They were from Germany and travelling together, like us.

'My knee is giving me a lot of problems. It is really painful, but I don't want to quit,' said the larger girl, her voice low and gruff, her eyes sad and tired.

Ali couldn't hold back. 'I'm a physio. Would you like me to have a look at it?'

A few minutes later she had investigated and strapped up the knee, leaving the curvy girl with some exercises and her smaller friend with instructions on how to strap it up.

They were smiling when we left them, plodding on.

For some time we walked across a wide, flat plain, but up ahead of us *Alto del Perdon* was looming, and I knew it wouldn't be long before we began to climb once more. About 11km into our walk we stopped for coffee in Zariquiegui, and I hoped the caffeine would give me the injection of energy I needed to propel me up the mountain. We had our passports stamped in the café and Jenny translated a prayer that had been painted onto the wall. It was the Irish Blessing and hearing it made me think of my mum, whose family were travellers:

May the road rise up to meet you.
May the wind be always at your back.
May the sun shine warm upon your face;
The rains fall soft upon your fields and until we meet again,
May God hold you in the palm of his hand.

On the way out of the village we bought some bread and tied it to the side of Jenny's rucksack. The marigolds, which carpeted the verges in this little town, were a perfect match for her orange fleece and her hat with the earflaps that her son had bought for her. So, never one to miss a photo opportunity, I persuaded her to sit amongst them.

'You look like the marigold fairy,' I said, hardly encouraging her to comply. But she did, and sat crossed legged, grinning up all rosy cheeks and crinkled eyes.

Later, under the revolving shadows of the wind turbines, we made our way up the mountain. Beehives skirted the almond orchards and, at the edges of the bean fields, herbs like fennel and verbena grew wild. The words of Yeats's poem, *The Lake Isle of Innisfree,* echoed in my mind, the beat keeping time with the rhythm of my steps.

> *I will arise and go now, and go to Innisfree,*
> *And a small cabin build there, of clay and wattles made;*
> *Nine bean-rows will I have there, a hive for the honey-bee,*
> *And live alone in the bee-loud glade.*

It's a poem about escape and discovery, escape from the routine of life that clouds our vision and makes us blind, and the discovery of the divine grace of simple things. *'And I shall have some peace there, for peace comes dropping slow...'* I repeated like a mantra, feeling a stillness settling on me, and a contentment growing.

I picked a bunch of fennel and was sniffing it as the Italian group from the albergue in Larrasoaña overtook us. I passed a sprig to the grey-haired George Clooney lookie-likie, who ate it, kissed me on the cheek, told me he loved me, and disappeared into the distance with his noisy entourage.

But if my heart and my head were enraptured, my body was anything but. The bloody hill went on forever. My pack was heavy and my feet were sore. No matter how beautiful, I wanted it to be over. Ali was right by my side, struggling silently and digging deep.

Jenny got to the top of *Alto del Perdon* first and waved her poles at us, cheering us on, her voice carried to us by the wind. Her smile gave us the jolt we needed and she guided us in like an air traffic controller. By the time we arrived at the summit we were on top of the world. Reaching the top meant we had walked 100km, and I pointed this out, breathlessly, triumphant.

From this high vantage point we could see the Camino mapped below us as the path snaked westwards across the plains, and it was beautiful. With Heather Small singing in my ears I forgot my sore feet and the weight on my back.

'I think this calls for a celebration,' said Ali, pulling three liquorice toffees out of her pocket. All through our training, she had lured me to finish lines with the promise of a sweetie and these were our favourites. She rationed them very carefully and we were allowed them only in extremis or as a reward. She clearly agreed with Heather that today, we really had done something to make us feel proud.

The vast wrought-iron monument at the top of the hill depicts medieval pilgrims battling against the fierce west wind and we were certainly feeling its full force as Jenny translated the inscription: 'Where the way of the wind crosses the way of the Stars'. A timely reminder to keep my eye on where I was headed when being buffeted by life.

As we skited down the steep, rocky path to the valley below, I was grateful for my poles. We could see the little villages ahead of us, each one a cluster of stone buildings built around a church and a town hall.

When the landscape levelled out we walked through vineyards and more almond orchards, stopping to eat bread and chorizo, oranges and dates outside a church in Muruzabal. Over lunch we spoke about our parents.

Ali's father had died the previous year and since then she had spent at least a week of every month up in Inverness, taking care of her mother and her brother. Jenny's father's health was failing and she tried to be in the Lake District as much as possible in the holidays, to support her mum. My dad had died 20 years before and my mum, who had lived with mouth cancer for five years, was told her diagnosis was terminal back in March. She was not in any pain, but we knew it was a waiting game, the outcome inevitable, the rest, uncertain. So many shared emotions, despite the differences in our experiences. All three of us carrying our responsibility carefully, like a dandelion clock we were guarding from the wind, for as long as we were able.

Before we set off again, we checked the map and opted to

take a detour to see the church at Eunate. I must have been feeling strong because, for once, the thought of additional miles did not fill me with dread. The church, when we found it, was octagonal in shape, but the handsome exterior was all that we saw as it was locked up until later. Being shut out of a church made me feel oddly rejected and I sulked a bit as the drizzle started.

On the last leg to Puente la Reina the weather closed in and the rain pelted down. We put on our waterproofs, stretched the rain covers over our rucksacks, and powered through the last 5km, heads down. As we were crossing the bridge that gave its name to the town, we met two Irishmen sheltering in an archway: one very old, the other not much more than twenty.

'We've been camping along the Way and we're just hoping that this rain will stop before we have to set up our bivouacs for the night.' The young man peered up at the heavy sky, willing the clouds to pass.

Every time I felt proud of my efforts I seemed to come across people doing truly remarkable things. This walk, I was discovering, was not a way to prove myself. Maybe it was time for my ego to simmer down.

Our chosen refuge for the night was up another bastard of a hill and I was using all the bad words I knew to power me up the last bit, which felt just too much at the end of a 28km day. By the time we got there we were soaked through and, as if that wasn't punishment enough, the barn of an albergue was completely freezing. Ali and I stripped out of our wet things and got into our sleeping bags to try to stop the uncontrollable shivering. While we warmed up, Jenny, who had found an extraordinary second wind, decided to head back to Eunate to see the church that had been closed. 'I'm unlikely to get another chance,' she reflected. For a nanosecond I considered going with her but came to my senses just in time. I justified my decision by telling myself that she would be glad of some time on her own and anyway, knowing Jenny, she would probably run.

'Leave me your laundry,' I said, in an attempt to atone for my lack of effort.

While she was gone, Ali slept and I did the washing. Waiting for the dryer I met some German ladies in their 60s who had been walking the Camino in stages over the last five years. They began in Munich and spent three weeks a year walking. I loved the idea that Jenny, Ali and I might still be walking together in 20 years' time.

Although, undoubtedly, Ali had her own, private reasons for being here, if I'd asked her she would have said, 'I'm just here to chum you along.' On that cold, wet afternoon I hoped she wasn't regretting her decision. I felt a responsibility for her. I had sucked her in and as payback I was determined she should have fun in Spain. Much as I might be feeling purged by the pilgrimage, for her, I didn't want it to be a penance.

Washing done, I tempted her out of her sleeping bag with the promise of a warm drink. I knew she felt far from her boys. She too was finding it hard to shirk the guilt that while we were here, all we had to worry about was ourselves. That freedom took some getting used to. She was cold and tired and her feet were hurting. Tea was clearly the answer. Tea and biscuits.

The only other patrons in the aircraft hangar of a bar were the American couple we had met in Pamplona, and Bernard the German. Just as in Pamplona, they were perched on bar stools, the lady looking elegant with a scarf thrown artfully around her shoulders. My hair was dripping and I felt like a sheep, just pulled out of the dip. Why hadn't I brought accessories?

Fortunately there were patio heaters in the bar and Ali and I huddled underneath one, cursing the day we decided to bring flip-flops as our only other choice of footwear, and laughing about the Horniman tea while Jenny braved the thunder and lightning.

An hour or so later she returned safely, enthusiastic about the church and pleased that she had made the effort. She was shivering and wet, but warmed up after her shower and joined us for dinner.

While we were eating our bunkroom had filled up with a group of French women and we tried to keep the noise down as we got ready for bed. By 9pm they were all fast asleep but we weren't quite ready to settle down for the night.

'Despite what that girl said this morning, we're not pensioners yet,' whispered Jenny, giggling that she was talking after lights out.

'Tell me a bedtime story,' said Ali. 'My boys used to love it when you read to them at school.'

I had taught both of Ali's boys and I smiled, thinking of my classroom in the prep school I had worked in ten years ago. I had a sofa in the corner and beanbags so that the children could stretch out to hear a story at the end of the day. I had worked through any number of curricular rearrangements but nothing could dissuade me from my belief in the power of the story. I was proud of the way my pupils had embraced reading.

'Are you sitting comfortably?' I asked in a low voice. I had downloaded *Harry Potter and the Philosopher's Stone* onto my phone, and in a whisper I began reading it to Ali, doing my best with the accents, not wanting to disappoint. But the funny voices made her chortle and the French women were starting to stir so reluctantly I put it away and Ali plugged in her headphones.

Day 4
12th April
Pamplona – Puente la Reina
Kari, Ali, Jenny
Today we made it past the 100km mark and we are feeling pretty proud of ourselves. At the top of Alto del Perdon *we celebrated with a toffee and posed for pictures with the epic iron sculpture of pilgrims battling the wind. Fitting really, as the weather today has been wild. Outside the storm is raging and the thunder and lightning has started again but as I type it looks like it will be a quiet night here in our all-women dorm. A treat after Dan's snoring last night!*

CHAPTER 6

Overnight the storm raged but while Jenny and I slept soundly, Ali spent a night that was anything but calm. By the time our alarms went off, she had hardly slept a wink. She had spent most of the night in the bathroom and she was drained and exhausted. It looked as though she wouldn't be well enough to walk and over breakfast, of which she did not partake, we tried to come up with a contingency plan.

'I couldn't help hearing,' said one of the German ladies who had walked from Munich. 'I have some medicine that might help.' She dosed Ali with the German equivalent of Imodium and gave her more to take later in the day. Although we had discussed what we would do if one of us were injured (if I was injured Ali would call it a day, but if Ali was injured, I would see her safely home and continue alone), we hadn't considered the possibility of illness. I could see that Ali was worried about holding us up.

'If you need to take a day or two to recover, that's not a problem,' I reassured her. 'We could book in here for another night and take things easy.'

Within a couple of hours, however, the medicine had taken effect, and Ali was insistent that she wanted to keep going. We gave it a little longer, just to be on the safe side, and then set off for Estella.

'We can call it a day in Lorca if you take a turn for the worse,' said Jenny, checking the map. 'We need to be in Logroño the day after next, but I'm sure we could chalk up the miles tomorrow if we needed to.'

'Or if the worst comes to the worst, we could always take the bus,' I said, shocking myself that those words had come out of my mouth.

'Bus!' said Ali, horrified. 'What kind of a lily-livered quitter do you think I am?' The very thought was enough to rouse her fighting spirit. She was more invested than I had realised.

Although the day before I had been swearing about the steep hill up to the albergue, I was glad we had done it as it meant we were spared the climb that morning. The yellow arrows took us through 'The nuns' neighbourhood' and skirted along the side of the river before heading uphill to Maneru, a village that sits on top of the first of three hills that we would tackle that day. The crosses carved into the walls spoke of the place's links with the Knights Templar and the Order of St John.

In the centre of a maze of sloping streets we found a church of orange stone and stopped at a café alongside. Jenny ordered while Ali flopped, grateful for the rest after her sleepless night. She had been raised to grin and bear it but I knew she was putting on a brave face. While Jenny was inside I checked how she was really holding up.

'I'm mostly just terrified that I'll be caught short miles from anywhere,' she said.

'Don't worry; today's walk is through a string of little villages. We'll make sure there are plenty of stops. And if you need to dive into the woods, I'll keep cavey.'

She smiled. 'Good to know you've got my back, buddy.'

'Look. I might just have found the world's biggest pork scratching,' said Jenny, coming out of the bar, holding up her purchase. 'The barman says it's a local delicacy and it seems rude not to try it.' The long piece of pork rind was curled in a giant, crispy bow and provided one of today's two taste sensations: salty, crispy and smoky-bacon flavoured, it was completely delicious. Ali quite sensibly abstained, silently waving it away, and averting her eyes. I'm sure the very thought of it did nothing to soothe her churning stomach.

As we left Maneru the view of Cirauqui opened up in the

distance. Another medieval village, its cluster of red-roofed buildings topped the hill ahead like a skullcap. From this vantage point, we could see the climb in front of us and once again it struck me as a pity to be going downhill, when before long we would be hiking uphill again. But the sun was shining, the sky was blue and Ali was feeling better so we were smiling pork-scratching smiles as we walked down through vineyards and cornfields.

Walking due west, our shadows were cast in front of us on the red dirt: one long and straight, two shorter and rounder. Looking ahead, I realised for the first time that as long as I was walking towards Santiago, my shadow would be on the road before me, showing me the way. The English teacher in me spent some time exploring this metaphor in my head. At times, the past throws our future into shade, changing how we perceive things, stopping us from seeing what's right under our nose. But sometimes, it's our history that helps us forge ahead, giving us the confidence that comes from experience. I decided against sharing my musings with Ali who would no doubt have given them short shrift.

At Cirauqui, while Jenny and Ali strode ahead, I stopped to take pictures of the heavy studded doorways, the narrow cobbled streets, the wrought-iron balconies and the big brass doorknockers. I found them waiting for me under an archway, and from here our path followed an ancient, well-preserved, Roman road. It was rough underfoot and we had to watch our step.

'It's not in very good condition, this path. I don't know why they haven't improved it,' said Ali, whose mind had clearly been elsewhere during the history briefing.

Jenny laughed. 'It's not too bad, considering it is 2,000 years old.'

And then we were heading downhill again and could see Lorca, our lunch destination at the top of the third and final hill. I burst into a chorus of 'The Grand Old Duke of York,' only to be told quite firmly, by Ali, that there was to be no singing today. Since she was poorly, I did as I was told. Not something which comes naturally to me.

On the way up the hill we saw, in the distance, a girl who seemed about my daughter Connie's age. She looked strong and energetic, happy to be on her own, walking in the sunshine with a bounce in her step. When she stopped to fix her headphones we caught up with her and said hello. Her Cleopatra bob and unguarded smile made her seem young, I would have guessed straight out of university, but it turned out she was in her late 20s and a lawyer in London. Her name was Harriet and she told us she was between jobs. She was walking from Pamplona to Burgos while she had the time. Something about her confident expression and purposeful stride reminded me so much of Connie that as I watched her head up the hill ahead of us, I felt an ache for home and family.

In the village of Lorca, we found some benches outside the little church and sat in the sun, eating our bread and cheese. For the first time, it was warm enough for me to unzip the bottoms of my walking trousers.

'Those are good Scottish legs,' said Ali. 'More blue than white, really.' Spain might not have been ready for them, but as we had hardly seen another living soul all day long, I felt safe enough to leave them exposed.

In the afternoon thyme, rosemary and lavender scented our way. The butterflies were out for the first time, as were the bees and the strange Spanish ladybirds. But, although the landscape was more gently rolling, the three peaks had been a challenge and the last 8.5km into Estella was a hard slog.

The path went on forever, conversation stopped and with every footfall I willed it to be over. Ali and Jenny pushed on ahead while I, exhausted and at the back, struggled to hold back the tears. Ashamed of my weakness I felt like an unwilling child being dragged on an excursion by her parents. 'Are we nearly there yet?' I called to Jenny, and it was only a well-timed liquorice toffee that kept my bottom lip from wobbling.

Ali was totally wiped out when we reached the town and as we hadn't decided on an albergue we headed for the closest one, located in a dingy back alley. We didn't get beyond the grimy front door. It looked horrible, and, although she was exhausted she somehow found the energy to keep going.

At our next choice, a parochial albergue called *San Miguel*, we were welcomed by two ageing hospitaleros who had walked the Camino many times. Bearded and tanned, they looked like they had spent their lives outdoors. They showed us to the outside store cupboards where we deposited our poles and boots, and with our feet breathing a sigh of relief, they led us into the dorm where about 15 bunk beds were crammed in at close quarters. The plastic bed covers didn't look all that appealing, but the place seemed friendly and we were glad to take off our rucksacks and head for the showers. To my deep, deep joy the bathrooms were not unisex and there was even a hairdryer. We may have had to queue and share the tiny space with six others, but it felt like Christmas.

While Ali nursed her feet and took a nap on her bunk, Jenny and I sat outside and watched the birds. Jenny pulled out the remains of the pork scratching and we lay on our backs in the sun, looking up at the vultures that started to circle as though they had caught a whiff of the meat.

'That's an Alimoche – the White, Egyptian vulture,' said Jenny, pointing up at the huge silhouette.

A woman with a mass of frizzy orange hair came to sit with us. She was from Bournemouth and had started her pilgrimage in Pamplona. Her feet hurt and she was struggling with the weight of her pack. Meeting a newbie, I found myself doling out advice like a seasoned *peregrina*. I felt proud of my blister-free feet and my proficiency in rucksack packing.

Milling around were clusters of young people who had met up along the Way and were now travelling together.

'Those kids, who come on the Camino as an alternative, cheap holiday, we call them '*Touregrinos*',' said the hospitalero later. 'They don't know that a pilgrimage and a long walk, they are not the same thing.'

But I disagreed. These young people seemed to be interested in more than a cheap holiday and they sat in small clusters, talking intently.

The striking, blonde woman in the orange jacket, who had been praying so fervently in Roncesvalles, joined us outside. Her feet were in a mess and she wasn't sure if she would be able to keep walking. Ali, feeling better after her sleep, got out her blister box and patched her up while we talked. Her name was Kate, and she told us she was a yoga teacher from Australia.

The albergue had a tiny kitchen and most of the young folk were cooking evening meals and sharing their food. They invited us to join them but once our feet had recovered we opted to explore the town a little.

Estella seemed large compared to the villages we had been in earlier that day, and everywhere we looked there was evidence that this was a town with a political agenda. From the 'Free the Basque Country' graffiti to the flags flying from windows of garret flats, it felt edgy and different from anywhere else we had been.

We walked up a stately set of steps to the Church of San Pedro de la Rua and were pleased to see that it was open, unlike so many of the churches we had passed. We arrived just as mass was beginning and Jenny and Ali went off to explore while I sat towards the back enjoying some time alone. It was cool and dimly lit inside and as the service carried on in Spanish, I had time to reflect. Although I have been a Catholic all my life, I am not a very good one. I have little interest in doctrine and rules: my faith is quiet, my spirituality instinctive.

As I sat, I considered what the hospitalero had said about the difference between a long walk and a pilgrimage. This, for me, was not about the walk. I was looking for more. Like the iron pilgrims at the top of *Alto del Perdon*, I felt battered by life. The velocity of the last 20 years (three babies in two years, three countries, nine house moves, eleven schools – six for the children, five for me) had blown me off my feet and left me uprooted and exhausted. I felt broken by a job that had asked too much of me and orphaned by sadness that my relationship with my mother had never been what I wanted and that time had run out on that hope. So there I was, at a turning point, knowing that some things change and some stay the same, trying to let go of the right things and hoping that when this sea change in my life was over, I would recognise the important things, and that they would still be in place.

When I came out of mass, Jenny and Ali were sitting on the steps, waiting to take me to a bar they had discovered. They were cheerful and their smiles relieved me of my introspection. I was glad of their company. Refreshed after a beer, we spent a while looking for a place for dinner, bearing in mind Jenny's rules, and settled (I'm not sure why) on a dark bar, where the walls were plastered with political posters and the only other patrons were hard-drinking men. Heavy metal music pumped through the speakers.

'Maybe, we should go somewhere else?' I said, but Ali looked exhausted and I could sense her reluctance to move. Just as we were considering our options, a waitress came to take our order. She looked beleaguered, tired of serving customers who only cared about their next drink. Jenny got her chatting in Spanish, and I smiled encouragingly, letting her know that we came in peace. It worked. She smiled back and told us not to worry about the menu, that she would bring us some good food, and we were so happy that she did.

Plates of delicious things arrived: patatas bravas, prawns in garlic, meatballs, calamari, and the highlight – and the second taste sensation of the day – a plate of skinned, charred pimentos. They were simple but completely and utterly divine. If I am ever on death row and they ask me what I want for my last meal – I am going to ask my jailers to send for them. I was in heaven and, as if to confirm this, the piped rock music was suddenly replaced by a live oom-pah band outside in the street, and all was right with my world.

Ali, who had soldiered all day on just bread and water, ate very little. She was done in but assured us that the worst was over. Whether this was down to the medicine from the German ladies or the dousing with the oil of chrism my sister insisted I pack, we will never know.

By the time we made our way back to the albergue, Ali was all but catatonic. She shuffled along the narrow streets with her eyes half shut, longing for her bed. When we arrived, the hospitalero was keen to chat and had opened up his bottle of local liqueur to share with us when we got in, but Ali headed straight for her bunk and I followed swiftly behind.

Day 5
13th April
Puente la Reina – Estella
Kari, Ali, Jenny
In a literal and metaphorical sense today has been full of ups and downs. Three hills were challenging enough, but worse still, poor Ali has had an upset stomach and soldiered on regardless. It can't have been much fun. As I type in the dark Jenny and the hospitalero are still nattering away in the communal kitchen. My sleeping bag is slithering around on this plastic sheet and Ali is out for the count: it's been a tough day. Here's hoping tomorrow will be a little easier.

CHAPTER 7

On the way out of Estella, Jenny filled us in on her late-night chat with José the hospitalero. Having her with us was like having a superpower: not only could we eavesdrop on conversations not intended for our ears, she could also mingle with the locals and wheedle out all kinds of information. That morning, as we overtook a group of Spanish women, she had heard one of them describe us as 'the sporty girls' (well that was a first!), and later, in a corner shop, the postman described us as 'good Christian women'. Thanks to Jenny and José we now knew a bit more about the symbolism of the shell, too.

Jenny held her shell up to the light. 'He told me that the grooves are like the sun's rays and that they symbolise the many ways to Santiago. They all converge at the cathedral, here,' she pointed.

'He said that the pilgrimage predates Christianity, and that for thousands of years, people have followed the Milky Way, west, to Finisterre – the end of the earth – to watch the sun set in the sea. Perhaps it was the liqueur talking, or maybe it was a line, but he told me "The Camino is eternal."' She paused. 'I'm not quite sure what he meant.'

I loved the mysticism that shrouded the Camino and soaked up these stories like a dry sponge.

As the days went by, the same faces popped up, and, despite our initial reserve, we enjoyed coming to recognise some of the pilgrims along the Way. There was Draggy Pole Man, who dragged his walking poles and smoked a lot (we tried to get past him as quickly as possible) and Mendicant Man who wore a loincloth and sandals and carried a crook and a golden gourd. There was Sara the Curvy German with the bad knee who Ali had fixed, and Lara her little friend. Elf was a Polish girl who worked as Santa's Little Helper, and was currently between jobs. Juan Camino carried his lunch in a carrier bag and had walked the Way countless times before. Valentino was the leader of the happy short-wearing gang from Italy (the one who told me that he loved me but never calls and never writes) and Dan the Canadian, who had turned out to be quite the snorer. Rivalling him in the decibel stakes was Joorst the cheerful Dutchman who was heard long before he was seen. Privately, we'd christened the yoga teacher from Australia, Holy Kate, and newer to the group were Harriet the London lawyer and Crystaltips from Bournemouth who had lent us her conditioner. These peregrinos were woven through the fabric of our days, giving texture and colour, building up the bigger picture. Many of them were glad that Ali was amongst our number, as she had taped them and bandaged them before sending them on their way.

'Have you considered charging?' I asked her that evening as she returned with her kit, having ministered to the footsore. 'I could be your manager. We could make a fortune.'

All day we had a spring in our step, perhaps fuelled by our early-morning stop at the wine fountain in Irache. Pilgrims were welcomed to drink wine from the fountain and fill up their water bottles with vino. Despite it being 7am we felt it was only right that we should christen our shells and give it a go, but we drew the line at filling our bottles. For a week now, our shells had been jangling on our backpacks, identifiers of which we were now proud, but this was the first time they had been put to use.

My shell brought back happy memories. The English Department at school had arranged a leaving dinner for our Head of Department, Mike, and me. Mike and his wife, Kath, my opposite number in the other girls' house, were moving out to Shanghai with their children, to take up new teaching roles in an International School. We were a close-knit department and had supported each other well. We knew how to have fun and we had been looking forward to our night out. I had ordered scallops as a starter and they arrived presented in a shell.

'This is the shell I need for my walk,' I squeaked, delighted.

Lauren looked confused. 'What on earth do you need a shell for?'

'I think it's just symbolic. You tie one to your backpack to let people know you are a pilgrim. If we were desperate we could use them to drink with and even eat out of I suppose.'

Not for the first time, my soon-to-be-ex colleagues looked at me as though I had taken leave of my senses. But always one to embrace the peculiar, Wanda asked the waitress if I could keep mine.

'Oh, I'm sorry,' she said, 'we're often asked that, but we always reuse. You may not think it, but they're expensive so we can't just give them away.'

'But she's going on a pilgrimage. She's walking 500 miles. She needs this one.' Wanda pleaded, two glasses of wine in, and with a flair for the dramatic.

The waitress returned to the table a while later, smiling. 'I'm really surprised, he never says yes, but the chef says you must be doing the Camino, whatever that is, and that you can have the shell with his best wishes.'

At 7am that morning I toasted my colleagues with the red wine, knowing they would be proud that I was putting the shell to such good use.

From here we opted for the less busy, scenic route that skirted Monte Jurra, and passed through woodland, hoaching with caterpillars, and onto open countryside via the little villages of Puente and Luquin. I was in love with the rough stone walls and the tiny shuttered windows with their flaking blue paintwork. The stone looked so warm it made me want to touch it, but my companions were yomping on at pace and with my sense of direction I couldn't risk getting lost, so I ran to keep up. Jenny and Ali hadn't known each other before this week, but now they were as relaxed as old friends. I smiled as I heard their laughter up ahead.

Eduardo's Mobile Café appeared out of nowhere just as we needed a drink and a rest. It provided a good spot for lunch and we had freshly squeezed orange juice that tasted like sunshine and shared a tortilla in the shade, happy to shirk off our rucksacks for a while. An abandoned walking boot filled with wildflowers adorned the top of a waymarker. Out of adversity, beauty.

We had been planning to spend the night in Los Arcos but were still quite fresh when we got there, so we decided to push on to Sansol which was just 7km further on. We stopped only long enough to spend a few quiet minutes in the church and to pay our respects to the statue of St James.

Saint Iago, Giacomo, Iacobus, St James the Greater – they're all the same person. He was one of the twelve apostles, the son of Zebedee, and brother of John. The Way of St James was originally a pilgrimage to venerate his remains. He was credited for bringing Christianity to Spain and was depicted all along the route, usually as a barefoot pilgrim carrying a staff and holding a gourd. At other times, unfortunately, he was portrayed as a warrior, the moor slayer, Matamoros. His name was used to call the 'faithful' to arms in the struggle to drive the Moors out of Spain during the Reconquista, although he himself was long gone by that stage in the game. The former depiction of the saint was the only palatable one of the two.

As always, the last 5km of the day seemed to be the hardest and I was dog-tired when I shrugged off my rucksack at *Albergue Sansol*. I showered, changed and sat outside with a beer in the little walled garden that had a small Romanesque pool for soaking tired feet.

I was in need of some time alone and after a while I called my boys, Alexander and Joss, and then spoke to Connie, who was working through the last couple of weeks of a ski season in Val d'Isere. Although she had loved much about her five months in the mountains, it hadn't all been bluebirds and après and there were times when she had been quite lonely. This gap year between school and university had been the first time that she and her twin brother had been apart and it had been hard for them. Sometimes they felt the separation like a physical ache and both had struggled to adjust to life as a one, not half of a whole. I had missed her terribly and was gently persuading her to join me here in Spain when her contract ended in the Alps. Although she was reluctant to commit herself, she wasn't ruling it out and this gave me a glimmer of hope.

At the pilgrim supper in the albergue, Dan the Canadian was sitting at the table next to us, talking with two Koreans. He looked as laid-back as ever, still taking it all in his stride.

'Hello, lovely ladies,' he said, hoping flattery would get him somewhere. 'That looks like a lot of wine you have there. If you have any left over, be sure and pass it this way.'

He underestimated us. We took our time and worked our way through the generous helpings of both food and wine, which made us surprisingly witty and a little mischievous. We persuaded Jenny to phone Finlay, Ali's son, pretending to be Ali, but speaking in Spanish. Finlay had his Spanish oral a couple of weeks later and Ali hoped he would have had no trouble understanding Jenny's impeccable Spanish.

In Spanish, Jenny said: 'Hello, Finlay darling. It's Mum. We are having a brilliant time and my Spanish is really coming on. I think I am almost bilingual now. How's the revision going?'

Silence from Finlay, who was never lost for words.

Then, to his credit, just moments later, he replied in Spanish, 'Good, good, how are your feet?'

She got away with it for a good few minutes but was rumbled when he asked a question about his granny. Smart boy. God, we're funny after two bottles of wine.

The next day would be Jenny's last on the Camino, but we had become such a comfortable trio that we really didn't want to think about that. I would miss her, and not just because she was so good at reading maps. Sometimes the three of us walked together, sometimes Ali with Jenny, sometimes Jenny with me, sometimes Ali with me, and sometimes we walked alone. The rhythm seemed natural and right. We'd laugh, talk, and put the world to rights but we were just as contented with silence, listening to the cuckoo who had been following us for days, and the water warbling in the streams.

Day 6
14th April
Estella – Sansol
Kari, Ali, Jenny
Tonight, this dorm is anything but silent! In pitch darkness we stumbled to our beds at the very back of the huge attic and fumbled through our rucksacks to find our wash bags. Now that I am in bed I'm not sure why we were so worried about keeping the noise down as the snoring is deafening – it's like sleeping in a train station.
For the second time in two nights, we are the last three people to go to bed but much as we would like to think of ourselves as the wild ones, it is still only 10pm. I say bed, but I am actually sleeping on two benches that have been pushed together, under a giant mural of St James. I am surrounded by snoring men and the noise is so loud that I have got the giggles a couple of times and have taken a recording on my phone.
I will have to fumble some more to get my earplugs.

CHAPTER 8

The *Albergue Sansol* with its beamed ceilings and whitewashed plaster was not without charm, but the dorm was packed full, and the snores continued to compete throughout the night like some testosterone-fuelled riff-off. When our alarms went off it was still completely dark and dressing was a real challenge, so I left packing my bags until after breakfast and headed downstairs, without my glasses.

As we were eating a fellow pilgrim came running into the breakfast room. 'Come, come, it's beautiful,' she said, and I ran out into the street in my socks. As the golden sun surged over the horizon, orange light flooded the narrow street and the valley beyond, firing rods of light across the mountaintops. Glasses or no glasses, I watched in wonder as the shafts sliced through the street where I stood until the whole sky was ablaze. When I finally turned back towards breakfast my leggy shadow stretched right up the street in front of me, some 50m long. In the albergue, Jenny and Ali carried on with their breakfast of coffee and crusty bread.

'It's a bit early for ecstasy,' said Ali, unimpressed by my enthusiasm. 'I'm more of an afternoon person, myself.'

We set off slightly later than usual as it took me a while to find my specs, but it was a shorter walk of only 24km, and we were all grateful for that. Ali's feet were in bad shape and she was well taped up. Although I had no blisters, my feet felt pounded and bruised and we were both relieved that the following day would be one of rest.

Despite our later start, it was still early when we walked through Torres Del Rio and down through a ravine to cross the Rio Cornava. The next long stint through the valley clearly took us into wine territory and the vineyards stretched out as far as the eyes could see. At this stage in the year the vines looked like twisted roots, gnarled and prehistoric. Planted row upon row, in the dry, red earth, it could have been a set for a sci-fi film. In amongst the vines, ancient beehive-shaped huts lay empty, and we wondered if these were still manned at night, by guards protecting the precious crops.

Reaching Viana at about midday, our first stop was the church. Inside we cooled off in the darkness and listened to *Panis Angelicus* surrounded by thousands of cherubs who brought Ali's curly haired son, Finlay, to mind. The German ladies who gave Ali the magic medicine were also inside the church: we often seemed to arrive at our lunch spot at the same time as them. They had walked over 2,000 miles in the last seven years, three weeks per year, and although we hadn't spoken much, we smiled and waved and kept each other going.

I noticed one of them sitting quietly, weeping as the music played in the church. Although the ornate decoration did nothing to stir the soul there was something invisible that seemed to touch us all. Often on this pilgrimage, I found myself moved for no particular reason, as if something deeper than my conscious thought was being stirred. Words seemed redundant and there was nothing for it but to be still, and feel.

We had our passports stamped beneath a poster for Radio Maria then sat in the square with our coffees while Ali tended to her now whopping blisters.

'For one not known for showing much flesh, you're certainly getting comfortable flashing your bod in public,' I said.

'This could be the beginning of a whole new me,' she answered. 'North Queensferry won't know where to look.'

Fully dressed once again we took a stroll around the town.

From the ruins of San Pedro we could see right across the valley to where we were headed – Logroño. This was our last stop in Navarre and we were looking forward to Rioja and all that it promised. Rich, red and fruity.

Later on, beside the Virgin of the Caves, we stopped in a meadow for lunch and stretched out in the sunshine for a while. I felt content, happy to have found a rhythm for our days, which combined the strenuous with the leisurely and relaxed. Now that she had a taste for it, Ali flashed a little more of her body, stripping off her merino base layer and giving a passing pilgrim more of an eyeful than he had bargained for.

'Ooh! It's the Madonna with the big boobies,' I said.

'More like the wicked witch of the Way,' she replied, pulling on her T-shirt. Apparently witches' covens met here in the 16th Century and the irony was not lost on us. We made ourselves at home. Our bread and jamon tasted good and Jenny filled the water bottles from the crystal-clear fountain.

She had a book that quoted a pilgrim from the 12th Century who complained that the day's route was very 'up and down'. Nine hundred years on, we could see his point.

The weather stayed glorious but the last stretch into the province of La Rioja was long and hot. The flowers did their best to keep up our spirits and eventually we arrived at Felisa's gatekeeper's stand where the eponymous Felisa's daughter now stamps passports and offers pilgrims metaphorical water, figs and love. To be honest, at this stage of the walk, metaphor wasn't really doing it for me and it was the literal prospect of an ice-cold drink that provided the incentive to power me through those last 4km.

After a bit of searching, and restorative cold lemonade (Ali went straight for the beer), we found an albergue in the slightly dodgy old Jewish quarter. Since the next day was going to be a day off Ali and I decided to treat ourselves and booked a room.

The sight of our two single beds with sheets and pillows made me clap with pleasure and I flopped on the bed, whooping for joy. Then, with wanton abandon we spread the contents of our rucksacks around the room before showering and changing into fresh clothes.

'Right, I don't know about you, but my mother didn't bring me up to be a quitter. There are churros out there, and we need to find them before this one abandons us,' Ali said, pointing at Jenny.

We didn't have to go far. On the tree-lined avenue, just round the corner from our albergue, we found a street café that sold the doughnutty sticks, freshly fried, and with a pot of thick chocolate dip. They were worth the seven-day wait.

Right in the heart of wine country, Logroño, the capital of the province of La Rioja, is a gastro paradise. Grouped together are four narrow streets, famous for *pintxos*, the little Basque tapas. Some specialise in only one dish. There is THE place for patatas bravas, THE place for squid, and THE place for mushrooms. It also seemed to be the hen and stag capital of Spain and by six o'clock the streets were full of parties of people dressed variously as animals, superheroes and cartoon characters. But we were in no mood to party and spent a rather mournful last meal with Jenny, reluctant to let her go back to Scotland.

One last time she took us to a winning restaurant and talked us through her golden rules.

'I hereby name Kari, The Keeper of the Kitty. Breakfast ordering will also fall to you. All other translation and language tasks shall fall to Ali, who is frankly much more of a natural in the parlez department.' And with that she passed me the sandwich bag, kissed us and left, satisfied that she had taught us all she could. We watched as her tall, purposeful figure headed off in the direction of the bus station for what would be an epic journey back to Scotland.

She was heading back to work, and as I waved goodbye, I thought, not for the first time, that my decision to resign had been the right one. For the next 14 weeks Jenny would not surface. When I was a housemistress, I barely left the remote, rural campus. I sometimes made it as far as Tesco, but usually that was to buy birthday cakes and weekend supplies for the girls. Otherwise I was on site and responsible, 24 hours a day, seven days a week.

There had been no mobile phone reception at the school, and friends and family quickly decided that in term time I was the human equivalent of a no-fly zone. The last thing I did at night and the first thing I did in the morning had been to check my emails. Parents sent emails at 2am. They saw nothing wrong with phoning at 11pm. Or 6.30am. And they always expected an immediate response. My first duty was to get the girls out of bed and off to breakfast, and my last duty of the day – at about 11.45pm – was to make sure that everyone was settled and the lights were off. In between those hours (and often after) anything could happen and often did.

It was not unusual to return from lessons to find a parent sitting in my kitchen (sometimes they had even made themselves a cup of tea). One evening, about 11.30pm, a mother wandered into our sitting room to let me know she had just dropped her daughter back. Thankfully David and I weren't shagging on the sofa.

The responsibility that parents handed to me, to know each of those 65 girls as they did, to monitor their moods and their eating, their periods and their relationships, their homework and their friendships, gradually crushed me. I hadn't even noticed it happening. I so wanted to be worthy of their trust but it left no space for anything else.

Alexander would call from university and I would say, 'I really want to talk to you. I miss you. I want to hear your news. But I have a girl who needs to speak to me now. Can I call you back?'

And he would say, 'No problem Mum,' because he is kind, and he understood. But he needed me too, and, often-as-not, I would forget to call back. In the night I would wake with a jolt and remember that I had let him down. Again.

Connie would sit down to supper, a supper thrown together between the end of lessons at 6pm and the start of prep at

7.15pm, and start to tell me about her day, or an essay that she was working on, and a girl would put her head around the door and shout, 'Mrs. G. There's a problem.' And Connie would look at me with her big eyes, and her mouth pulled up in the corner, willing me to say, 'I'm just having my supper. I'll be with you in half an hour.' But I never did. I was working on the 'What if…' principle and I always jumped straight to catastrophe.

Looking back, I had spent those years consumed by guilt and anxiety. Guilty that I was never doing enough. That I could never do enough. I could barely mother my own three children in these circumstances. How could I possibly mother another 65 at the same time? Anxious that I would miss something crucial. Miss the child who was underachieving. The child who wasn't eating. The child who was being bullied. The child who was quietly suicidal. Of course, I spotted plenty. I was good at my job. I helped girls to achieve their potential and follow their dreams. I helped them through bereavement and divorce, relationship break-ups and depression, but I missed some too. And the misses never left me. Would never leave me.

Jenny and I had barely spoken about school while we walked. But I knew she was heading back into the thick of it and the familiar surge of adrenaline gripped my stomach when I thought about what she would face. I thought about poisonous emails from parents who were looking for someone to blame, and fire alarms and bells, and lists. So many lists.

Here on the Camino, Jenny had been a touchstone. While she was with us I felt secure. She knew what she was doing, what was right and true, and walking back to our albergue as a duo, I felt suddenly vulnerable. Jenny was the person who made me believe I could do this and I wished she could have stayed.

'One thing's for sure, there will be far fewer eavesdropping opportunities now that she's gone,' Ali said quietly.

When we got back to the albergue the little kitchen was lit with lamps and three Spanish men were sitting on the sofa. One of them was playing the guitar. Two Americans, university professors from the West Coast, were sharing a bottle of wine at the table.

'We bought this wine skin last year,' one of them said, holding it up. 'We fill it up every morning and it spurs us on.'

Perhaps not a tactic I would be adopting as the wine just made me want to sleep. 'What I want most in the world is a cup of tea,' I said. 'If only there was some milk.'

Enrico, the boss-eyed hospitalero, who had seemed a little distracted when we arrived, jumped on his moped and bombed off to pick up some milk from his own home so that we could have a cup of tea before bed.

'I like this place,' I told Ali as we settled into our single beds. 'I think we will be OK, just the two of us.'

'Me too,' she said. 'Mmmm… sheets.'

Day 7
15th April
Sansol – Logroño
Kari, Ali, Jenny
Today, we made it to Logroño, the first of the cities we pass through on our way to Santiago. Arriving here meant it was time to say goodbye to Jenny who has been the best of guides, the best of interpreters and the best of friends. We will miss her.
We have covered 189km in seven days and are almost a quarter of the way in so we have rewarded ourselves with a private room. It feels like heaven to be lying between clean sheets in a room with no snorers. Everything hurts but we are happy. Happy, and looking forward to a day of rest tomorrow.

CHAPTER 9

The revellers of Logroño partied well into the night, the noise of merrymaking finally giving way to the sound of bells at dawn. We could see the church tower and the bell from our window and we could feel the reverberations in our bones. My legs had started to twitch in the night and Ali told me hers were doing the same. I think our muscles were in shock.

It felt like such a treat to leave our rucksacks unpacked and we took our time getting ready. Our tiny room with its two single beds and small chair had space to spread out our belongings and to reorganise our dry bags. Seven nights in and we had got used to the confines of the albergues. Whether you are on the top or the bottom, bunk beds mean that you are permanently bent over, sorting while you sit on a bed. Bottom bunks are dark but have the advantage of the floor for extra storage. Top bunks have more light but things fall off in the night and, worse still, if you need to go to the loo, you risk standing on the person below you. Jenny, being the lithe and agile one, always opted for the top bunk. Ali, on the other hand, a closet diva, would only take a top bunk if there were no other option. I liked to mix it up a little.

In our twin-bedded room, enjoying the space, I was waltzing about with carefree abandon and stubbed my toe on the chair. Within minutes it was blue and looking very unhappy. I am a world-class klutz and over the years it has been my poor toes that have suffered the most from my total lack of coordination.

Ali looked at it with her serious medical face on. 'I don't

want to alarm you,' she said, instantly alarming me, 'but I think you've broken it.' She made me lie back down on the bed and raise my foot on the pillows.

A broken toe might put a serious dampener on our plans to reach Santiago but rather than worry about it, I concentrated on willing my toe better. Despite some serious eye-rolling from Ali, Patsy's oil of chrism was applied and healing prayers were said over my puffy, blue, chipolata of a toe. We gave it an hour or so, but the call of coffee was strong so I limped out to the café where we had found our churros yesterday afternoon. Like many places, they offered a pilgrim breakfast of white, crusty bread, served with olive oil and a fresh paste made from tomatoes and a little garlic. Sprinkled with salt it tasted wonderful and with a cup of coffee and a freshly squeezed orange juice it had fast become my favourite way to start the day.

The weather was overcast, and we were hoping it would stay dry, as we were both in our still unseasonal flip-flops. Although the pain in my toe was fading, there was no way I was prepared to put my feet in boots again that day.

Ali had done a bit of research and discovered, to her delight, that Logroño had a municipal swimming pool with a spa. Enrico, the hospitalero, pointed it out on the map and after a bit of grumbling about the fact that we were on our feet again, we set off to walk the couple of kilometres to the pool. Somehow, despite the flip-flops and the toe, it just didn't feel right to take a bus.

The Spanish take their hydrotherapy seriously and we discovered locals aged 2 to 92 taking the waters. For just a few euros, the facilities rivalled the best luxury spas back home and we were soon looking forward to working our way round a circuit of water treatments.

'Put this band round your wrist and show it to the... em... Baywatch men at the pool,' said the girl at the desk, who was struggling to find the right English words.

'I can hardly wait,' I winked.

I'm not going to lie, the lifeguards were a bit of a

disappointment but the spa more than met our expectations. We bubbled, steamed and stretched, the water pummelling the knots in our necks and shoulders and soothing the soles of our poor, poor feet.

When I first imagined the Camino I pictured myself walking alone. Not because I wanted it that way, just because I didn't think anyone else would be mad enough to join me for five weeks.

Ali and I had known each other since our boys, my Joss and her Saunders, had teamed up in primary school. We, and they, had been friends ever since. It was Ali who listened when I reached breaking point at work, and she who helped me to see that there were choices to be made. When I moved back to Edinburgh, we walked together a couple of times a week and I planted the idea of the Camino, feeding it and watering it as we went. It didn't take long for her to agree to a week, and then two weeks, and as we grew fitter her resistance weakened. We came to know Edinburgh like the back of our hands and walked the Fife Coastal Path, the Water of Leith, the Pentlands, and the John Muir Way. Eventually I broke down her resistance and she was hooked.

'I'm in,' she told me just before Christmas, 'and I'm coming all the way.' But like a rock star she came with a rider. She was not really a demanding sort, but she liked her home comforts. High on the list was finding a jacuzzi and a sauna so that we could soak away the pain on our days off.

It was gone 2.30pm by the time we finally dragged ourselves out of the water; bad timing as Logroño shuts down on a Saturday afternoon and we were a bit too late for lunch. All the inviting cafés we had passed on our way to the pool were closed and the only place we could find was a seedy bar where old men with trousers belted just below their armpits were drinking Rioja at the counter.

The waitress looked pleased to see us.

'I recommend the goat's cheese salad,' she said. 'One will be enough. You can share.' She was right. It was enormous. Toasted walnuts, a warm glaze and about half a kilo of goat's cheese was delicious, and more than enough for two.

After lunch, Ali was on the lookout for a pharmacy as her supply of tape, Compeed and ibuprofen was running low, but nothing was open so we headed back to the albergue. Reluctantly, we moved out of our little room and into the bunkroom downstairs.

We were sharing the dorm with a retired couple from Minnesota. They were both tall and lean, he greying and she well-coiffed. They were kitted out in high-tech gear but she was sporting a compression sock and had the other foot bandaged and raised on a chair. He introduced himself to us as Jerry but didn't tell us his wife's name. Between ourselves we called her Mrs. Jerry.

'She's not in shape and she fell on the gravel coming down from Alto del Perdon. She's sprained her ankle. We've had to take the bus since then.' He gestured at his wife, talking about Mrs. Jerry as if she wasn't there.

They had just come back from the hospital in Logroño where she had had it x-rayed to make sure it wasn't broken. Something about his tone made us want to take Mrs. Jerry under our wing.

It turned out they had spent a bit of time with PJ and Duncan (our nickname for the good-looking priests we met back in Roncesvalles) and at about 6pm they headed to the huge gothic cathedral where the priests were attending an ordination. Tempted as we were to see the hot priests in action, we opted for more secular pleasures and headed out for *pintxos* and wine. Well, when in Rioja…

The tapas bars in *Calle del Laurel* were tiny and in most there was standing room only. The counters were covered in trays of pintxos – tiny portions of food presented either on bread or on a stick. There seemed to be rivalry between establishments to see who could produce the most spectacular gastronomic displays. We were tempted by shards of Serrano ham, triangles of Manchego cheese, skewers of croquettas filled with ham or fish, and little glasses with cold soups, but we settled for a bowl of fish stew and some calamari bravas (our new favourite).

Once again, the waitress took a shine to us, perhaps spotting that we didn't quite belong in this city of revellers. 'I ask the cook to make you something special,' she said, and the aproned woman in the hot kitchen waved at us from the other side of the pass. A while later she presented us with two bowls of a milk pudding that looked a bit like custard.

'Oh no,' whispered Ali. 'Custard makes me gag. What will I do?' Hiding it in her napkin was not an option so she pretended to eat until the cook turned her back. Then, surreptitiously, we swapped bowls. I finished hers too, and the big Spanish Momia smiled at the empty plates and gave us encouraging nods. She was looking after us and I felt warm and glowy inside.

The day felt like a normal day on a normal holiday. One where you treat yourself to something indulgent, wander around and eat ice cream. We walked back slowly, window-shopping, laughing. The sombrerero had a double-fronted display of men's hats and in the underwear shop stuffed bras that must have been there since the 50s were pinned up alongside y-fronts big enough to keep an elephant tidy. By the time we were back at the albergue and ready for bed, the partygoers of Logroño were just getting started.

Day 8
16th April
Rest Day – Logroño
Sitting in the bubbles soothed all our aches away. Despite a suspected broken toe (mine) we have had a restful day in Logroño. No singing Spaniards inside the albergue tonight, apparently they are all on the streets outside our window. Jerry and Mrs. Jerry got back before us and Jerry is already snoring at full volume. Funny really, as he already warned us that 'she' is a snorer.

CHAPTER 10

Our day off did us good. With the exception of my toe, which had turned a right royal purple, my bones felt better when I got out of bed that morning. Ali was ready in record time and, rested and recharged, she had a spring in her step. Jerry and Mrs. Jerry were up early and had left us the remnants of a large box of cereal and a tray of strawberries, which made a pleasant change from bread.

'Do you think they have been carrying this box around with them?' I asked Ali.

'Well, I suppose it's easier to carry your shopping if you've been travelling by bus,' came the reply. Her irritation at the '*touregrinos*' was starting to grow.

The noise of last night left us in no doubt that Logroño was a city which liked to party, and on the way out of town we inadvertently stumbled into the morning after the night before. Two men followed us down a quiet lane and for the first time we felt uneasy.

'Do you think this might be time to put Joss's self-defence lessons to use?' said Ali in a low voice.

My younger son, Joss, had been worried about the trip, sure that two sturdy, middle-aged women might be plagued by unwanted male attention. I hadn't known whether to be flattered or indignant. But Ali and I had come up with a more verbal self-defence tactic of our own.

I swung around. 'Piss off, Pedro,' I hissed at our stalkers and, deflated, they turned tail.

'Impressive,' said Ali. 'Shame you didn't get the chance to

show them your moves.'

A seedy fog lingered and we were keen to get out of town. Walking fast up a narrow street, we held our breath when a white Transit van hurtled between the parked cars on one side and us on the other. His wing mirror caught my shoulder at a fair speed, leaving me shaken and nervy. Revellers lay strewn in doorways and when I went into the foyer of a bank to get some cash, bodies littered the floor.

'It's like *Night of the Living Dead* round here,' Ali said.

I tried not to show how uncomfortable I was feeling, but Ali must have felt the same as, without saying anything further, we stepped up the pace. Within an hour we had reached the *Parque de la Grajera,* an expansive nature reserve, where finally we slowed down, relieved to have left Gomorrah behind us. The Way took us through pinewoods and past a lake, the still water soothing my anxiety.

My toe was bearing up well but when a café appeared at the side of the lake, it seemed a good opportunity to stop. A quick check on the mileage showed us that we had just crossed the 200km mark and we did a little happy dance to celebrate. Down by the lake we took a selfie and sent messages to David and Guy so that they could share the moment. Though I hadn't spoken to him, I could hear David's voice in my head telling me he was proud, that I was doing well.

'You're a superstar, Devs (a nickname that has stuck since university), keep going!' it said.

My critical inner voice is all mine; my encouraging inner voice sounds just like him.

The café had an old-fashioned bar-football table and tiny tin men in stripy red and blue tops were facing tiny tin men all in white. Barcelona v Tottenham. The little men were chipped and worn, but it had a vintage charm that took me straight back to my first term at Oxford. I had fallen for David as I watched him play table-football in the beer cellar. I could still see him leaning over the table in his 501s, black polo neck and Chelsea boots, long fringe covering one lens of his little round glasses. I was 18 when we met, in my first week at university. I was an impressionable fresher and he a worldly wise second year, or at least that's what he thought. For the next two years we barely spent a night apart and it felt good to remember those days, and us, before life took over.

As Ali and I drank our coffee, Jerry and Mrs. Jerry arrived and while he ordered, we chatted to Mrs. Jerry. It turned out, away from him, she had quite a bit to say for herself. Two weeks earlier she had retired after 30 years in the same job, and just two days later they had flown to Spain. She hadn't had much time to join Jerry on his training walks and she clearly felt she was holding him up.

'We don't go very quickly,' I said. 'Why don't you walk with us for a while? Jerry could wait for you in Navarrete. That's only 7km or so.' She seemed keen.

'Oh no,' said Jerry, who overheard us on his way back to the table. 'It'd be better if she stuck with me. She's not a great walker and I don't want her to hold you up.'

We left them to finish their coffee and carried on uphill to Alto de la Grajera. Before long the silhouette of a giant bull, the symbol of Rioja, appeared on the hill ahead of us. There was no way a person could forget they were in wine country round here.

Walking through miles and miles of vineyards we became quite the amateur viticulturists and noticed that while most fields were planted regularly, others seemed more haphazard. Some of the vines were coming into leaf but the majority were still in their dormant winter state. They reminded us of the mandrake roots in Harry Potter and we decided that if we pulled one out of the ground the screams would reverberate around the valley.

'The cry of the mandrake is fatal to anyone who hears it,' said Ali, doing a fine impression of Hermione Granger. 'You'd better put your fingers in your ears.' And since there was no one for miles around she ran into the field and pretended to pull up a vine while I giggled helplessly on the side of the road. It'd been years since I had last been this silly and it felt good to be playing like children, our sensible heads for once, left to one side. I felt free and unshackled, with no one and nothing to bother about but our walk, our meals and where we would sleep that night.

A few miles on we started to think about lunch.

'I wish we had a knife,' I said. 'I really feel like a tomato and my spork is just not cutting it.'

'Boom, boom,' said Ali, rolling her eyes.

In Navarrete we picked up some food from a grocery shop, including the desired tomato. But we didn't linger, deciding to push on to the next town before taking a break.

At points today, the path edged close to the busy N120 so when a sign for a detour appeared, promising 'a kilometre of art,' I persuaded Ali that we should take it, to get us away from the noise of the traffic. The art, however, was difficult to spot. We stopped to consider whether a bit of artily stacked rubbish might be a sculpture of some sort, but that was as close as we came to a cultural experience. By then, Ali was cursing me as even without the detour this was a long walk.

'And I'm not the one with the broken toe,' she pointed out.

'Look!' I said. 'The Camino has provided.' There, right in the middle of the path, just waiting for us to take this detour and find it, lay a classic Victorinox tomato knife, serrated, clean and orange handled. Our tomato would be sliced after all.

I smiled to myself, thinking that as gifts from God go, a knife might seem somewhat unspectacular. But I was opening my mind to all sorts of mystical possibilities and if God wanted to give us a little practical help I was a willing recipient of His grace. I opted not to share my thoughts with Ali, but even she was impressed by the find.

The next town wasn't much to write home about and Navarrete would have been a much prettier lunch spot, but we were happy. And we had a knife.

We found a bench on a side street behind a rather bland housing estate and never had a tomato tasted so good. There is a truth in the adage 'hunger is the best kitchen' but somehow the food on the Way just tasted so much better.

Bread, tomato, salami and a banana and we felt as if we had eaten like queens.

'I do like a firm banana,' sighed Ali, not for the first time, and she wasn't disappointed that today.

While we ate, three little boys emerged with sticks: brothers in matching green hand-knitted jumpers and purple trousers, and a mean boy who was clearly harbouring a grudge. They looked as though they had endured a long Sunday lunch and had finally been let down from the table while the grown-ups finished their wine.

They ran up and down the street shouting like savages, the mean boy hitting the smallest one on the head with his stick. The wee man, undaunted, roared back at him, giving as good as he got, as his big brother remained staunchly oblivious to his plight. The look of furious indignation on his face was priceless. Ali and I were torn between staging an intervention and enjoying the free entertainment.

The last stage of this big, 31km walk, was a killer. By now my toe was pulsating and my shoulders crying out to be released from under the rucksack.

'OK, this calls for a distraction technique. For one day only, singing will be permitted,' said Ali, knowing there was only a short window before I had a melt-down.

With no one around for miles, we sang with gusto. Spontaneous bursts of *Men of Harlech* and *Heart of Oak* roused our fighting spirit. David liked a bit of history and had suggested we pass the time by playing 'Wellington and Napoleon'. This was a game all of his own invention, created to entertain the children when we dragged them on hillwalks. The rules were known only to him but it seemed to consist mostly of hiding in hedgerows and leaping out at unsuspecting family members crying, 'Ambush!' Jenny had vetoed the game early on, but the songs would have made David happy if he could have heard us.

When we felt we could go no further without one, we ate the last of the liquorice toffees, savouring every last bit.

Careful sampling in a sweetie shop in Logroño had resulted in the purchase of eight sweeties. They were usually sold by the kilo so the shopkeeper was not impressed, but Ali only wanted enough to tide us over until our friend, Tinker, arrived with emergency rations in four days' time. He tried to shake in a few more, but she was adamant. She wanted eight. One each for four days.

'No one could ever accuse you of being wasteful,' I said, wishing I could eat a whole bag of liquorice toffees in one go and sit surrounded by wrappers sticking my tongue out at her.

By the time we finally arrived in Nájera I couldn't have cared less what it looked like or what its history was. All I wanted to do was take my boots off. If someone had told me that Napoleon, the Knights Templar and the Duke of Wellington himself were having a giant orgy on the medieval bridge I would have replied, 'That's nice, dear,' and walked on.

In our albergue, *Puerta de Nájera,* the beer in the vending machine was cheaper than the water and the showers were hot. And that was enough.

Once we had showered and changed Ali lay on her bunk and shut her eyes and I went down to the sitting room to watch the pilgrims arrive. Joorst, the cheerful Dutchman and his less cheerful wife fell in through the doors. His voice was so loud you couldn't miss him. He called his wife his 'better half' and he was beginning to grate on my nerves. They seemed to have teamed up with Sara, the Curvy German, and Lara her little friend, who arrived half an hour after them, taking it slow and steady.

'The race is not to the swift,' Sara called out to Joorst.

When Ali came downstairs we decided that after all the itty, bitty morsels we had scoffed in Logroño, we felt like a proper meal. We hadn't forgotten Jenny's advice, but the rain was pelting down so we ran to the first place we saw and flagrantly disregarded golden rule number two – *avoid places where there are pictures on the menu.* Jenny would not have been surprised to discover that the food was decidedly average, but a big bowl of pasta was just what we needed so we weren't complaining.

Much as we missed Jenny, it was fine to be just the two of us. I understood Ali. The things she didn't say were often just as telling as the things she said. And she knew me just as well. Now that it was just us, I felt completely unguarded, as if I was with family. A bit of me had wanted to impress Jenny, to show her that I was fitter and faster than I had been before. There was something to prove. Now that it was just us, we were finding our own pace.

Day 9
17th April
Logroño – Nájera
Kari, Ali
It was a long haul today but the miraculous discovery of a tomato knife gave us a much-needed boost. My purple toe is throbbing, but when it's laced up in my boot, it's quite secure. Our dorm is small and I am hoping for a quiet night. We are missing Jenny today but, if we could just draw a veil over the dinner, I think she would have been pleased that we had found our way by orienting the map to the ground and topped that off by asking for two beds in Spanish.
Oh, and one more thing… A man (albeit a very old man) called us 'chicas guapas, peregrinas guapas' today and I didn't need Google Translate for that one. Take that, girl who called us pensioners.

CHAPTER 11

It was early afternoon when we arrived in Santo Domingo de la Calzada. The walk had been a short one, just 21km, so we spent a lazy afternoon with our feet up in the sunshine in the pretty garden of an albergue run by the Spanish Confraternity of Saint James.

The previous night, Kathleen, an Irish woman in her 30s, had joined us in our small dorm. 'I've been looking for a blanket, but there are none to be found,' she said. 'I sent my sleeping bag home last week 'cause my pack was way too heavy. There's been blankets everywhere else, but it looks like I'll be sleeping in my clothes tonight.' I had noticed that chat about bedbugs was beginning to hot up, and was glad it wasn't me sleeping on a bare mattress.

As we sat in the garden that afternoon, the man next to us stripped off and his friends examined him for evidence of bites. Ali regarded me with narrowed eyes. She had been horrified to read that bedbugs might be a feature of the Camino, and I had done my best to reassure her that our walk would be bug free. 'Apparently the German word for bedbug is 'bedbug',' she said through pursed lips.

'I'll be sure to let Jenny know,' I replied, not raising a smile.

That morning, the self-same vending machine that had served us such fine beer, delivered the worst cup of coffee we had had so far. It's astonishing how dispiriting a disappointing cup of coffee can be. Muttering, we left the ancient capital of Navarre at dawn. I don't do well without food and I found myself struggling to be cheerful when all I could think about was sustenance. Ali sensed my struggle but knowing better than to try to distract me out of that one, she kept quiet and left me to it.

Nájera butts up against red, red cliffs and in the glorious light of the sunrise the medieval streets seemed to radiate warmth. This was an illusion: the morning in fact was so cold we could see our breath and my thumbs throbbed as they gripped the tops of my walking poles.

'I wish I hadn't sent my gloves and hat back with Jenny,' I whinged as I waited for my central heating system to kick in. Ali would never part with her gloves. She wore them to bed in August back home in Edinburgh. Even with them, it was lunchtime before she warmed up.

The Way took us past the Royal Pantheon where the Kings and Queens of Navarre were buried, straight into the *zona natural*. At first, pine trees lined the deep, red pathway but these soon made way for miles of vineyards in a wide flat landscape that took us all the way to Azofra.

I was still smarting about the vending machine so when we reached the village Ali suggested we stop for a decent coffee to erase the memory. 'And why don't we have one of these giant pastries?' she said, in placatory tones. 'I think it will make you feel much better.' She was right, it did. And later we were glad we had stopped as this was remote, agricultural territory and there wasn't another café until we reached Santo Domingo.

We had planned to stop for lunch about two-thirds of the way in, but Ciruena turned out to be a ghost town. Devastated by the recession that had hit rural Spain particularly hard, hundreds of modern houses stood empty with the shutters down, the grass in the gardens grown high. *'En Venta'* signs plastered the windows and an eerie stillness seemed to have becalmed the town. We passed playgrounds, where the swings groaned quietly in the wind, and the slides stood unused. But there was no sign of life at all – not even the ubiquitous *abuela* with her wheelie shopping basket.

Ali raised her eyebrows. 'I don't like this place at all.'

'OK, Scooby, let's split,' I said. And with our imaginations getting the better of us we ran out of the town without looking back at the army of zombies that was chasing us.

Tall wooden waymarkers, which counted down to Santiago, appeared on the path-side in this stretch of the Way, and we found it satisfying to spot them and tick off the kilometres.

'Another one bites the dust,' I sang, feeling more cheerful since the pastry.

This was a gentle walk and we were not dazzled by the views or delighted by the villages we passed through. Instead, we found an easy, relaxed rhythm that suited us very nicely, and I felt as if we had moved beyond the excitement of the first stage of the walk, onto a different level where a calmness had settled.

The following day we would be skirting along the roadside and we were expecting it to be noisy, so in preparation, we experimented with iPods and earphones. It's certainly a different experience walking with noise in your head and Ali began listening to *Game of Thrones* on audiobook, while I had a bit of a boogie to Dolly Parton and a bit of a cry to Johnny Cash. On the whole, I didn't enjoy the distraction. When you walk without earphones you hear the birds and the water and there is room in your head for your thoughts, but maybe tomorrow I would be glad of the noise.

We were hoping to stay with the Cistercian nuns in Santo Domingo but there was no sign of them when we arrived at the convent. We shirked off our rucksacks in a café nearby and ordered a salad and some tortilla while we consulted our guidebook and came up with a Plan B.

And Plan B – the municipal albergue – turned out to be pretty comfortable. Although the dorm was a bit of a pilgrim squash, the communal spaces gave us room to stretch out and relax. In the garden we ran into the small lady with the elegant scarf, whom we had met back in Pamplona and Puente la Reina. Her name, it turned out, was Jean and she chatted to us while she did her washing in the big outdoor sink.

'Is your husband staying here too?' I asked.

'Oh, I'm not married,' she laughed. 'I just met Richard and Bernard in Saint Jean. Which one of them did you think was my husband? They were just too fast for me. I was almost on my knees by the time we got to Los Arcos and I asked myself, Jean, what are you trying to prove? This is not a race to the finish.' She had a gentle east coast American accent and there was a warmth about her that immediately made me feel like her friend. Her big brown eyes were shining like chestnuts as she wrung out her laundry with her quick little hands. 'It was a tough decision to leave them. I felt we had become good friends in that week, but I told them it was time for us to say our goodbyes. Bernard went home when he got to Logroño and Richard is already in Burgos. He's really pushing himself.'

She told us that Richard was Canadian, but she was from Boston, like our friend Lynne who would be joining us soon. Jean had been walking alone for a couple of days, but she had made lots of buddies along the Way and seemed comfortable with her own company.

'It has been my dream to walk the Camino for the last ten years, but things just kept happening that made me put it off. Now, I'm finally here.'

She told us about her father, who had died recently, having survived a stroke that had left him severely disabled for a number of years. She ran a food bank in the Boston area, one of the largest in the world, and seemed utterly committed to her work.

'I didn't grow up wealthy,' she said. 'But we always had enough and every night we sat down to a family meal. When I finished university I worked abroad with an aid agency and I thought International Development would be my life. But when I realised that there were people going hungry in my own country, I felt a tremendous sense of responsibility and knew I had to channel my energy there first. America is one of the wealthiest countries in the world, but the level of inequality is enormous, and I felt I had to help those who didn't have the voice, or the strength to help themselves.'

I felt humbled by Jean's sincerity, by her openness, and for a moment I saw a glimpse of the person I had been. The person I wanted to recover. Perhaps it was an effort at self-preservation, or maybe I had to protect myself from the slingshots, but in my last year at the school, I had put up my defences, battened down the hatches. I had retracted. And speaking to Jean I could see that now.

When our feet had recovered enough for us to do a bit of exploring, Ali and I headed out. We scouted out the tallest bell tower in Rioja, the cathedral and a dark, quiet chapel. Saint Dominic is the patron saint of pilgrims and in the town which bore his name he was everywhere in evidence. We had some fun sticking our head through the hole in a large wooden cut-out of him, in pilgrim garb, like the fat lady in the frilly swim-suit at the seaside, only browner, and in our case holding a chicken. Ali, in her mirror shades, brought the look bang up to date.

While I went into the chapel Ali chatted to a dog in the square. As I sat in the twilight interior I pictured the faces of my children, the touch of their skin. I imagined them in St Andrews, Val D'Isere and London, working in the library in sweatpants and stubble, ironing napkins into origami folds for clients with more money than sense, sitting in a café with friends talking Stella Adler and Pina Bausch. I sent kisses to the tops of their heads, hoped they were happy. *Thank God they have grown up interesting,* I thought.

Giving thanks felt important, but my thoughts drifted to things I could have done differently in my life, to conflict, and resentment, and wasted opportunities. There were still ripples in the calm I was finding on this journey. Still a long way to go. Perhaps atonement was a necessary element of the pilgrimage after all. And suddenly I felt a connection with those ancient pilgrims who had walked to seek forgiveness.

As I was leaving the church, I bumped into a gorgeous

young priest (think Il Divo) at the doorway. He smiled and switched on the lights, but before I could make my exit, 40 chattering children processed in, single-file, crisp packets in hand, for what I imagined was first communion preparation. I stood to one side while all 40 of them took turns to bless themselves with the holy water by the door, giggling and munching crisps all the while.

'I thought you'd got locked in there, you've been gone for so long,' said Ali, when I finally emerged into daylight.

Later, sitting outside in the sunshine, we ate the best dinner yet. A local cannelloni made with stuffed red peppers instead of pasta followed a hearty bean and chorizo soup. We washed it all down with a bottle of Tempranillo from a vineyard that we had walked through earlier that afternoon. As we ate we worked on *The Times*, quick cryptic. David had sent us a photograph of the clues and we drew out the grid on the paper tablecloth. By the end of dinner the table looked like a scene from *A Beautiful Mind*. We didn't finish but we got pretty close; perhaps the Tempranillo helped.

Day 10
18th April
Nájera – Santo Domingo de la Calzada
Kari, Ali
Our dorm really is cramped and there are maybe 15 bunk beds in one fairly small room. There is no room to store anything and you have to jump over the rucksacks that fill the spaces between the bunks. A young French girl and her granny are in the beds next to us, so close I can hear their breathing from my top bunk.

'We are walking for one week every year until we reach Santiago,' the granddaughter tells us as Granny gets into bed in her men's striped flannel pyjamas. A German couple that, rather infuriatingly, walk hand in hand, are here, and I am trying to be nice, as is Joorst, the cheerful Dutchman, whose guffaw is getting right on my nerves. A multitude of students from America, Slovenia, Hungary, Australia, Germany, Romania and Italy are having a party in the communal kitchen, and Jean is right in the midst of them, making friends. You don't need

television for entertainment; pilgrim watching is much more fun and like a couple of old crones Ali and I like speculating about the burgeoning romances.

CHAPTER 12

Ali and I were up before most of the crowded dormitory had started to stir. My platypus water system had leaked all over the floor and as I mopped it up, a good-looking young man from Brazil whispered a heartfelt goodbye to Ainslie, a 20-year-old from Nova Scotia. She had been keeping pace with us on and off since Saint Jean, and was one of the 'Camino Kids'. Looking on from his top bunk was Tim, a round, bearded Australian, in a dirty vest.

'I'm here for you, Ainslie,' he said, though nobody heard but me.

Love triangle or no love triangle, we had 7km to go before breakfast and the day was a-wasting. The road out of Santo Domingo was flat and straight and this made for an easy start to the walk.

The ploughed fields to our right and left caught the early morning sun, the furrows radiating from the vanishing point like the grooves on our cockleshells. The road climbed a little as we approached Granon, and a sturdy wooden cross, Cruz de Los Valientes, stopped me in my tracks. My breath caught in my chest. Its heft stood out against the landscape that was pieced behind it in strips of greens. Day by day my sense of wonder was being reawakened and at times, I felt the beauty, like electricity, tingling through me.

When I was working, I used to enjoy watching the girls' sports fixtures. Hockey in the winter, then lacrosse, and tennis. One day I was out watching the hockey, chatting to a woman who was cheering on her niece. She was there with her own little girl who must have been about three. The wee one, perhaps inspired by her big cousin, was keen to play ball and I was rolling a hockey ball to her and she was kicking it back. It gets dark early in the winter months and we were starting to lose the light on what had been a rainy autumn afternoon. The sun broke through the clouds but the woman and I carried on watching the match and chatting. Suddenly the little girl let out a gasp and ran over to pull her mother's sleeve.

'Mummy, Mummy. Look at that. The sky is full of colours. There is pink and green and other colours too. Oh Mummy, look at it.'

A rainbow had appeared over the hills and the child was hopping with excitement as her mother knelt down to explain what it was.

She turned to me. 'Libby was born with cataracts in both eyes. She was blind until just two weeks ago. Her surgery has been completely successful and she is seeing things for the first time. I can hardly keep up with her excitement.'

I thought then, if only we could see the world as Libby did, new and freshly created, what a gift. It was a gift I felt I was now receiving.

Coffee in Granon was worth the wait and the chalkboard outside the café promised music. The young Peruvian woman, who single-handedly managed the café and the shop, remembered everyone's names and sang as she took the orders. The tiny café was full of pilgrims, and four dashing Frenchmen broke into a spontaneous rendition of *What a Wonderful World*, urging the rest of us to join in, conducting us with flamboyance. The pretty waitress flashed them her gorgeous smile and called them her 'peregrinos caballeros'. Life felt good. Simple and happy.

There, we caught up with Sara the Curvy German, and Lara her little friend. Sara was getting less curvy by the day and her determination was inspirational. Neither Ali nor I had thought she was going to make it beyond Logroño and she had certainly confounded us.

'Cigarettes and paracetamol,' she told us. 'The secret of my success.'

Grandmère et grandfille from last night's albergue nodded their hellos as they came into the café. Grandmère had been wearing her stripy pyjamas on top of her walking clothes so that she could make a quick, modest getaway this morning. When she walked she rarely raised her head and she was so stooped that she looked like a pilgrim's staff, but slowly and surely she was getting there, with her granddaughter by her side, walking at her pace – the women of the Way.

After the colourful start to the morning, the green, white and blue soon turned to grey as the fog set in just before lunchtime. Aware that today's walk would be a bit of a slog we assumed we would plug in and plug on. But the Way was gentle on us and we came upon old villages every couple of kilometres, making the time pass quickly. Lots of these little towns reminded me of the place in *The Godfather* where Michael Corleone flees after he kills McCluskey – the village where he meets Apollonia – and I pictured him walking with the goatherds and stopping for coffee and grappa in the bars. Spooky then, when we heard the Nino Rota theme music playing through an open window.

Often, as we walked, I stopped to take photographs. Nothing spectacular, mostly doors and windows. Ali walked on rather than waiting, but I loved the layers of faded paint on the thick wooden doors, peeling like the bark of a London plane tree, and couldn't seem to pass one without stopping. Most of the paintwork in this area was green, but that afternoon we passed through a village where the doors and shutters were cornflower blue and all along the street, paint cans, oil drums and buckets were painted in washed-out iterations of the same shade, all planted up with straggly geraniums. Ali was ahead of me and pointed at the doorways with her walking pole, just to be sure I didn't miss them.

We seemed to be the only people on the road for much of

the morning but as the fog came in we caught up with a woman who was walking on her own. Kathy began her pilgrimage in Le Puy and had been walking in stages over the last 15 years.

'We started walking when my daughter was about 13,' she said. 'But this time she and my husband are too busy with work, so I decided to go it alone.' I was amazed when told us she was almost 70 as her funky cropped hairstyle and nimble gait made her seem much younger. For the rest of the morning we had no need for podcasts or audio books. She told us stories of her wild days studying languages at Oxford in the 60s, and about working in Paraguay and travelling round South America in her 20s. She told us about returning from Brazil by boat, flying fish and all, and about her current quieter life in rural Oxfordshire.

She had researched the area and, clearly a woman passionate about food, she had earmarked *Restaurante León*, in Villamayor del Rio as a lunch stop. It was a funny place that seemed to offer either expensive speciality dishes or bocadillos (sandwiches), but nothing in between. She took her time asking the waiter about various local delicacies before ordering a chickpea stew with Morcilla – the famous blood sausage.

'We usually just make a cheese sandwich,' I said, feeling singularly unadventurous. There was a delicatessen at the back of the restaurant that sold local produce but the prices were exorbitant, so rather than picnic we opted to share a bocadillo and kept Kathy company while she tucked into her stew. I felt like a child eating from the kiddie menu and envying what was on the adults' plates. As we ate we were watched over by five instrument-playing cherubs who had been caged behind bars in a bizarre wall display.

Kathy joined us on the last challenging 5km into Belorado. Once the rain started, conversation was no longer an option. Worse than the rain was the thick fog that had settled, making it hard to stick together and to follow the waymarkers. I dawdled at the back and the gap between us widened until I could no longer see Ali and Kathy who had disappeared into the fog. Fearing my own terrible sense of direction I felt anxious and petulant about being left behind. The route ran alongside the infamous N-120, the busy motorway that crosses the North of Spain, and I reasoned with myself that as long as I kept the road to my right I couldn't go far wrong. I put on my headphones to drown out the noise from the lorries, but losing another of my senses only emphasised my feeling of dislocation and I soon switched them off. There was no pleasure in this walking. Eventually I escaped into the rhythm of my footfall and the strike of my poles, my breathing eased and I found a sense of calm. Ali and Kathy had waited for me at the next waymarker and we walked close together on the home stretch.

The rain had stopped by the time we reached the village of Belorado where there were a number of albergues to choose from. We headed for the Santa Maria, a *donativo* where pilgrims paid what they could afford or what they felt was appropriate.

In the doorway stood a longhaired Frenchman with more than a passing resemblance to the Jesus in my Children's Illustrated Bible. He was berating the Swiss hospitalera. 'What do you mean you don't speak Spanish? We are in Spain!' Speaking in fluent English, the hospitalera was trying to calm him down. There was nothing wrong with his English; for him this was sport and he was clearly in the mood for a showdown. Over his shoulder we could see that the albergue was dark and gloomy so when Stanley, a tall, bald Puerto Rican waded into the argument, we seized the opportunity and scarpered.

Down the road we plumped for the albergue, *Cuatro Canton,* and landed with our bums well and truly in the butter. A converted house, it was painted in warm, earthy colours and instead of dorms, there were bedrooms that were small and warm. The icing on the cake would have been an all-female bedroom, but instead we found two men comfortably settled into our room by the time we arrived. One was curled in a sleeping bag, talking on the phone, and the other sat on a top bunk, looking at a laptop.

'*Addio Mamma, addio Mamma, ti amo,*' said the small Italian, dropping his phone on the bed. 'I am 30 years old but I have to call my mamma every day. She thinks I have gone crazy!' His accent was thick, like the papa on the Dolmio sauce advert.

'Ciao, I'm Stefano,' he said. 'My mamma and papa can't understand why I have given up a good job in London. I tell her, I'm finding myself, Mamma, but she thinks I am poco loco!' He tapped the side of his head.

Stefano told us that he had found himself on the bunk next to Mike in the albergue in St Jean Pied-de-Port and the pair had been together ever since. Mike was pushing Stefano to walk faster and further every day, despite the dramatic protests.

'I am dead, I am dead. He has killed me,' Stefano moaned, flopping back on his bunk.

He was a short, round Roman and Mike a tall, gangly Australian, the Luigi to Stefano's Super Mario. Although Mike may have looked the more naturally adapted to the challenge his feet were in bad shape. Before long Ali was fixing him, taping up his feet and showing him some exercises for his sore knees. Still full of energy, and keen to test out his strapping, Mike left Stefano to sleep while he went off to explore the troglodyte dwellings behind the church and climb up to the castle ruins on the top of the cliff.

We found it remarkably easy to resist the temptation to join him, and instead Kathy joined Ali and me downstairs in the kitchen where we tackled the quick cryptic and shared a cold beer. Here the four French caballeros were slicing garlic, opening tins of foie gras and drinking red wine. Tim, the hairy, lovesick Australian was sitting at the kitchen table and when I asked him how he was doing, his story tumbled out of him. I think he was missing his mum and I must have seemed a good substitute.

'Ainslie's blisters are really bad so she's staying in Santo

Domingo for a couple of days. She really likes Alex from Brazil, but it's complicated, y'know. He really likes her too, but he's kind of seeing someone so he's gonna go on ahead. Yeah, I'm fine. She's a good mate. She'll catch up in a few days.' And then he told me all about a very long story he had written in the sixth grade and about the film he was making with his sister.

Day 11
19ᵗʰ April
Santo Domingo de la Calzada – Belorado
Kari, Ali
Kathy joined us for a carb-loaded but delicious pilgrim supper in the albergue (salad, pasta, risotto, pudding and wine for €10) and we were all in bed by 9pm. Ali and I are on bottom bunks of two beds which have been pushed together to make a double so we are doing our best Morecambe and Wise impressions. It has been a great day and the rain that has just come on again is not dampening our spirits. Life is indeed good.

CHAPTER 13

Mike and Stefano turned out to be quite the double act and from the moment we woke up they had us laughing. Our room must have been a dance studio at one point, as there was a barre and one wall was mirrored. Mike showed us his sleeping bag dance entitled 'Caterpillar to Butterfly' and did a bit of barre work before Ali checked the strapping on his feet.

Ali spent a good fifteen minutes every morning sorting out her own tootsies and she finally seemed to have got her blisters under control. Initially I had been impatient, keen to get going as soon as I was dressed. But I had got used to our routine and slowed my pace, giving her the time she needed. She snipped her tape with the surety of an expert and wherever we went, there was no shortage of patients waiting for a consultation with Dr Foot. Sometimes they formed a queue. Today was such a day. My feet were bearing up well, and other than a bit of strapping on my pinkie toes, both of which had developed callouses, they didn't need much attention. The purple Logroño chipolata had made a miraculous recovery.

When we were finally ready to go it was absolutely tipping it down and the pilgrims in the albergue gathered by the boot racks, bracing themselves for the deluge. Strangely the downpour seemed to lift everyone's spirits and we all appeared struck by a sense of the ridiculous. The French Caballeros were singing again and Kathy joined us, rustling, as we all were, in her wet-weather gear.

As usual we had pinpointed a spot for coffee, but when

we got to Tosantos everything was locked up, so on we plodded. The mist came down like a blanket and we saw a new landscape as a result. The teasels on the verges, the soft palette of greys and browns, suggested a return to winter, when only a few days before the greens and oranges had promised us spring.

The rain pelted down hard, and by the next village, where again everything was closed, we were starting to feel uncomfortably cold and wet. Finally we found a place in Espinosa del Camino where we offloaded the rucksacks and took off our jackets so that we could dry off for a bit. The café was packed and steamy as several other pilgrims had stripped off and were changing into dry socks.

'This Gore-Tex Berghaus jacket is not bloody waterproof at all,' Ali muttered, looking at the lining of her coat which was just as wet as the outside. Generally slow to rile, she hated to feel ripped off and once the bit was between her teeth I knew there would be no stopping her. Her righteous indignation unleashed a splendid burst of activity and before I had finished my coffee she had taken photographs of the wet interior and fired off an email to Berghaus.

Ali grinned. 'Be afraid Mr. Berghaus, be very afraid. Hell hath no fury like a middle-aged woman from Scotland who doesn't feel she has got her money's worth.'

I knew who the smart money would be on.

We trudged on through the unrelenting rain until, at about midday, we reached Villafranca de Montes de Oca. Kathy, like many others, decided that enough was enough. She would call it a day and stop there. While she explored the accommodation at the *San Anton Abad*, Ali and I sat on an old cart and chatted to the Jesus look-alike from Paris who had been causing trouble in the donativo yesterday afternoon.

'Before I saw you guys, I spent the afternoon drinking a bottle of red wine in one of the caves behind the village. I was hoping someone would pass by and join me for conversation, but I was out of luck.'

He had started his pilgrimage in Paris and was planning to walk home after he reached Santiago. He had the bluest eyes and carried a guitar on the back of his rucksack. By the time he suggested we warm up with a cup of tea in the café next door I think I was a little bit in love with him.

'The fire is on. You will like it,' he said. Then he went on his way. He was right. The café was an oasis – there were comfy sofas, a big log-burning stove and Gregorian chant playing on the loud speakers. We stripped off our wet things, dried them by the fire and got a bit of lunch, fortifying ourselves for the 13km hike up Montes de Oca.

As we sat, socks steaming in front of the fire, Harriet, the young lawyer we had met earlier came in with James, a pilgrim who walked with a staff covered in wild flowers. She told us that she was newly married and was spending a fortnight walking before heading back to find a new job in corporate London. She had walked the Camino before and she said that, for her, it was magical, something that had to be experienced to be understood. She looked for the lessons of the Way and spoke with such enthusiasm and positivity, that it was a shock when the tone of the conversation changed.

'James is walking through the forest with me. I don't want to be on my own.'

'I thought you were enjoying the solo experience,' I said.

'I was. When I first saw you I felt invincible. I loved being by myself, with my music playing, choosing when I stopped and how fast I went.' She paused. 'After I left Estella, I took the alternative route through the woods towards Luquin. I was feeling great, and then I saw someone coming towards me on a bike. He didn't look like a pilgrim, I don't know what it was, but something seemed wrong. He was heading in the wrong direction for a start, but I told myself that I shouldn't make snap judgments and said hello when he passed.

'He got off his bike and came right up to me. Invading my space. He was hassling me. Telling me he wanted to take pictures of me. That he wanted naked pictures. And that I had to do what he said. He was right in my face, aggressive. I pushed him off with my poles and just ran. I knew he had a bike and I was terrified he would catch up with me. I didn't look back, but for the rest of the walk I was sure he was behind me. I had felt so strong, and he made me feel so vulnerable.

'When I arrived in Luquin I was a mess. I sat down on the roadside and just cried and cried. These Dutch evangelicals found me and took me to their prayer house. They were so kind. They really looked after me and prayed with me. I mean, I'm not even religious, but it made me feel so much better. They called the police and made me tea and after I had made a statement they ran me a bath. I stayed with them for the night.

'I thought about going home, but I couldn't let him spoil the Camino for me. I still want to walk on my own, but James has said he will stick with me through the woods and keep me in his sights the rest of the time. James is looking out for me. I'll be fine.'

Her wide smile returned to her face and she nodded, convincing us that she was happy to continue. Like Harriet, I had felt invulnerable on this walk, almost as if I had left reality behind and was in some wonderful parallel universe where only good things happen. I felt jolted back into the real world, and worried for Harriet, as I would have for Connie.

We hugged her and swapped numbers, telling her to contact us if she needed anything at all, or if she just wanted some company. She smiled at us again and she and James headed off into the woods.

Finally warmed up, Ali and I said goodbye to Kathy and headed up the hill. Although the rain had eased off, we felt trepidatious: the path was slippy and it was a steep climb through the mountains to reach San Juan. We had been warned by a group of American walkers that the main path was flooded and we took a much steeper route into the oak forest.

Although the going was tough, we were more than rewarded for our efforts as the second half of our journey felt like a medieval mystery play with a whole cast of characters stepping into our path. David, a 66-year-old ski instructor from

Aspen, asked if he could walk with us for a while and told us about digging up Mastodons and hermaphrodite frogs. Peter told us he had walked all the way from his home town in Denmark, and Andy from Calgary told us he was walking in memory of his son who had died two years earlier. He would have been 21 this year.

Huge bushes of pink heather lined the pathways and, as we climbed through the woods, flooded streams rushed past us down narrow gullies. At times the whole path became the streambed and we had no choice but to wade through it, ankle deep. The Way turned from red to yellow, opening out where the stones spelled *Buen Camino*. We stopped for photographs and a chance to get our breath back. At about 4pm we walked past a gang of escaped donkeys, through the tumble-down ruins, into San Juan de Ortega, Saint John of the Nettles – a tiny town dominated by the monastery where we were planning to stay.

The albergue was very basic and freezing cold but despite this we felt relieved to have shelter. The dormitories were huge and looking around we recognised lots of our fellow pilgrims. Joorst, the cheerful Dutchman was in the other dorm (thankfully), as was Wee Jean from Boston and Stanley the bald Puerto Rican. Harriet and James were in our dorm where the radiators – which were not on – were covered with wet socks. Ali was so cold she got straight into her sleeping bag and decided to give the shower a miss. This was a good choice. The shower was a mistake. The room was so cold that every surface was wet and with nowhere to put my fresh clothes, they ended up wet too.

By the time I arrived at the pilgrim mass I was still dripping and as I sat in the pew, I was so cold I couldn't control my shivering. A Korean film crew was there and I worried they would think I was in the grip of some sort of religious convulsion and zoom in on me. Stanley, the tall, bald Puerto Rican (a man so wild about goodwill that he shook hands with the entire congregation at the sign of peace) told me later that he thought I was 'very afraid'. At the pilgrim blessing the priest asked me to read a passage and I could barely stop my teeth from chattering. He gave each of us all a small wooden cross on a black shoelace and I put mine around my neck with shaking hands.

As I left the church I saw Stefano. 'I know you don't know me very well, but would you mind hugging me? I think I'm hypothermic.'

He grinned at me and wrapped me up in his warm arms. He saved my life and I knew we would be friends forever.

Ali had warmed up in a more conventional manner and as I came out of the church she greeted me with a big smile and another hug.

'Come with me, you're going to like this,' she said, taking my hand. She had tracked down a wood-burning stove and we stood by it for a while before supper. We ate our garlic soup and pasta as close to the stove as we could manage. I would have sat on top of it if they had let me.

After dinner we couldn't bear to leave the fire and Ali and I sat on for an hour or so warming up while I dried my hair. Harriet and Stefano, Wee Jean, Sara the Curvy German, Lara her little friend, Bald Stanley and Joel, a US Marine from Puerto Rico, pulled up their chairs. It didn't take long until we were sharing stories and laughing like old friends.

Just two weeks ago the thought of interacting with a bunch of strangers had filled me with dread. Two travelling companions had seemed more than enough for me. But on that evening in the monastery, I could see that this crowd of pilgrims, my Camino cohort, was not extraneous to my journey, it was central. We were part of each other's story and impermanent though our bonds might be, for now they were strong and binding.

Day 12
20th April
Belorado – San Juan de Ortega
Soaked to the skin for most of the day, I am shivering still as I type in

my bunk. Once again the dorm is unbelievably noisy – it's vibrating, I swear. A snore, like a loudmouth in a bar, is competitive, it likes to be noticed. If there are other snores out there, noisier and more exuberant, it ups its game until the noise is thunderous.

There were two firsts today:

1. I was washing my hands in the bathroom and was surprised to see a very tall German man in his pants. He looked a bit surprised to see me too and led me to the door. It said 'Caballeros' which apparently means 'Men.'

2. I am sleeping in my clothes, as it is too cold and damp to strip off.

Tomorrow we reach Burgos and Lynne and Tinker will be joining us there. They are old friends from the days our children were all in primary school together and a reunion is long overdue. I am looking forward to seeing them, but this doesn't feel like a holiday, or a girls' week away and I am worried that the peace that has settled on me this week, might be disrupted by the excitement of their arrival.

CHAPTER 14

It wasn't yet dawn when Ali and I hauled on our rucksacks. Most of the other pilgrims were still in their beds, their limp socks zig-zagging the corridors like dour Camino bunting. It was so damp in the monastery that the walls were dripping.

'If they're holding out till their washing dries, they'll be in for a long wait,' I muttered, heading for the door.

'Hang on,' Ali whispered. 'I'm going to pull out my anorak.'

The shaven head of Joel the Marine popped out from his bunk. 'I have a feel for the weather. It'll be a clear day,' he said. 'Trust me. I've been in the military for twenty years. Forget the waterproofs.'

And it was dry, for the first twenty minutes, we had to give him that. But by the time we reached the forest, it had started to drizzle. The scrubby pines were ancient and gnarly and tattered ribbons of lichen hung from their branches. It was muddy and slippery underfoot and in the eerie gloom of first light, the mist clung to the undergrowth. Out of the darkness the yellow eye of a horned cow glinted, watching us from the woods. We were about to pass her when I spotted her calf on the opposite side of the path. Ali, a farmer's daughter, was pretty brave when it came to livestock but there was no way I was going to pass between mother and child. Instead, we ducked into the tangled woodland behind the cow and scrambled through brambles and over ditches until we were sure we had passed them. As we looked back, the terrifying beast, who hadn't taken her eye off us, flicked her tail, mooed and sauntered away.

The drizzle soon turned to downpour and by the time we stopped for breakfast, I was soaked to the pants. Inside a busy café, Stefano and Mike, our favourite Camino buddies, were buying empanadas, fresh from the oven. The ample Spanish Momia who was running the place told us about this local speciality – giant pasties filled with chorizo, potato, bacon and tomatoes. How could we resist?

'One is enough for two,' Momia said, as she wrapped an empanada in tinfoil. We would have it for our lunch.

Then, much to the entertainment of everyone in the café, a pilgrim pulled up with a donkey and cart. The red cart looked like a bubble-lift from a ski resort and sitting in the 'driving seat' was a shaggy little dog. The pilgrim and the donkey were covered from head to toe in blue ponchos and only the man's white beard and rosy cheeks were visible. We had seen him before, in a square somewhere: a one-man band, with a mouthorgan, an accordion, and a belly that wobbled in time to the beat. It was too wet for the accordion, but he winked at us as he came into the café and I half expected him to chuckle, 'Ho, ho, ho!'

The next point of interest was Atapuerca, a UNESCO world heritage site. The earliest human remains in Europe had been discovered in some caves outside the village and everywhere we looked adverts invited us to visit the museum. The poster boy, *Homo antecessor*, bore more than a passing resemblance to Jim Morrison from The Doors, but despite his allure, we weren't up for a detour. The walk was 26km as it stood, and we wanted to reach Burgos by mid-afternoon.

As we approached the village centre a busload of school children spilled out onto the Way. 'Maybe they're just visiting the museum,' I said hopefully. But just as we stopped to take a picture by the statue of Jim Morrison the noisy mob ran past us, snapping selfies on the hoof. They were definitely walking the Camino. My heart sank at the thought of being stuck in the middle of a school trip and I resolved to overtake them. Unfortunately, the path ahead of us led straight up to the Cruz de Matagrande at 3,543ft. Pushing in front of this herd of children was not going to be easy.

Teaching had been such an important part of my life for so long and yet I had turned my back on it without so much as a glance over my shoulder. Over the course of my career I had taught all age groups, but my passion lay in the secondary school classroom, teaching English. Young people are spontaneous, unguarded, honest and provoking. Their bullshit detectors are highly tuned, and they have not yet learned the platitudes that make adult life run so smoothly, and so inauthentically. But in recent years I had spent less time in the classroom, and those moments that kept the fire alight – the flashes of brilliance from a child who lacked confidence, the sparks of understanding when a poem unfurled – those moments had become too rare.

In my pastoral role, I was responsible for the wellbeing of 65 teenage girls and I was available for them day and night. All of the girls needed me to listen and provide support, but at any given time there might be a handful who were experiencing problems so significant that I held them in mind all the time. In the early days, I seemed to cope with the responsibility, but gradually my ability to manage it faltered. Those girls were under my skin and in my head and before long I was having nightmares almost nightly. I used to cry out in my sleep, and awaken, heart pounding out of my chest, struggling to breathe. Frequently I dreamt that a child was trapped in a locked room and that I couldn't find the key. In my dreams my own babies lay helpless and abandoned. I knew they needed me, but I couldn't get to them in time.

It had been eight months since I left my job, and the last nightmare was just days before I left for Spain. And now I was surrounded by schoolchildren, and I didn't want them there. Full of raucous energy at the start of their walk, they were quick on their feet, and I was trapped. In front of me, behind me, pushing past, they shouted to each other, oblivious. Music blared from someone's phone, teachers yelled to keep them in check, and inside my head a hard-won peace was shattering.

Panting, I speeded up and pushed on, but Ali was struggling with sore feet.

'I just can't go that fast. You'll have to slow down,' she called after me. I ignored her; I couldn't stop to explain that the children's clamour was shrill to my ears and that I needed to be free of it. Anxiety was tinged with anger. I deeply resented this intrusion into my Camino and just had to get past them.

While we easily overtook the girls who were gossiping and flicking their hair, it was harder to overtake the sporty kids at the front. My breathing was laboured and the rain was pelting down as I swerved into the outside lane (the verge) and pushed ahead into pole position.

Ali was swearing at me under her breath as she too made it to the front, sweaty and unclear why I had forced her into this manic dash. And then, before we had time to appreciate the silence, the air was filled with the sound of bells, hundreds of bells. There ahead of us, a shepherd was moving his massive flock. My herculean attempts to beat the crowd had failed. We had no choice but to slow down to a meander and as we slowed, the kids caught up. Once again we were surrounded.

I tried to concentrate on my breath, to quiet the frantic voice in my head.

Yesterday as we'd sped past the four French Caballeros, one of them had called out, 'Slow down or you'll miss Santiago!' And I'd felt proud that he'd commented on our speed. But now, stuck between the sheep and the kids I wondered what he'd meant. What was I really doing here? Surely it wasn't a race to the finish.

Freezing and very wet, we stopped for a loo break at a café just a few kilometres on. I sighed as the school children piled in after us and while we waited for our order, they occupied nearly every seat in the café.

Ali and I pushed through the tables to reach the last two

spaces and found ourselves, once again, surrounded by children. Within moments, a Spanish boy introduced himself. 'Hello. My name is Herman, and I am twelve years old.' His English was confident, like he'd prepared for an oral exam. Outsized incisors flashed in a broad grin and his big brown eyes looked directly at me. 'My class has been walking one stage of the Camino every year since we were ten. We will reach Santiago by the time we are fourteen.'

My stiffened frown relaxed, and I smiled as he proudly showed me his pilgrim passport, pointing out his favourite stamps. The girls he was sitting with huddled in, leaning over the table to tell us about the albergues they had visited.

'Would you like a strawberry? They are delicious,' one of them asked, wiping juice off her chin and offering me the punnet. I took a berry and bit in, grateful for its freshness, its ripeness. These children were utterly present in this place, at this time. They were not looking back or forwards, they were open and responsive to the experience of now. But I had been so intent on my own journey that I had closed myself off from the moment. Herman and his friends had been my teachers that day and I felt ashamed of my anger at being stuck in their midst. Their pilgrimage was not just about silence and reflection, it was also about joy and friendship. These children were looking out, not in.

Despite the weather, we could see Burgos from a long way away, but although the end was in sight, we were wrong to hope that today's journey was nearly over. It was a long, hard slog into the city and the industrial hinterland went on forever. We walked past the airport, industrial estates and other uninspiring features of the urban landscape until we found ourselves at a huge intersection with a large café.

'Well, if it ain't Ali and Kari,' came the greeting from David the ski instructor from Aspen. Talking to him, and pondering his map, we figured out that we had missed the option of a more scenic route and feeling deflated, we took our coffee outside and ate our empanadas under an awning, in the rain. We were just wondering which way to go when we spotted the flock of school children up ahead. We followed them, their bright ponchos showing us the way.

Although she didn't know it yet, Ali now had blisters on her blisters and she was in a significant amount of pain. She is not one to complain, being more of a 'suck it up soldier' than a princess type, so I knew to take her seriously when she said she couldn't go much further. The last kilometre was a killer, and Ali walked as though her feet were bound, every short step considered.

I tried to distract her with the promise of an ice-cold beer but she was immune to her own tactics and only the thought of Tinker and Lynne encouraged her over the finishing line. It was sheer joy to check into our private albergue where we had treated ourselves to a room for two, with an en-suite bathroom. There was a bed, and sheets, and towels and everything. For €20 per night, it might not have been the Ritz, but it certainly felt like it.

The manager greeted us at the desk.

'The Camino is a beautiful thing and you are beautiful pilgrims,' he said. And who were we to disagree?

Day 13
21st April
San Juan de Ortega – Burgos
Kari, Ali
Ali and I collapsed on the double bed as soon as we got to our room. Although we have slept at pretty close quarters for the last 14 nights, we haven't yet been bedfellows. I think the pair of us might be suffering from some bizarre exhaustion-induced hysteria, as despite the sore feet and the aching legs, we lay side by side on our double bed, and laughed until the tears rolled down our faces.

CHAPTER 15

Yesterday, we took our boots off and lay on the bed for an hour or more. When the feeling finally returned to her feet, Ali examined her toes only to discover they really were in quite a mess. She soothed them in the tiny bath in the micro-ensuite that we were so ridiculously excited about. For the first time my travel-plug was put to use, and I had to eat my words since I had told David that it would be a space-occupying waste of time.

Cleaned up and wearing what we now referred to as our 'play clothes' we called home and spoke to our families. I found myself struggling to put the walk into words, usually restricting myself to basic information about distances covered and places visited. It was easier to ask them about what they were doing and catch up with their news, and they seemed happy enough with this, not pressing me for more.

Guy, Ali's husband, was planning to join us in a week's time, and, truth be told, she wasn't wild about the idea. Guy is a super-fit, action hero of a man, always cycling to Paris, or pedalling across the Alps with a group of equally gung-ho chaps. Although she hadn't said as much, I think Ali felt he had plenty of adventures of his own and wasn't entirely sure why he was joining us on ours.

'Great... yes... super... that'll be lovely,' I heard her say with a singular lack of enthusiasm.

At about 5pm, we heard Tinker and Lynne coming down the corridor. They arrived like two Beroccas dropped into a glass of water, and fizzed about, recharging us with their sparkle. Lynne, who had flown from Boston, showed no signs of travel fatigue, and Tinker distributed presents, clipping flowers into our hair, and replenishing the liquorice toffee supply. They moved into the double room next to ours and we lay on their bed and flicked through the magazines Lynne had brought, while they freshened up.

The four of us had been pals for a decade. For years we had seen each other on the school run every day, our children slept at each other's houses and our husbands were friends too. Lynne, Tinker and I had a little craft business called Cotton Thistle when the children were small and I have never had a lovelier or less remunerative job. After we had dropped the kids off at school we would spend happy hours round my kitchen table making doorstops and notice boards from vintage fabrics.

We went camping with the kids every summer, usually without the dads, and sat on cold beaches wrapped in blankets while the children went feral, burying themselves in holes and living on crisps. Lynne was a 'new mum' at the school at the same time as me. They had moved to Edinburgh from Boston just as we moved up from Jersey. Her daughter Lauren quickly became Connie's best friend and we too hit it off from the start. She had the gift of seeing things from an outsider's perspective and her 'smart mouth,' as she called it, helped us see the funny side of almost anything. We were bereft when she returned to Boston four years later but we visited each other every couple of years so we had never felt out of touch.

Tinker, the most generous of friends, with the biggest heart, would do anything for anyone but the strain of running her own business and putting her own needs at the end of a very long list had taken its toll this last year. She needed time to recuperate and I hoped the walking would give her some peace.

Our albergue was on a quiet street near the library in the Plaza San Lesmes. Just around the corner was a stone archway into the old city and we stopped just short of that to pay our respects to San Miguel.

'Well, now we have a patron saint to bless us on our journey,' said Lynne as we clinked our bottles. Her time in Scotland had in no way converted her to the more European pastime of wine drinking. She was a beer drinker through and through. And Spanish beer would do her very nicely. One beer became two and before we got too comfortable we took the smart decision to move on.

We made our way to the cathedral so that we could get our bearings for more serious sightseeing the following day and stumbled on a street full of bars and tapas restaurants.

We settled on a place called *Los Herreros* and turned our attention to the tapas and the Rioja. In the main the food was a beautiful mystery, as with Jenny gone, we no longer knew what we were eating. We pointed at the tapas along the counter of the bar until we had a good selection including the famous Morcilla de Burgos. And every plate was delicious.

With nine children between us, there was a lot to catch up on. Between the food and the wine, the chatter and the laughter, we barely drew breath.

But we had all had a long day and it was still early when we started to flag. Ali and I were in bed before 10pm, promising to keep our hands to ourselves, and hoping that neither one of us had become a snorer.

We slept like babies, in blissful silence, and woke feeling like new women. Sadly our bodies had not recovered quite as efficiently as our minds and the feet were still suffering. There was no way we would be putting our boots back on today, and that left us with a problem. It was cold and rainy outside and although no one would describe us as fashionistas, vanity dictated that it was a step too far to resort to socks and flip-flops.

'I would rather freeze,' I said, like some wannabe Anna Wintour. 'Camino fashion is pretty alternative and that's fine when you are out in the boonies, but Burgos is a sizeable city, and I already look peculiar enough.'

'You're not wrong there,' said Ali, looking at the stripy dress I was wearing over the top of my leggings and the puffa jacket I had zipped up over the top.

But before we could go shoe shopping, we were headed to the municipal swimming pool.

'Ooh, bubbles and steam. My poor feet will be so happy,' Ali cooed with utter, utter delight. Given the state of her 'poor feet' we opted to go by taxi and felt like cheats as we travelled for the first time on the pilgrimage by any means other than legs.

The spa was even better than the one in Logroño and we spent an ecstatic couple of hours unravelling the knots and laughing like the children who had come for a Saturday morning play in the pool. The circuit in the ice pool took a full two minutes to complete and it was only with a gargantuan effort of will, and a lot of encouragement from my friends, that I was able to stay in the perishing water for that length of time. When I climbed out, though, it was as if someone had pressed the boost button on my circulation and my muscles surged with warmth.

A glass-fronted shower cabinet on the poolside offered a hydrotherapy that involved pummelling the occupant with ice-cold water sprayed from a series of jets that made their way slowly from feet to head. Standing outside and watching the faces of the poor victim inside was the best entertainment we'd had in days and feeling revived we headed off to do some sightseeing.

In the Catedral de Santa Maria many of the side chapels were too ornate for my taste, but the building itself was deeply inspiring, and the huge star lantern in the middle of the transept, sublime. In a little side chapel I found myself crying as I looked at a sculpture of Saint Anne, Mary and the infant Jesus, and my thoughts turned, as they so often did, to my mother.

I had telephoned a couple of times and sent postcards whenever I found them. Although postcards seem to have gone a bit out of fashion in an age where it is now so easy to keep in touch, Mum still pinned all her postcards onto a noticeboard in the hall. She loved to show visitors the places her children, grandchildren, nieces and nephews had been, travelling vicariously through all of us from the comfort of her armchair. She was supportive of my plan to walk the Camino. While we were training, Ali and I struggled to find circular walks that were long enough to build our stamina. The Heritage Trail round Loch Leven proved ideal and we usually popped in to see Mum, who lived in Kinross, at the halfway point.

'Och, you girls are doing so well. Imagine being able to fit everything you need in that wee bag. Go and cut yourself a nice bit of cake. A bigger slice than that. You'll be walking it all off.'

She was happy to hear my voice when I rang, but she was not keen to chat for long. I was sure my sister was worried about her, but when we spoke, she moved off the subject quickly, preferring to tell me about the preparations for the wedding. Her son, Greg, would be marrying Charlotte, just a week after I returned and I had been saying a prayer for them in every church that I visited.

In the cathedral in Burgos I felt far from home, and far from my responsibilities. For the most part, that freedom from responsibility was a lightening, a gift. I was starting to remember who I was before I became someone's teacher, someone's wife or someone's mother. That person laughed more and worried less and I was enjoying being just me again. But I had always been someone's daughter and I wasn't ready to imagine a future without my mum. Especially when so much was unresolved.

Our relationship had always been complicated. A 'late baby', I came into her life uninvited and too late. She loved me fiercely, of that I was in no doubt. But her life had moved past the childrearing stage when I arrived and I had to slot in to an adult world. She and Dad bought a hotel when I was an infant and their life was hectic as they built the business. I needed to be looked after by somebody other than them. Sometimes it was the 'women', as we called the squad of local ladies who cleaned the hotel. They allowed me to trail behind them as they cleaned the bedrooms and mopped the floors. Sometimes it was Aileen, a young girl from Aberdeen, or Kay who worked in the hotel in her holidays and died tragically in a climbing accident when I was just four. Sometimes it was Eddie the barman who took me home to his house on Sunday afternoons. Sometimes it was my Uncle Willie who worked in the public bar and brought me sweeties every day. Most often, though, it was my sister, who was 19 years my senior and already at college by the time I came along.

Mum and Dad juggled two busy bars and a thriving restaurant. Every weekend there was a wedding or a dinner dance. Business was booming and they worked flat out. I enjoyed the company of the adults around me, became a precocious three-year-old who sat on the bar stool and chatted with the punters, who played dominoes with the old men in the public bar. But I didn't do toys or play dates and I don't remember board games or family days out. I grew up thinking that the reason I couldn't ride my bike till I was nine, or swim till I was ten, was because I was useless at sport. It was some years before I realised that no one teaches themselves to swim, no matter how sporty they are.

I'm not complaining. I had a privileged life. Boarding school when I was nine, cruises with the old folks and holidays abroad: I was a lucky girl. Dad's health was poor and they moved to Florida when I was ten. I visited sometimes, and joined the blue-rinsed ladies in the pool at the retirement condominium where I wasn't permitted to be resident. But in the holidays, when they didn't manage to get home, I stayed with my sister and her young family. I had Christmases at her house. And I didn't mind. Because her house was full of children and toys and books. Not antiques or alcohol.

My mother's drinking had been the greatest sadness in my life. It hung over me like a dark cloud, a nasty secret I kept to myself. As a child I couldn't make sense of the difference that came over her, of the Jekyll and Hyde nature of the game. Mum could be the kindest of women – she saw the good in people and never spoke badly of anyone. She was a generous host, an excellent cook, the life and soul of the party. My dozens of cousins adored her. She was everyone's favourite aunt. And sometimes she was like that at home too. But I could never be sure. There was always a risk. Sometimes her face contorted and she hissed at me, spitting venom. I hid in cupboards and prayed for invisibility. I kept so still I wanted my breath to stop, so no one would know I was awake, and listening. By the time I was ten I had learned not to rely on her. It limited the disappointment. And I had my sister. Who was always there.

When I was away at boarding school, I kept my secret. I would call home to share my news and by the first word I would know that it was the wrong time to call. Sometimes before a word was spoken, the delay and the breath was enough. I learned to end the phone call quickly with a well-chosen lie. Reducing the risk of conflict. Keeping things sweet. 'Got to go, Mr. Williams is looking for me.'

Over the years I considered my options. I went to counselling at the drug and alcohol dependency unit in Jersey where I learned that some secrets are best not kept. I came to see that there was a border between my mother and me. It was my choice to step into her world; it was my choice not to let her step over into mine. I could pull up my drawbridge. I could keep myself safe. I held my tongue when I could. Which was not often enough.

Later on, when I had children of my own, I timed my visits, maximising the good time I could spend with her, reducing the risk. And this brought a fragile truce, a sad sort of peace. At arms' length I could mitigate the damage, but the price was the intimacy for which I so longed.

That day, standing in front of the sculpture of Mary, nursing the infant Jesus with her mother, Saint Anne, looking at her with such love, I felt a surge of grief. Motherhood has been the most important aspect of my life. That visceral, gut-wrenching love that I had for my children, that would make me run into the flames or stand between them and the lion; and that tender, flickering love in my fingertips as I touched their sleeping faces, or nursed them in my arms, this love, this love that has seemed so vital a force in me, where would it go now my children were grown? And why, at 47, did I still crave that love so badly, and feel its loss so deep?

While Lynne and Tinker explored the cathedral, Ali, who in a vain effort to keep warm was wearing all her clothes, seemed to have fallen into a trance and I found her wandering through the museum like a wee lost soul. It was time to get her warm and find her some sustenance. And shoes. We both needed shoes.

By the end of the day we had found some ultra-lightweight trainers, and overdosed on tapas: padron peppers, Morcilla, tiny eels piled high on slices of crusty bread, octopus, calamari, and costillas, the speciality ribs of Burgos. Harriet, the lawyer from London, called from *Los Herreros* and asked us to join her, and by the time we arrived there was a great gathering of pilgrims, many of whom we had met along the Way. James the wood nymph, Tim the love-struck Australian, Sara the Curvy German and Lara her little friend – they were all there. We shared blister remedies and bedbug stories until our beds finally beckoned.

Day 14
22nd April
Rest Day – Burgos
Kari, Ali, Tinker, Lynne
Burgos: we love you, but Santiago is calling and we still have 25 days to go.

CHAPTER 16

As there was a fiesta in Burgos we hit the road slightly later than usual having wasted a bit of time looking for a breakfast spot near our albergue. Unsuccessful, we followed the yellow arrows past the back of the beautiful cathedral that dominated the city.

Here we stumbled on a café near the municipal.

'Good morning, lovely ladies.' Harriet and James waved from their table. Grandmère et Grandfille and Sara 'n' Lara were here too. The place was buzzing. A father-and-son team were pressing oranges and toasting crusty bread at pace and all too soon it was time to say a second goodbye to Harriet. Despite knowing her for only a few days, she felt like a friend. Her courage and enthusiasm had touched me and I felt sure our paths would one day cross again.

'Come on, girls, get your flower clips in your hair,' Tinker insisted, and Harriet snapped a picture of the blossom ceremony before we parted. We were nothing if not colourful as we headed out past the cathedral for our first walk as a quartet.

'We should be thanking our lucky stars that she didn't have T-shirts printed with *The Sturdy Girls do the Camino*,' Ali whispered. She understood how I felt.

We were usually a quiet duo for the first hour or two of the morning but with the arrival of our fittie friends, there was no hope of a gentle start to the day. Tinker danced her way out of town, shaking her legendary bootie and trilling away with far too much eagerness, while Ali and I kept our heads down, looking for waymarkers. They led us through El Parral with its many sculptures and out by the university of Burgos, until we had left the city behind.

Before I left Edinburgh I didn't know the difference between a long walk and a pilgrimage. I wasn't yet sure I fully understood, but I knew that for me, this was no longer about the walking. The stillness of the Way and the rhythm of my steps were almost hypnotic and often the walk became a kind of meditation. In some barely perceptible way, my consciousness was altered. This morning, I wondered if the arrival of our friends would interfere with the gentle unravelling that seemed to be taking place in me.

The weather was misty and at first the Way was busier than we had seen it, more pilgrims having started the walk at Burgos. We were conscious of groups of day-packers for the first time and kept pace with seven Spanish women, about our age, most of the way to Hornillos.

'No wonder they can go faster than us,' Ali said, as the women overtook us. 'They're cheating. They are not carrying their rucksacks. And they're going to get to the beds first.'

Back home at the beginning of our training, we had both been quite taken with the idea that we could have our luggage carried on to our next destination. It was a good option for pilgrims who were injured or less able to walk, but for those who *were* able, carrying everything you needed on your back was a daily lesson in moderation and simplicity, and one I would not have missed. I had – despite the discomfort – enjoyed discovering that that I needed very little and was made of strong stuff.

There were no coffee stops for a good long way but the first stretch out of Burgos was flat with plenty to see. We passed through some traditional villages where the adobe walls were the colour of warm sand, and the weathered wooden doorways showed just the ghost of blue paint. A washing line pegged with white vests and blue checked napkins, looked like a painting, strung as it was across an ancient vine that wound up the yellow building.

In Tardajos an old lady in a pink padded dressing gown, leaned out of her top floor window and wished us *Buen Camino* as so many had on our journey. I was glad that Tinker and Lynne's first walk had started so beautifully, and that in the quiet of our surroundings, their excitement had gradually abated.

Mid-morning, and before we started the climb to the Meseta, we stopped at a bar for a cold drink and the waiter wrapped us up some bocadillos as the local shops were shut for the fiesta. We had heard mixed reports about the flat, featureless landscape of the Meseta and were not quite sure what to expect. Birthplace of Cervante's Don Quixote, the Meseta is a place of visions. A treeless high central plateau, it is lush in springtime but blisteringly hot in the summer, and freezing in winter, exposed as it is to the elements. We had picked the right time of year to come.

We climbed to about 1,000m, Ali and I struggling to keep pace with Lynne and Tinker who were both runners, and on fresh legs. From the high plateau the fertile plains stretched out as far as the eye could see. All around us, fields planted with wheat and beans had just sprung into life and the nascent greens looked so satiated with moisture I felt I could drink them. We couldn't see a road or a village for miles and the only sound was birdsong.

The weather closed in around lunchtime, but conveniently, we found a tumbledown hut with a stone bench where we could sit and eat our bocadillos. Stanley, the Puerto Rican who shook hands with the whole congregation in San Juan de Ortega, joined us. He told us that Joel, the military man with the terrible weather forecasting skills, had gone home.

'His gout got the better of him. It was not God's will that he should complete the journey this time.' Full of Camino wisdom, Stanley's enthusiasm for evangelisation was definitely best in small doses. He told us about walking the northern route, delivered a short sermon on the dangers of following the dollar and then he was on his way.

'I don't think he asked a single thing about us,' observed Ali.

I watched him go. Very tall, and bearing more than a passing resemblance to Uncle Fester, he wore a bright red jacket and walked with a big silver umbrella to protect his bald head from the sun. He would be easy to spot should we wish to avoid him in future.

The final stretch into Hornillos, down a path known as Cuesta Matamulas (mule-killer slope) was fabulous. Ahead of us the Camino stretched like the yellow brick road in the Land of Oz. The sun had come out again and the walking could not have been more lovely. I was keeping up with the fitties, my legs felt powerful, and the breeze was at our back. My sense of satisfaction vanished quickly, however, when on reaching Hornillos, we were turned away from three albergues because they were full. Inside, I groaned, not relishing the thought of walking on to the next town, but I put on my game face and smiled, not wanting to worry Lynne or Tinker on the first day of their pilgrimage.

'Don't worry. The Camino will provide. She always does,' I chirped.

'All right, Pollyanna. Say a prayer to St Anthony or whoever it is that finds things,' said Ali.

Our last option, the municipal, had five spaces left.

I smiled at Ali. 'You owe him another fiver when we get home. I'll add it to your tab.'

The hospitalero welcomed us with a terracotta beaker of cold water and we were allocated bunks. Wee Jean from Boston arrived right behind us and got the last bed.

Once we had showered and settled in, Jean and I went to sit outside. Stefano, our little Italian friend, paid us a visit and the three of us sat on white plastic chairs, warming ourselves in the afternoon sun.

The albergue had a kitchen so I thought it might be fun to make supper and we headed to the tiny local shop to gather a hotch potch of ingredients. Lynne spotted a Rioja that her husband, Tim, liked (although I suspect he usually paid more than €5 per bottle) and we drank that while she sipped her San Miguel from a teacup. Cooking in the tiny communal kitchen with six or seven others was a challenge, particularly as there was only one chopping board and two wooden spoons. Jean joined us for our supper of tomato risotto and salad: no culinary masterpiece but after all the tapas we were craving a big bowl of something hearty and this hit the spot. Food really did taste wonderful on this walk.

Mary and Meyrick, the mother and daughter from Boston who had been in the cubicle next to us on that first night in Roncesvalles, were staying here. Jean had got to know them both in the last few days. Mary was about our age, a diminutive Italian-American with black hair tied back in a ponytail and soft brown eyes. She seemed to be looking after a brood of young people she had gathered on the Way.

'OK everybody, move on now. These ladies need a table so they can eat their dinner,' she said, clearing a space for us in the kitchen. She set the table and joined us for a glass of wine. Looking after people was clearly what she did, and she made me feel cared-for instantly.

'I'm so glad to sit with adults for a change. These kids are great, but enough is enough.' Meyrick, her daughter, was a dancer who moved with effortless grace. She wore her walking gear with a stylishness that looked like she was advertising Ralph Lauren. She was gorgeous: perfectly toned, tanned, with wavy black hair and dark brown eyes, it was perhaps no surprise that she and Mary had gathered a retinue over the fortnight.

Mary had lost her wedding ring and after supper we helped her look.

'Don't worry; it's my third one. Third ring, same husband. I guess I'll just put in a claim when I get back home.'

Supper eaten and washing up done, it was still early, so we headed into the village to explore.

'I'm so glad we're not in our flip-flops, Kari,' Ali said, shivering.

'I know. These trainers are the best things I have ever

bought,' I said.

The temperature had dropped and we were lured into the first bar we saw by a fire and the promise of hot mint tea. On the way back the wind picked up and Tinker, the Kit-Queen, produced from a pocket a lightweight, translucent-green jacket that, with the hood up, looked like she was wearing a giant green condom. We sniggered all the way home.

'Wind is our enemy,' she told us, her little mouth peeping out from a tiny breathing hole. That's as may be, but I'd rather take my chances.

Maria-Manuela was in the bunk next to me, and when we returned she was pleased to see us. A little Puerto Rican girl who talked ten to the dozen, we had been running into her on and off since the start. She greeted Jean like a long-lost relative.

'If it wasn't for this amazing woman, I would have gone home at the end of day one.' She had been part of the group of noisy young people that had set off from Saint Jean Pied-de-Port on the same day as us. Stefano and Mike had also been amongst them. She had a backpack so heavy she could hardly lift it off the ground and that killer day in the mountains had nearly finished off both Maria-Manuela and Stefano. It was Mike who had kept them going during the walk with his unique brand of comedy and that evening they had met Jean, who was kind and encouraging.

'Oh, I didn't do much,' said Jean, 'I just went through your rucksack with you and helped you decide what you really needed to keep and what we could ship home.'

Maria-Manuela continued, 'A few days later, my so-called best friend, left me behind. My blisters were really, really bad and I needed to take a day off, but she said she couldn't wait and ditched me.'

It would have been easy, and understandable, for her to throw in the towel at this point, but Maria-Manuela had kept going. Like Sara the Curvy German, she didn't seem built for long-distance walking, but what she lacked in natural

120

athleticism, she made up for in determination. She had taken the bus a couple of times, had spent a few nights in more salubrious accommodation and now she was back on track, determined to make it to Santiago.

'The funny thing is… well not funny really, but you know what I mean… the friend who dumped me has just flown back to Miami. She ended up in the hospital, her blisters were so bad.'

Day 15
23rd April
Burgos – Hornillos del Camino
Kari, Ali, Tinker, Lynne
It's only 9.30pm but I seem to be the only one awake in the municipal albergue in Hornillos. We are in a tiny room and as I type a snorer who sounds like a revving motorcycle engine is rattling the bedsteads. I'm not complaining, we are lucky to have beds: many who arrived after us were turned away and faced a 10km walk to the next albergue.
Today I am feeling pretty proud of myself. I have kept up with Tinker and Lynne and my rucksack felt light as air. We have heard stories of soldiers who have had to fly home, and young people who have taken the bus, or called it a day, and although I keep telling myself this is not about the physical challenge, I have to admit to feeling a little bit pleased with myself. Who'd of thunk it?
As I lie on my top bunk the original snorer has been joined by two more – it's like the frog chorus in here. Early start tomorrow so best sign off.

CHAPTER 17

It was pitch dark when we woke, so we gathered our belongings in silence and crept downstairs to repack our rucksacks. Simone, the charming Italian hospitalero was making toast and there was coffee ready and muesli on the table when we appeared in the kitchen.

Wee Jean, the Bostonian woman, joined us on our walk and we were a quiet five-some when we hit the road before dawn. The moon was still high as we climbed steadily up onto the Meseta and gradually the group dispersed. Ali and Lynne, their tongues setting the pace for their feet, sprinted on ahead, while Tinker, Jean and I followed them, taking our time.

The sky was heavy and a thick band of black, ominous cloud obscured the sunrise directly behind us. We were walking, as always, due west, and everything was cast in the dark shadow of the cloud. As we reached the crest of the hill the sun broke through behind us and the hillside was suddenly flooded in brilliant, golden light. The green of the crops seemed improbably bright and, instantly, the sky ahead of us was a deep, cloudless blue. The intensity of the light stopped me dead in my tracks and as I looked up I saw a red iron cross, staked in a pile of rocks at the top of the hill. Unbidden, a wave of pure joy surged through me and the breath caught in my throat. Jolted by the current, it was as if something elemental in me had connected with a life force beyond, electrifying and sublime. I looked at Tinker and Jean and saw that they too had tears in their eyes, overwhelmed, like me, by the convulsive beauty of the moment.

Behind us everything was silhouetted against the sun and we could see two dark figures walking towards us, one tall and thin, the other small and round. Their poles were in the air and they were whooping as they made it to the top of the hill. It was Mike and Stefano and we hugged each other, celebrating our good fortune at being together in that place, at that moment, in all that impossible light.

Ali and Lynne were ahead of us and had already started the steep descent to the San Bol river valley. As we came over the hill, our enormously long shadows were cast ahead of us on the fields and I noticed that a brilliant halo of light seemed to have surrounded my shadow and was following me down the hill. Tinker said she could see it too, but to her, it seemed as though the halo was around her own figure, pursuing her. All the way down the hill the light tracked us and although I now know this to be a type of Brocken spectre, the experience was mystical to me: I felt swaddled in light, held in everlasting arms. And as the euphoria subsided I was left with a profound feeling of peace, like the stillness of a child who had cried until there were no tears left.

The Way was full of surprises and sometimes I felt as if I was a knight in a medieval quest, challenged to overcome the obstacles that blocked my path. Just as I processed one experience, another, quite different, came along to test me or teach me. Just a mile or two along the road we regrouped as we faced a quagmire.

Mud. More mud than I had ever seen. Thick, sticky, grey mud.

'Well, we can't go over it, we can't go under it... Uh oh, we'll have to go through it,' Ali quoted. And in we went. And if we had to be in it, we might as well enjoy it.

When my son, Alexander, was not yet two, and I was pregnant with the twins, we planted tomatoes. It was a hot day in our garden in Jersey, and he was wearing just a nappy. He was digging with his little trowel, helping me fill the tubs and I sat down for a minute to watch him play. He felt the mud in his fingers and it was cool and damp. He pushed his chubby hand in further until it was up past his elbows and paused. I could see his thought process, his face expressive, his brow furrowing in concentration. He took his nappy off, and climbed into the big flowerpot, wriggling his toes, burrowing them deeper. Then he sat down in the compost and buried himself like a tomato plant, lost in the moment, loving the smell of the damp earth and the coolness on his perfect little body.

His younger brother, Joss, when he arrived, had a less thoughtful, though no less appreciative relationship with mud. He too felt the need to strip off to appreciate it fully and loved nothing more than painting himself, and sometimes his sister, from head to toe in its sticky glory. Faced with this field of Spanish mud I kept my clothes on, but channelled my inner child, relishing the squelch of the mud and the ooze under my feet. Once your boots are that dirty you might as well go for it.

Just before we reached the muddy stretch, Mike had presented Stefano with a branch of blossom.

'A symbol of our friendship,' he said. 'Prickly, but with some pretty decent flowers.'

Stefano was clutching his bouquet as they waded into the mud, Mike wearing sandals, as his feet were too sore for boots. Then, with a primordial howl Stefano slipped in the swamp, all pedalling legs and flailing arms. He landed flat on his back, somehow keeping his arm straight up in the air, holding the flowers aloft. The little Italian beetle, weighted down by his rucksack, lay for a moment admiring his bouquet, until Mike took pity on him and helped him back onto his feet.

Laughing, we made it through the mud and the Meseta fell away once again to reveal Hontanas, a little village with a welcome coffee stop. Looking like a creature from the swamp, I visited a tiny shrine to Santa Brigida complete with a finely painted dome ceiling before stopping to wash the mud off at a hosepipe stand.

Lynne and Tinker queued for the loos while Ali and Jean charmed the waiter who brought them free doughnuts to have with their coffee. Outside in the sun, Jean introduced us to Luis, a pilgrim she had walked with a couple of days before. He was Spanish, but had worked in Kendal in the Lake District for a couple of years so his English was excellent. He was small, like Jean, and I guessed he was in his mid-twenties. His twinkly hazel eyes and wide smile made him look like he was ready for mischief. My teacher's spidey senses turned out to be spot on.

'Last night in Hornillos, I went up to the castle after dinner. It was all locked up but I was sure there would be a way in. I found a small door that was open and crawled through it. I was all alone in there and I climbed up onto the battlements and shouted, "I'm the King of the Castle!" That's what you say in England, no?'

By early afternoon my legs had started to feel the strain and I broke off from the group to walk at my own pace for a while. Lynne found it hard to slow down, and Ali had become turbo charged and was keeping up with her. 'You know what she's like,' Ali said. 'She's chatting away and I get caught up in her stories and forget about everything else.'

We reconvened at the towering ruins of the *Convento de San Anton*, where a man in a van was stamping passports. We bought wooden Tau crosses, made by the nuns, to hang on our rucksacks. In the empty rose windows of the ruins we spotted the Tau, the ancient symbol of healing and resurrection. My shin was feeling oddly tight so maybe a healing cross would come in handy.

I took the last 8km slowly and Ali, who was paying for her burst of enthusiasm, joined me at the back, flagging. Keeping up with Lynne had been a bad idea.

She had her game face on. 'Don't talk to me. I'm gritting my teeth and bearing it.'

Her rictus grin slipped as we walked past a perfectly acceptable looking albergue in the hope of something better. 'What if the one in town is full? We might have to walk back to this one,' she said, sounding like the very thought was too much to bear. But the others were too far on to hear our calls and we had no choice but to plug on. I knew she felt as I did, that had it been just the two of us we would have been taking our boots off in the first place we saw.

Fortunately we were in luck and there were beds for us in the *Casa Nostra* so we shrugged off our rucksacks and flopped onto our bunks.

Castrojeriz was a long village that traversed the hillside so that everywhere you went there were wide views across the valley. The stone was cosy and hospitable and this felt like a vibrant community, unlike so many of the deserted towns we had walked through.

Just after 2pm we ate our picnic in the square, as a happy family celebrated the Baptism of a baby girl in a bar next door. The bearded man with the donkey and the red cart pulled into the square as we ate. The little dog, who had previously been in the driver's seat, now stood on the donkey's back and the man got out his bagpipes and entertained us all for a while.

Tinker and Lynne were on the lookout for a chemist so Ali and I made the most of the afternoon sun and lay feet-to-feet on the low wall opposite our albergue. The silence was soothing and I think I must have fallen asleep as I was sunburnt when I came to. Maybe I was dreaming, but I swear a man in a cloth hat and a roughly woven tunic walked past, a bushel of sticks tucked under his arm – it could have been 1,000 years ago.

Our bedroom in the albergue had two huge windows, which looked right out across the valley. The blue sky was clear and gave an illusion of warmth, but indoors it was so cold Ali's fingers turned deathly white and the freezing showers left us dripping and chilled. The four of us huddled in our bunks to warm up before dinner. An Australian woman and her teenage son didn't move from their spot in front of the Calor gas fire and a man on a top bunk went straight to bed at 5pm and was in the same position when we returned from supper.

Jean was staying in the municipal albergue up the road with Donkey Man and his dog (the donkey had to stay outside) and we met up with her, Stefano and Mike for supper. The pilgrim menu in the bar in the centre of town was excellent and we were a raucous crowd. When my fish, a hake steak, arrived, I stared at my plate, aghast.

'My fish… it has a face,' I said. And they couldn't disagree. The parsley and the bones created a perfect line drawing of a woman's face, quite a pretty one, complete with eyelashes. And she was winking. I had heard of people seeing Mary on a slice of toast, but this floozy was no Madonna.

Day 16
24ᵗʰ April
Hornillos del Camino – Castrojeriz
Kari, Ali, Tinker, Lynne, Jean
Wherever we go now we are greeted by fellow peregrinos who know us by name and whose stories are unfolding to us by the day. Ali and I are pleased that Tinker and Lynne have met these Camino characters; we were worried people might think we are making them up. Today has been extraordinary and this village so peaceful that I am almost reluctant to move on – but I'm freezing cold and the snoring has started up so maybe I will be ready by the morning.

CHAPTER 18

And just as everything was going so beautifully. . .

We left Castrojeriz before daybreak on a cold, cold morning. The streetlights, like the old gas lamps in Edinburgh, were still on and behind us we could see the first shaft of sunlight at the end of the long, cobbled street. The sky was clear and the ground frosty so we set off at a fair crack to warm up.

We walked through farmland, crossed a narrow causeway and paused for a moment on an icy wooden bridge. The light was rosy and under hoods and hats, Ali, Tinker, Jean and Lynne were glowing pink. The crystals of hoar frost glinted in the sun and I stopped to take some photographs while the others pushed on, up the dauntingly steep Alto de Mostaleres.

I preferred to tackle hills alone, not wanting to waste precious breath on conversation, enjoying the silence of the morning. When the going got tough I paced myself with 'Hail Marys'. I took them slow, matching the rhythm of the prayer with my footfall. This was a whole rosary hill. The sun was coming up as I reached the top, and breathless, I stopped for a moment to take in the spectacular panorama. Tinker and Lynne, having got there some time before me, had already been chatting to a pilgrim who had just emerged from a frost-covered tent at the summit.

Our walk continued across the Meseta and we began a short, steep descent to the fertile plains below: ahead of us, the hill cast a deep shadow. As the sun rose behind us a spotlight of brilliant white crested the arc of the shadow and remained just ahead of us, leading us down through the fields. The stillness was hard to express, the only noise was birdsong. The cuckoo kept us company and later frogs added to the chorus. The crops surrounding us were extraordinarily lush, greener than green, and in the silence our thoughts turned, as they often did, to home and family.

All five of us walking today had lost our fathers. Ali's dad had been a farmer and this landscape made her feel his presence. How envious he would have been of these wide, open fields and of the fertile, rock-free soil. The farm in Invergordon, where she grew up, had not been so yielding.

'When we first moved there, I was eight and David, my brother, was ten. Dad used to pay us 50p an hour to pick stones out of the fields. I was saving up for a pony and would stick at it for hours, long after David had given up and gone home.' If anyone can defer gratification, it is Ali, and it came as no surprise that she saved every penny to buy her first pony. Her dad, of course, must have paid the bulk of the bill but he allowed his small, determined daughter the pleasure of believing she had earned and paid for it herself. He was wrapped around her little finger, the default position for all of our dads, it seemed.

Jean's father was the principal teacher of a school for children with Learning Difficulties and instilled a strong sense of responsibility and duty in her and her brothers and sister. She painted a clear picture of him when she described his short stature and his immense charisma. As a young man, he had served in the military.

'One day he was returning home on leave and he was wearing his uniform as he walked down the main street. A woman pulled up her car and said, "Sonny, would you like me to drive you home? My son was a Boy Scout."

'He smiled at her and replied, "Why thank you, ma'am, that's a mighty kind offer, but I'm in the US Army and I'm looking forward to the walk home."'

Tinker's father had died when she was in her early 20s. He had been an action-man dad and had instilled in her a love of skiing, sailing and the outdoors. He had died too soon, at a time in her life when she was stretching her wings and finding her own way, before she had a chance to come back to him. This saddened her still.

My own father was my hero. He died when I was 28, a year and a half after our son, Alexander was born. Although I saw him the week before he died, I was at home in Jersey when the phone call came to tell me that he had gone. He had always been my greatest champion and he made me believe there was nothing I could not do if I set my mind to it. We had been through a lot together and I missed him terribly.

Lynne, a great storyteller, got us smiling again when things turned a little sad.

'My dad sounds a lot like yours, Jean. He was a teacher too, and he tried to bring us up with a social conscience. He liked to make sure we did the right thing. He would send me down the street to pick up beer cans. "Lynne," he would say, "those darn kids have been drinking again, go get the empties and put them in the trash."' She imitated her father's gruff voice.

'So when I was a teenager and my friends and I were drinking I'd say, "Don't worry about hiding the empties, just leave them at the bottom of our road and my father will send me down to get them tomorrow."' Hiding the evidence in plain sight worked a treat.

The walking seemed easy and we sang in the sunshine, deciding that life was just about perfect. Every couple of hours the real world reared its head when the infuriating clown horn ringtone of Tinker's mobile burst our bubble. But, for the most part, I escaped into the timelessness of the pilgrimage, feeling connected to the thousands who had walked that way since pagan times, and the four friends who were right by my side.

I passed a field where bushels of sticks tied up with blue twine were stacked in bundles, used for kindling, now, as they would have been then. In this landscape it was not hard to picture how things would have been; many of the buildings we passed were more than 800 years old. Every now and then

I checked the compass that dangled from my rucksack thanks to my loving, anxious husband. We were, invariably, heading due west, following the moon that set in the late morning, and the long shadows that pointed out the way.

It was early when we stopped for lunch in Boadilla del Camino. Curious, we followed our noses through a little arched entrance into an albergue run by a sculptor. Evidence of her skill was everywhere and the secret garden in the middle of this stony village, was a haven. We sat in the garden for two hours, eating soup and salad, chatting, and watching the storks that were nesting on the church steeple next door.

'Who wants a chocolate biscuit?' Jean asked, delving into her bottomless rucksack. She had been walking with us for just a couple of days, but she already felt like an integral part of our team. She had even started contributing to the kitty. We were constantly amazed by the things she produced from her bag in moments of need and decided she was our Mary Poppins.

Tinker bought us all yellow arrow stickpins for our rucksacks and as I was attaching mine I dropped it. A search of the garden ensued. The waiter joined us on his hands and knees as we ran our fingers through the grass searching for the tiny arrow. Finally, we had to admit defeat. It was lost.

He handed me a replacement. 'I promise I will keep looking for the one that is lost,' he told us. 'I will find it one day.'

The tiny pin had no real monetary value, but his sincerity was striking. At home, if things are lost, I buy a new one. If something is broken I replace it with a newer and better model. Our house in Scotland was overflowing with stuff, and just thinking about the cluttered cupboards and study crammed with cables and redundant technology made me feel uneasy and burdened. I resolved to purge when I got home. To shed excess weight like an aircraft jettisoning fuel.

We arrived at our destination, Frómista, in good time and settled on the municipal albergue as the guidebook promised small bedrooms. Stefano and Mike had a few cardinal rules, a bit like Jenny's but with more swearing. Rule number one was: 'Fuck the municipal'. It wasn't subtle, but it was to the point and, you would think, easy to remember.

We knew the rule, yes, but we were fearless middle-aged risk takers and we would take our chances. What could go wrong?

It didn't start well as Ali got off on the wrong foot with the hospitalera. Pointing at a photo on the desk she asked with a grin, 'Is that your daughter?'

'No,' came the tetchy reply. 'That's me.'

Without a smile she showed us to our room, which seemed reasonable enough. All of the beds were made up with bottom sheets except Ali's, and as she looked weary I stepped in to make it for her. And that's when it happened.

There... in the sheet... was the creatures of our nightmares... a bedbug. No. Not one, but two ladybird-sized, round, hard, brown, obviously dead, beetly bedbugs. Knowing I had to get them away from Ali quickly, before she about turned and went back to Scotland, I bundled up the sheet and took it straight to the tetchy hospitalera on the desk.

Instantly she was on the defensive.

'No, no, no. That no bed bug. We 'ave no bedbugs. No bedbugs here!' she shouted at me.

'They look like bedbugs,' I insisted.

'No! No bedbugs. This ees very clean place.' She snatched the sheet from me and indicated that I should follow her to the laundry where she provided me with another sheet.

'The problem,' I said, 'is not the sheet but the bed. I think perhaps we will move on to another albergue.'

At this suggestion she became distraught and marched me up to the bedroom shouting in Spanish that we must stay there tonight and that she would be ruined if we left. She was drawing attention. And I was mortified.

By the time we reached the room the girls had found more bugs in the other beds. The whole albergue had, by now, got wind that something was up. Mary, the dark-haired lady from

Boston who had looked after us in Hornillos, looked out from her top bunk.

'Bedbugs? Did someone say bedbugs?'

At the mention of the word hysteria broke out. Several pilgrims walked, nay ran, out of the albergue as if it were anthrax, not bedbugs, that we had discovered. Others gathered in the doorway of our room just to look at us. People were pointing. The hospitalera was in a complete fandango and we, rather bemused by the storm we had unleashed, followed her to another room where she shut us in, telling us that we must stay there or she would lose all her business.

Feeling like we had no option but to remain, whilst wishing we were anywhere else, the girls inspected every bed thoroughly and found no more evidence of the little critters. Ali, who had been freaking out about bedbugs before we'd even set off from Edinburgh, became a picture of composure; whereas I, initially quite brave, froze, trying to make sure that no part of my body, bar the soles of my shoes, was making contact with anything in the room.

'Let's head into town and buy some bug spray,' Lynne said. She kept a spotless house but I could tell she was squirming at the idea of sleeping on those bunks. If she had called home, Tim, her husband, would have booked us in to a five-star hotel in the blink of an eye; but she knew, for us, that wasn't an option so she stepped into 'fix it' mode, making the best of it. We willingly followed her out, heads down as we passed the judging eyes of our fellow pilgrims resting on their bunks.

In a street café, we found Mommy Mary and her daughter Meyrick and waited with them until the farmacia opened.

'Wine will help, ladies. Really it will,' Mary said. It helped a bit.

The chemist must have been rubbing his hands when he saw us coming and we bought every one of his anti-bug potions for the beds, and for our bodies. He also gave me an ointment for my now rampant cold sores which he said he had made himself.

Tinker was perhaps the hardiest amongst us. She was used to sleeping in mouldy bothies on the edges of mountains or in the back of a camper van with a gaggle of smelly cyclists. The odd bedbug, for her, was not worth getting her thong in a tangle. She sprayed the beds and our sleeping bags, while the rest of us sprayed ourselves. I was itching all over when we headed out again for supper, my mind playing tricks on me, as it used to when there was an outbreak of nits at school. Everything and everybody smelled of tea-tree and I found some comfort in that.

Stefano and Mike who were staying in a fabulous private albergue, shook their heads when we approached. Bad news travelled fast on the Camino.

'I don't believe it. Did I or did I not tell you to stay away from the municipals? You are crazy women. Crazy. Leave the municipals to the teenagers,' Stefano berated us.

'Say the rule after me. All together now…'

Rule firmly committed to memory, we joined them for beer and pizza before reluctantly heading back to Bedbug Central.

Day 17
25ᵗʰ April
Castrojeriz – Frómista
Kari, Ali, Tinker, Lynne, Jean
The Bed Bug Incident has left us all squirming. Ainsley and Tim, 2 sides of the love triangle that has kept us so entertained, have joined us in our quarantine quarters. Ali has her silk sleeping bag liner pulled up round her head with the drawstring tied under her chin and Jean is sitting outside distributing love and wise counsel to her 'Camino teenagers'. Tim has now abandoned most of his kit, including his sleeping bag, and is travelling very light. Perhaps he should have kept a change of clothes, as he is a little ripe. I think it might be a long night.

CHAPTER 19

Long before my alarm went off I was awake and itching to get out of bed. Fear of the bugs had kept us firmly tucked inside our sleeping bags and much to our relief, nobody had been bitten. We were eager to leave the municipal far behind us, but took the time to check all our kit before we packed it into our rucksacks.

Like fugitives we sneaked out past the sleeping pilgrims.

'Where do you think you are going? I have reason to suspect you are smuggling bedbugs,' came a voice from behind the desk.

Jean had taken up residence in the tetchy hospitalera's chair and was sitting with her feet up, hands behind her head, in a final act of defiance before we high-tailed it out of Frómista.

The sunrise was glorious and I stopped to take pictures of seed heads covered in cobwebs, glinting in the dew. There was something magical about the early morning light and it seemed to draw my attention to things I might otherwise have overlooked. My nerves were soon soothed and the high drama of the night before forgotten.

Many of the rural churches we passed were perfunctory rectangular buildings with elaborate bell gables facing the street. 'Fur coat and nae knickers,' my mum would have said. Bells swung through a trio of simple openings and the ledges below the bells were the favourite nesting spots for storks. In the morning sunshine shafts of light shot through the openings, and I was caught by the sight of the birds and their giant nests, silhouetted against the sun.

There is nothing like walking for building up an appetite and we were looking forward to that first coffee of the morning when we came across signs for the Hermitage of San Miguel.

'It's a sign. We have to make a mini pilgrimage to pay our respects to our patron saint,' said Lynne. 'It would be rude not to.'

Although it was a little early to chink beer bottles we took a detour and made a metaphorical toast: he had certainly been good to us. And our efforts were soon rewarded with an enormous pastry known as a Napolitana de Chocolate (a big Spanish pain au chocolat) and a fine café con leche grande.

We had expected the day's walk to be a bit dull as, for the most part, the main route was on the *sendas* – rather uninspiring footpaths that ran alongside the road. So over breakfast, we consulted the map and opted for an alternative route that ran alongside the Rio Ucieza. It was longer, but promised to be quieter.

The five of us seemed to be the only pilgrims on this 'road less travelled'. High on the fact that we had survived the bedbugs we were in a buoyant mood and Jean and I split a set of headphones and sang along to some John Denver. David had made a 'Camino Playlist' for me and I had been saving it for a moment when I needed an emotional boost. Life was so good that it didn't feel like I was ever going to need that boost so we stuck it on and joined in with such show stoppers as *You've Got a Friend*, *Feeling Good*, *Shut Up and Dance* and the old classic *Ca Plane Pour Moi*. It was like Guru Dudu's walking disco from the Edinburgh Fringe all over again, and as we wiggled our booties, waved our poles and sang at the top of our lungs. I felt on top of the world. We caught up with Ali, Tinker and Lynne in time for a whole group rendition of the Camino tune to end all Camino tunes – The Proclaimers: *500 Miles*.

'Yes, I will walk 500 miles, but I'm buggered if I'm going to walk 500 more,' said Ali.

Then, thoroughly spent, like a toddler who had overdone it in the soft-play area, I was happy to return to the calm of the Way, the birds, the noise of the river and the ever-changing landscape. Today the low, flat scenery reminded me of the Netherlands with its red barns and stripes of fields in green and yellow.

A short stretch on a quiet road took us to Palomar del Camino – an ancient dovecote with a café alongside. The immaculate, white dovecote was cylindrical with no windows, and inside the light came from the small holes for the birds just below the roof. Warmed up by the coffee and the impromptu disco I unzipped the bottoms of my trousers.

Camino fashion is a wonderful thing and we felt we could carry off one or two looks that might have been a little too 'out there' back home. Ali rocked the 'gilet as a skirt over leggings' look but I particularly enjoyed unzipping the bottoms of my walking trousers and leaving the calf sections loose round the ankles, like baggy gaiters. This was cooling and added a certain relaxed elegance to the otherwise rigid boot. The effect could be enhanced by tucking the sock over the top of the redundant trouser bottom to create a cuff in a contrasting colour. This look was not for everybody and I would recommend it only for the more experimental of Camino fashionistas. This morning we followed a sandal-wearing pilgrim in a cape who clearly drew his fashion inspiration from St James himself. Great close up, but from a distance he looked more like Darth Vader or perhaps Severus Snape.

As we rejoined the main path, our expectations were low, but we found the Way quiet, the company good and the sunshine warming. Our cuckoo was back.

Yesterday over wine, Mary had told us that it was in fact her cuckoo and that it was following her. When I begged to differ, Ali broke the news to us that there might, be more than one. Mary was in raptures about the 'sweet little bird' and was somewhat deflated when I told her a few facts about the nasty little interlopers. As we drank our wine, she

Googled 'cuckoo' and was horrified to see pictures of the giant chicks, demanding food from stepparents half their size, step-siblings long since pushed out of the nest.

'They sound so friendly. Who knew they were such little monsters?' she said.

About midday, Stefano and Mike caught up with us and we walked together for a while. Mike could play Stefano like a fiddle and he used statistics to get the little accountant moving faster. 'Today we are going for a personal best,' he called as they sprinted ahead.

Mike's tactics seemed to be working. We too made good time and arrived at about 2pm, some in our party having a more strongly developed competitive streak than others. Jean and I were happy idling along, smelling the flowers and stopping every couple of hours for a coffee. Ali was always worried about not finding a bed and became twitchy when I dawdled. Lynne didn't have a slow setting and when Mike sprinted off it was all we could do to stop Tinker from running after him. Sometimes she calculated how quickly she could reach Santiago if she was running or on a bike.

'It's not about the destination, it's about the journey,' I said, full of Camino wisdom.

Ali rolled her eyes. 'You won't be saying that if we end up sleeping in a hedgerow.'

As place names go, Carrion is not the most inviting, but we liked this quirky place and there was not a dead animal in sight. Our first stop was *Santa Maria del Camino*, a dark and twinkling church that pleased Ali because it smelled old and fusty. It was still and cool and a good place to spend some time at the end of a fast walk.

These church stops were important to me. It gave me a moment to settle myself, to return to the here and now. In the stillness I sat alongside Lynne and gave thanks for the friends I was walking with and the friends who were following our progress back home. She held my hand briefly, and gave it a squeeze, letting me know without any need for words that she was glad to be sharing this with me, that our friendship was precious.

I gave thanks for my husband and each of my children in turn, picturing their faces, imagining the smell of their hair. I heard the words, 'Let go,' and repeated them in my head. 'Let go.' For the last few days these words had come to me. 'Let go,' I prayed again.

I prayed too for my mother. Last night my sister had told me that Mum enjoyed hearing about our walk, and that she perked up when she read her my posts. At other times, Patsy said, Mum seemed unusually quiet, as if she was wrestling with something she was not ready to share. For most of her life Mum had believed she was invincible, I had believed it too, but since she was first diagnosed with mouth cancer the fight had gone out of her. She deeply resented this illness that forced her to accept her own mortality, as well as help and care. For someone used to being in charge, it was a struggle to relinquish one iota of her power.

Ironically, for me, the last four years had perhaps been the most harmonious in our adult relationship. Although there was no intimacy, we spent happy afternoons visiting the Scottish Antique Centre (where she demonstrated that she had not lost her keen eye for quality or her skills in negotiating), doing the crossword puzzle and talking about the old times, before I was born. Passing on stories was important to her and she wanted us to know about our heritage.

Until I was 40, I hadn't known that her family were travelling people, but once this secret was out, she had plenty to say on the subject. Her father had become a 'flattie', a settled person, before she was born, but she spoke words of de Gammon Kant and kept herself somewhat distant from the settled community. Her sisters were her best friends and family was everything to her. Now she was the 'last of the Mohicans' as she liked to put it. All of them were gone, and she missed them terribly.

After the night with the cold water, and the night with no heating, and all the nights with the snoring, and of course the night with the bedbugs, we were reluctant to take any chances with accommodation. We had picked up a flier for an albergue on a waymarker just before the town and although this was evidently the work of an enterprising hospitalero, we were happy to be persuaded that this was another 'sign'. Jean was not so easily defeated and braved the municipal yet again.

'I love you, Jean, but this time you're on your own,' I said. 'We'll see you at dinner time.'

The saying is that 'The Camino will provide' and that day we needed a clean dorm, hot water and a room for four. Thank you, Camino. We got just what we asked for.

The boys headed to a convent where a tiny nun, half Stefano's size (and he's not tall), greeted them and showed them to their room. Meanwhile, the four of us, like corpses laid out in a funeral parlour, lay stretched on our four single beds and waited for the feeling to return to our feet. Then it was showers all round and what a treat it was to have an ensuite bathroom.

'Don't tell Tim, but this is better than sex,' shouted Lynne from under the power shower.

Back last November, when I had been trying, not very subtly, to persuade Ali to come with me on the Camino, I had made promises. We had just finished climbing Arthur's Seat and I had bought her a 99 from the van at the bottom of the hill.

'Imagine. We will be burning off so many calories we can have an ice cream every single day,' I had said, playing to her weakness.

Sadly, there had been very few opportunities for gratuitous consumption and I felt I'd let her down. Today, the sun was shining, we were in Spain, and surely there would be ice cream.

Clean and refreshed we set off on a *helado* hunt but much to our disappointment a Magnum was the best Carrion had to offer. Disgusted, we bought some prunes and headed down to the river. Moments later, Jean, Stefano and Mike strolled past and joined us on the benches in the park, sharing our prunes, and chatting. Mike and Tinker entertained us by trying out the exercise equipment that must have been installed to help the inhabitants of Carrion embrace a healthy outdoor lifestyle.

Stefano had the soul of a poet and talked a bit more about the choices that faced him. He had built a life in London, but his family lived in Rome and these two aspects seemed irreconcilable. He had given up a good job because he knew it was not making him happy, but, as yet, the future was uncertain.

'I feel like my life is a painting and I have found myself with only a small piece of the canvas left still to paint. I like what I have painted, it is beautiful, but it is not the painting I wanted to create. I want to start the canvas again before I get to the end, and put my signature to it.'

Later, with flagrant disregard for Jenny's Rule Number 1: Never eat in a square, and Rule Number 2: Never eat in a restaurant with pictures on the menu, we sat in the playa mayor and made the most of the evening sun whilst eating a disappointing deep-fried dinner. Children played on their scooters, pregnant ladies met to attend an antenatal class, geezers in souped-up cortinas revved up and down the narrow streets and an old man tried to steal Tinker's calamari – all good.

Day 18
26ᵗʰ April
Frómista – Carrion de los Condes
Kari, Ali, Tinker, Lynne
I love our quiet little room. I have the light on while I type and no one is snoring. Tomorrow we reach the half way stage and I feel both proud to have made it this far, and a little sad that this incredible adventure is no longer beginning. I don't want it to end.

CHAPTER 20

Some days were harder than others. Despite the luxury of the private albergue I woke with aching feet and for the first time in nearly three weeks I didn't want to get out of bed. Tinker and Lynne, still relatively fresh and brimming with energy, were much more enthusiastic than Ali or me, and I struggled not to let my grumpiness show.

The hospitalero from our albergue, which boasted many fine features like hot water and sheets, had told us about three places where we could get breakfast on the way out of Carrion. His timings, however, were way out, and all three were still closed when we passed them before 7am.

We had arranged to meet Jean by *San Zoilo*, once a monastery and now a swanky 4* hotel, and we thought we might as well see if they would serve us coffee. Their café didn't open until 8am and they suggested we try a petrol station nearby. The petrol station was also shut.

Normally this wouldn't have been a problem as there was usually a little town within a couple of hours of our starting point, but today we had been warned that it was 17km before the first shop or loo.

Wee Jean dug around in her magic rucksack and produced an enormous box. 'I have some cereal bars,' she said, distributing one to each of us. We ate them in the garage forecourt, washed down with water, before carrying on, grateful but somewhat despondent. David would vouch for the fact that I don't do well without caffeine. And that I don't do well when I'm hungry. This morning I was struggling to keep 'Bad Kari' in.

The walk was straight and the scenery flat and featureless. When we were planning the pilgrimage back in January, I had marked that day on the planner as 'dull'. And dull it was. I took hardly any photographs and I speeded up considerably as a result. Knowing I needed a bit of time to myself, and not wishing to inflict my grumpiness on the others, I plugged in my headphones and listened to the Archers for a while. Poor Helen.

Ten miles in, my mood was at an all-time low, the lack of coffee and the need for a loo stop having kicked in with a vengeance. Al fresco peeing is all well and good but the landscape was flat, the road was straight and the verges were sparse. With pilgrims dispersed at about five-minute intervals, if a person *was* game enough to attempt it, they would need to time it carefully. Jean devised a plan to use her green poncho as a screen so that we could preserve our dignity. But only in extremis would this be an option for me. I was the child who, as a weekly boarder, could go from Monday morning till Friday night without a poo.

The other night, Mary told us, she had been walking with PJ, the hot priest.

'Would you like to say the Rosary with me, Mary?' he had asked. She said she would and they walked together for an hour or more, praying.

'Forgive me, Father,' she said, as they finished the rosary. No doubt he thought he was about to hear her Confession. He must have been a bit surprised then when she continued, 'I have to go to the ladies' room.' By which she meant, dive behind a tree: not something people often do in the presence of a priest.

At an uninspiring concrete picnic table we pooled our resources and shared a modest second breakfast of one orange, some dried apricots, nuts, and a bit of leftover cheese. Holy Kate, the Australian yoga teacher, identifiable from miles off by her orange jacket, joined us for a while.

She was a convert to Catholicism and her fervour was intense. Blonde and strikingly beautiful, she looked an unlikely evangelist, and when she told us about her rock-and-roll past it was easier to picture her as a rock chick. But she was utterly sincere and it was this that made her enthusiasm bearable.

'Back in Burgos, I managed to gatecrash the beatification ceremony of the four martyrs of the civil war,' she told us, looking so thrilled you would have thought she was telling us she had sneaked in backstage to a Rolling Stones concert circa 1969. 'At first, I was turned back by security, but I grabbed onto the back of this old nun's habit and told the doorman I was with her. The old dear didn't mind, and we got great seats.' This was how she got her kicks these days. Crazy cat.

As we were talking to Kate and eating our meagre smorgasbord, a German woman walked up to the side of our table, pulled down her pants and peed right there beside us. Being British we averted our eyes and said not a word, but it took the edge off breakfast somewhat, and we packed up our things. We should have held up Jean's poncho.

When you learn about Roman roads in primary school they tell you they are long and straight and this one was exactly that: long, straight and stretching out interminably in front of us. The grey gravel path we were walking on was laid on top of the 2,000-year-old Via Aquitana, a Roman trading road that led to Astorga. We passed a small preserved section where you could see the stonework of the original, which would have been raised above the surrounding fields. Although it was humbling to think of the history of our journey, for the most part, long and straight is dull indeed and we had to make our own entertainment.

We sang the songs we used to sing to our babies to keep them from falling asleep in the back of the car and Tinker and I made up an extra ten verses of *Green grow the rashes, oh*. We sang hits from the musicals and all the 80s pop songs we could remember. We sang hymns from school and jingles from adverts, Christmas hits and dirty rugby songs. And then, when there were no songs left to sing we played a marathon game of 'In my Camino Rucksack I packed...' Yes, it was a long, hard road.

Then, in the distance, almost like a mirage, a building came into view. My heart leapt as I dared to hope that this place might offer both coffee and a loo – an answer to my prayers. The closer we got the less appealing it looked. Pilgrims were huddled in what could best be described as a bus shelter and they confirmed my fears that there was no loo and certainly no coffee to be had here. I did not hold back on sharing my disappointment.

Behind the 'bus stop' hundreds of pilgrims, unable to hold it in any longer, had used the field as an open-air privy and we had no option but to do the same, one at a time. In front of the shelter, Stefano and Mike were standing up eating sandwiches, feeling similarly despondent. Lying on the ground beside Mike lay a pair of tights filled with sand, perhaps used in some sort of penitential flogging ritual. Certainly it all felt pretty punitive today. We stepped back onto the path disappointed: for once the Camino had not provided.

Or had she?

Just as we hoisted our rucksacks onto our backs, it happened – *The Miracle of the White Van*.

'There's our coffee,' Tinker said.

'No, it's just a white van,' I replied.

'Let's see.'

And lo, it stopped right in front of us and a man with a generator hopped out. I looked at the huddled pilgrims sitting in the shelter behind me, not sure what they were waiting for and turned to the man.

'Café?' I asked.

'Si,' came the answer we were all hoping for. The seven of us burst into a spontaneous rendition of the *Hallelujah Chorus* and the hunched pilgrims uncurled, smiled and cheered. Miracles, it seemed, came when you least expected them, and in the most practical of forms. And gratitude filled us, happiness spilt over.

Five minutes later we were caffeinated and ready to go. And then, just two kilometres further on, we were caffeinating again at the 17km café, which had seemed apocryphal for so long. We stocked up on lunch supplies and Jean made friends with another shopkeeper who brought her yet another free doughnut and wished us *Buen Camino*.

Despite these moments of euphoria, the last 10km were a complete slog. Ali's blisters were throbbing, Tinker's bunion was giving her grief and my shoulder was tingling with the cold needles and pins sensation which had been bothering me for a week or so now. We soldiered on, not chatting so much now, just listening to the rhythm of our feet and the poles on the gravel. Sometimes I recited poems in my head, or said my prayers in time with the beat. We passed through the town of Ledigos and were tempted to call it a day there, but the place smelled of lamb and we were not keen.

On the final stretch the landscape became more interesting and we saw houses with walls made of mud and straw and wild flowers on the verges. In truth, we were too tired to appreciate much, our eyes fixed, as they were, on the prize – a bed for the night. As we took the risky decision to walk straight past the first of the two albergues, Ali caught my eye, letting me know she was done in. For the second time in two days, the thought of backtracking was almost unbearable but to our relief they had room for us at the second and it had been worth taking the risk.

Passports stamped, the hospitalera showed us to our room and we collapsed on our bunks. A little voice from Jean's bed declared, 'I'm so happy!' and we all knew just how she felt: the release at taking the weight off our backs and the boots off our feet was immense.

This was our first two-beer day and as we enjoyed the last of the sun in the courtyard we felt we deserved them. We were even able to get some washing done before supper.

Terradillos de los Templarios was an unassuming little

place with a grand history, but although no buildings of historical significance still existed, the legacy of the Knights Templar was everywhere in evidence. We were staying in the *Jacques de Molay Albergue*, named after the last Grand Master of the order. Red Templar crosses adorned the walls and a huge mural of a knight looked over the courtyard.

We had reached the halfway mark and celebrated with a bottle of Cava over our pilgrim supper. Tinker ordered minestrone soup that had to be eaten with a knife and fork and consisted almost entirely of green beans, and the rest of us had roast chicken – delicious.

Day 19
27ʰ April
Carrion de los Condes – Terradillos de los Templarios
Kari, Ali, Tinker, Lynne, Jean
Our dorm is all women and after supper we sat on our bunks and talked for a while. We are sharing with a Dutch woman called Ingrid who is travelling alone and has brought a hot water bottle with her, and a young English artist, who came on the Camino on impulse. She is walking in a pretty skirt and her only waterproof is a flowery anorak she borrowed from her granny.
For the last few days, my thoughts have been less inward looking. Instead I have been caught up in the camaraderie of the walk and the joy of friendship. I am plagued by a niggling worry that I have drifted further from my purpose, rather than drawing nearer to any kind of resolution. Another 27km tomorrow. Oh boy. What the hell was I thinking?

CHAPTER 21

On the way out of Terradillos de los Templarios, we were treated to the most glorious sunrise. The wide mackerel sky seemed to be on fire and the great, corrugated expanse of oranges and pinks was edged with a gold that glistened like it was molten. It was freezing, but our faces glowed and the fields of bare orange earth gave an illusion of warmth. Our va-va-voom was most definitely va-va-back.

We walked as a group, chatting all the way and before we knew it, we were approaching Moratinos. In the distance we could see large, grassy hummocks, almost like burial mounds. As we got closer, we spotted chimneys poking up from the tops and closer still, we picked out little doorways, curved like eyelids, cut into the hillside. My curiosity was piqued and Jean went with me to investigate while the others stayed in the village, ordering desayunos.

The doorways, just big enough for tiny Jean to stand up in, were entrances into the Bodegas of Moratinos. An information board nearby told us that these cave-like structures had been around for 2,000 years. They looked just like hobbit holes, and the tiny, shell-decorated doorways were welcoming and inviting. They were traditionally used as cellars and for winemaking, but nowadays they are used mainly as cold stores. The TV aerial attached to one of the chimneys hinted at an alternative use – in Britain our menfolk may retreat to the garden shed, but here in Spain, the 'man-cave' seemed to be the real deal.

Curiosity satisfied, we rejoined the girls in a café where the owners clearly had a taste for the macabre. Although it was April, the place was decorated for Halloween. We were somewhat disconcerted by the bowl of eyeballs near the till and the terrifying scarecrow in the garden. But we had clearly been drawn here for a reason. Jean and Lynne had, for some days now, been craving peanut butter, and the breakfast chat often turned to this favourite protein-rich snack. In this unlikely place, the Camino provided yet again, and on the counter an enormous tub of peanut butter was for sale. Not only did Wee Jean buy it for the group, she also insisted that she carry the extra weight. What more could this little woman fit into her tardis of a rucksack?

With the morning light still rosy we opted once more for the scenic route, a good choice, as the path proved quiet, with hardly another pilgrim in sight. Jean and I walked together, the slow coaches at the back, and she told me a little more about her family. They were close, and nursing her father after his stroke had made them an even tighter unit. Her sister was bringing up her daughter on her own, and Jean was close to her niece, sending her messages most days to keep her updated on her progress. Just before her father had passed away, Jean's brother had been killed in an accident and she told me about the terrible course of events and the devastating impact it had had on them all. She spoke with such calmness and acceptance, but her losses had been shattering and as she spoke the tears rolled down my cheeks. Hearing her talk with such love about her brother made me think of my own. My relationship with him had been fractured for years.

As she spoke I felt a deep, deep sadness that I had allowed things to come between us, and for the first time I felt my brother's pain at being on the outside. Something in Jean's quiet compassion, in her own honest disclosure, helped me put into words how much I wanted to make things right.

My tears had dried by the time we crossed the sleepy Rio Valderaduey and the girls were waiting on the narrow humpback bridge. Just beyond stood Our Lady of the Bridge, a 12th Century church built in the Mudejar style. Outside, we could see the Moorish influence in the geometric patterns of the brickwork and I wanted to get inside to have a closer look.

We tried the door. It didn't budge so we went round the back to see if there was another way in. Absorbed in our hunt for an entrance, we jumped when we heard a voice.

'No luck today, ladies,' said Luis Pilgrim, the Spanish breaker-and-enterer from Hornillos. He came round the side of the church. 'All the doors and windows are locked. It has beaten me.' He bowed like Zorro, gracious in defeat. He had been squeezing through cat-sized openings all across Spain, so if he said there was no way in, there was no way in.

We walked on, chatting while Luis smiled and nodded, his eyes twinkling, and his white teeth flashing. The matchmaker in me was already hoping that he would still be around if Connie joined us.

Before long, we came to a stone gateway with a carved knight on one side and a rustic farmer on the other. It looked as if it belonged on the set of *Indiana Jones: Raiders of the Lost Ark*.

'Rub the knight's left knee. It opens a portal which takes us straight to Santiago,' I suggested.

Jean gave it a go, but we stayed put. Halfway there.

The carving on the gateway claimed this spot as the geographical centre of the Camino, and whether it was or not, we did a small victory dance to mark the moment.

Sahagun, variously miscalled Shangri-La, Chagrin and – my personal favourite – Shogun, was our next stop. We entered this town through a desolate industrial area that looked like it should feature a giant eye on a billboard and a garage with a girl named Myrtle looking out of an upstairs window. There were swastikas graffitied on the walls and this place gave me the chills.

'There was a shoot-out in that pink hotel over there,' said Jean, who had memorised the guidebook. And, five abreast, we walked down the Calle Mayor, whistling the Sergio Leone theme tune from *The Good, the Bad and the Ugly,* looking out for tumbleweed.

It was too early for lunch, but we stopped for a coffee in a bar full of locals who watched us over their coffee cups, frowning at our bulky rucksacks and muddy boots. Out the window, Jean spotted Alex the Brazilian as he emerged from the giant, red municipal albergue, and she ran down the street to say hello. Alex was waiting for Ainsley, who was travelling with Tim. Tim liked Ainsley, Ainsley liked Alex, and we weren't sure who Alex liked, so we sat for a while, wondering if she was about to get off the next bus, and waiting for the drama to unfold. She didn't get off and Alex settled down on the roadside for a long wait.

A hostile town, there was nothing to keep us here except our curiosity, so we decided to get the hell out of Dodge, pausing only for Ali to admire the big tractor that was parked right on the Main Street. We had taken the farmer's daughter out of Invergordon, but we hadn't got her past a tractor yet.

Over a bocadillo lunch we decided that rather than following the main route to Bercianos, we would head for Calzadilla de los Hermanillos. This took us back onto the Via Romana, the longest existing stretch of Roman road left in Spain: Caesar Augustus used this route long before the peregrinos.

At first, the alternative path seemed peaceful with the sun shining on us once again. We saw a procession of millipedes and heard the loudest of frog choruses, stopping to watch their mating antics in the waterways that ran alongside the path.

As the road went on our group dispersed along the straight, flat, empty road. The solitude started to get to me. It was eerily quiet, and after a couple of hours without seeing another living soul, Jean and I passed a wide, low house, set back from the road. The garden was full of broken statuary and decapitated gnomes had been cemented onto every fence post. Weirdest of all, dozens of cats, positioned in every window, stared at us, like the gnomes would have, if they still had their eyes.

Just then a small engine, like a lawnmower, started up. Startled, we caught sight of the occupant in the barn at the end of the property. A moon-faced, lumpen man in faded denim dungarees, was pulling the starter rope of a chainsaw. I looked at Jean, my eyebrows raised as high as they could go, my mouth articulating, 'Oh. My. God.'

With adrenalin coursing through our bodies, we legged it – rucksacks bouncing, sticks cycling in mid-air. Only when we had put a safe distance between Chainsaw Man and us did we finally double up, in the laughter of relief.

But our experience had unsettled me and I was glad when we caught up with the others. As we walked on I was even more conscious of our isolated surroundings and it was a relief when we stumbled upon some fellow pilgrims sitting in the woods. We joined them on a bench which curved round a large stone fountain. The three men looked like hippies from the 60s. One was playing a ukulele and his friend, who wore beads, yellow harem pants, and round John Lennon sunglasses, welcomed us to the grove.

'Hey, guys,' he said. 'Wanna cookie?'

We sat in the shade and shared their snacks, enjoying the music, breathing out. We didn't speak much, just smiled and nodded and communed in the woods. As you do.

'You're a long way from Morningside now, Mrs. Gillespie,' said Ali.

I was footsore and weary when we staggered into Calzadilla just before 4pm, the holiday mood of the morning having long since dissipated. The docile town was deserted, few pilgrims having chosen this route. Since the town was so quiet, we thought it would be worth trying the municipal, ignoring yet again Stefano's golden rule.

The hospitalero looked bored, and grunted a welcome at us as he showed us to our bunks. We were prepared to look past the hole in the stairs and the toilet in the kitchen area, but the filthy sheets were just too much for us. I looked over at Ali who was sitting on her stained mattress, checking for bedbugs. Her shoulders were down and she sighed, looking far from happy. I gathered up the sheets and went to see the surly hospitalero.

'Could we possibly have some clean sheets?' I asked, trying to sound chipper.

'Turn them over,' he suggested without looking up from his book, a Wilbur Smith.

The decision to follow Stefano's advice was unanimous so we packed up our things and got the hell out of Dodge for the second time that day.

We must have looked like a motley crew, boots slung over our shoulders, and towels draped over our packs, as we set off in search of beds for the night. We walked from one end of the long town to the other, but the second place we came to was a hotel and out of our price range. Reluctantly, as going backwards seemed quite, quite wrong, we turned tail and headed back to the first place we had passed as we entered the town.

Lynne, Tinker and Jean forged on ahead, leaving Ali and me on our own at the back. Things had been straightforward when it was just the two of us: making decisions that suited five people seemed a lot more complicated. My sense of humour abandoned me, and Ali, sensing my decline tried to chivvy me along.

'Look at that pretty doorway, Kari. Why don't you take a picture?' she said.

I told her what she could do with her doorway.

She smiled and dangled a liquorice toffee knowing I was close to breaking point.

'It's the last one, and it's just for you,' she said.

Raising her boys had made Ali a master in the art of diversion and I was putty in her expert hands. The sweetie, and her arm around my shoulder, gave me the boost I needed to stagger to option three – the last chance saloon. Like the bears in the story the first bed was too dirty and the second bed, too fancy, but the third bed was just right – so we stayed.

But I was finished. I struggled not to cry when I finally lay down. Everything hurt: my shoulders, my feet, my calves, but most of all my lips, which were a throbbing mass of evil cold sores. I'd had enough of people and when Tinker and Lynne offered to go to the shop to get some supplies, I took the chance to decompress. I shut my eyes for a while, not sleeping, but thinking about home. Home. Struck by a thought, I rummaged in my rucksack, pulling out a wrinkled envelope that had been squashed in an inside pocket. I read: 'For Kari – for when you're wet, tired and completely demoralised.' I ran my finger over the message, imagining David writing, awkward and left-handed.

No.

Today was not the day.

I put it back, and pulled out a postcard which read 'Dream it, believe it, achieve it.' I turned it over and read his message, heard his voice speaking to me: 'If anyone can, you will. You have more determination and vision than the rest of us put together. I expect a lot of this will be very hard, both physically and mentally. It will put you to the test. Expect that and in those trying times focus on your dreams and your beliefs, and you *will* achieve... one step at a time.'

By the time they returned, I had showered and was fit for human society again. They made me laugh, telling me about the shopkeeper with the cross eyes who appeared to have forgotten where he had put the bread and kept looking in different cupboards. Instead, they bought an enormous hunk of cheese that must have weighed about a kilo. We'd have supplies for tomorrow's 24km walk, which wouldn't take us past any services or cafés. Cheese and peanut butter, and plenty of both.

Later, the pilgrim dinner was served in a small dining room with a log fire. Ingrid, who had been in our dorm last night, joined us and we tried all the different starters and shared them family style. A bit of risotto, a bit of pasta, some soup, and plenty of salad – it was good to have some fresh vegetables for a change.

Ingrid had a mop of short blonde curls and her cheeks were downy, like peaches. She had an expression of surprise and never seemed to know where she was going or how she got there, but she oozed good health and kindness. She proudly showed us photos of her son and daughter, and in turn, we did the same. We were all missing our children and the photographs made it harder sometimes. Tomorrow though, Ali's husband, Guy, would be meeting us in Mansilla and he would be bringing a bit of home into our Camino world.

Day 20
28th April
Terradillos de los Templarios – Calzadilla de los Hermanillos
Kari, Ali, Tinker, Lynne, Jean
Today was the hardest yet. The walking was punishing and my spirits low, but tomorrow, Guy arrives with a bundle of quick cryptic crosswords and a fresh supply of liquorice toffees. Tonight, instead of typing in the dark as I normally do, I have the light on as Tinker and Ali are my only roommates and they are not yet asleep. The low wooden ceiling above our single beds smells wonderful but there is something scratching in the eaves – Tinker thinks it's a stork. I hope she's right.

CHAPTER 22

We fuelled up with a cooked breakfast in our albergue, the eggs and ham making a welcome change. There were no facilities on the Via Romana and 24.5km without a chance to refill our water bottles or stop for the now customary coffee meant that we had to be well stocked with supplies. Thankfully, the hospitalera sold us some of her delicious bread so at least we had something to go with Tinker's rock-sized hunk of cheese.

It was gone 7am when we hit the path and soon it was as silent and remote as yesterday. It had only taken Tinker and Lynne a few days to adjust to the Camino mindset, and our walk first thing this morning was meditative once more. Yet again we seemed to be the only pilgrims who had opted for the alternative route but there was no chance of getting lost, as there were few turn-offs on this straight Roman road. The landscape was flat and featureless but the prairies on either side of the warm, yellow path were full of wild mustard and the birdsong kept us smiling.

This was our last day with Lynne and Tinker, and we slowed our pace, in no hurry to reach our destination. Being together on the Camino reminded me of when our families were young and time was on our side. As our children grew they headed off to different secondary schools and work had taken over, leaving no room for those idle hours, watching the kids play and talking about nothing and everything. I had missed the afternoons spent sitting in each other's kitchens or standing at the side of a pitch, touching base with the women whose support was so vital and whose validation gave me strength. We talked, but we also made each other laugh and when I went back to teaching it was the laughter I missed most of all. We knew each other's stories, we had shared the best and the worst, and this time spent together had felt like a gift every day this week.

The sun was shining and mid-morning we stopped by the side of the path to rest our feet. Jean spread out her poncho and we plonked ourselves down, Tinker and I leaning on each other, back to back, with our faces up to the sun. This week, the old Tinker was back and a calmness seemed to have settled upon her. The worry had gone from her face, her brow had relaxed.

'Jean, guess what? I'm so happy,' she said.

Tinker's husband, Gordon, and my eldest son, Alexander, had both sent us Proclaimers songs and we had a sing-along to *Sunshine on Leith* while our toes had a stretch. We saw butterflies aplenty and birds of prey hovering over wide-open fields. *Life doesn't get much better than this,* I thought to myself.

There had been some challenging days and the long, flat walks had been not only physically but also mentally demanding. The ache to see family might have been overwhelming if it was not for the well-timed arrival of the girls. Lynne, for all her joking, is the most grounded person I know. She is a force of goodness and since she moved back to Boston I had missed her positivity and her ability to pull me back to the centre when I was in danger of veering off track.

I told her I had been writing about her in my posts. She doesn't 'do' social media, so there was no chance of her reading it. 'If you must write about me, be sure and say I'm the leggy blonde with pneumatic breasts and eyes that you could drown in.'

'No problem, my frizzy friend. I will turn all 5ft 2" of you into a sex bomb,' I said.

The five of us had laughed and cried and danced and sung for almost 200km and I knew I would miss them when they left.

As we continued on what felt like our own private Camino, the road took us through wetlands and alongside irrigation canals where the frogs were out in force again. Poplars planted in regimental rows provided some shade and added vertical interest to an otherwise horizontal landscape. The bridge over the *arroyo Valle de Valdearcos* gave us a good vantage point and through the crystal-clear water below we could see the streambed, formed of tessellated flat rocks, like the floor in a cathedral.

We were set to continue on the diversion all the way to Mansilla de las Mulas (hands on the saddle of the mules) but an old man and a dog appeared at the only crossroads of the road so far and advised us to go through Reliegos as he promised it would be prettier. He told us the hospitalera, Laura, would look after us when we got there. Whether he was paid by Laura to stand at the crossroads and send people her way, or not, we took his advice and headed to Reliegos in search of a spot where we could eat our picnic.

A concrete table in a municipal park, was not that pretty to be honest, but we spread out our provisions, the massive hunk of cheese and chorizo from the potty shopkeeper, the bread from the albergue and the peanut butter, as if we were at Henley. Just as we were tucking in, Stefano and Mike appeared, joined by a young guy we hadn't seen before, Emmanueli, from Italy. It was good to see them and they told us they too were stopping in Mansilla. As we walked the last 6km together I noticed a twinge in my right shin and attempted to ignore it as best I could.

Guy was arriving later in the afternoon and we had been teasing Ali that she would be booking into the bridal suite at the albergue that night. Guy had made it clear that after years in the army sharing basic accommodation with other soldiers, he would not be roughing it when he joined us. There would be no snorers, sleeping bags and shared showers for him.

Ali was torn. She wanted to be with us for the girls' last night, but equally, she didn't want to leave Guy by himself on his first night in Spain. Finally, knowing that she would be staying in a hotel in León, she agreed to a private albergue where she and Guy could have a double room and the rest of us could stay in a dorm.

'Oooh, I do hope the room with the waterbed is available,' Lynne said.

'And that you packed your silk negligee,' said Tinker.

Ali rolled her eyes. 'The only silk I have is my sleeping bag liner and there's definitely only room in there for one.'

Once in Mansilla we headed straight for the place recommended by the man and the dog, and struck gold. The hospitalero said that they were full in the main building, but that he would show us to their overflow accommodation as soon as he could. In the meantime we should wait in the bar. Music to our ears.

Just as we were sorting it all out, a familiar Scottish voice boomed out from across the quiet street.

'Helloooo sexy ladies! Lookin' good!'

Guy had arrived.

Ali ran into his big, manly arms while we hummed the tune of *Love Story*. A moment later, Guy seemed to be indicating that she should get something out of the back seat of his rental car, and, looking a bit puzzled, she opened the door. Hiding in the foot well was all 6ft 4" of Saunders, her eldest son. Ali, unlike me, is not a crier, but tears came quickly as she buried her head in his chest, smothered in a bear hug. Saunders had been working as a chalet host in the Alps since November and she had missed him terribly. She held his face in her hands, drinking him in, his long shaggy hair, his stubbly chin, his psychedelic fleece – her boy was back. In an instant Ali understood Guy's insistence that he come out to visit – they had been planning this all along.

They came full of stories about the people following my posts and told us about the abundance of good will flowing our way from the hundreds of friends and family following our progress. Guy made us feel like heroes and we were floating on air by the time we reached the beer garden at the back of our albergue.

The sun was shining and right on cue the pilgrims appeared and joined us at our table. Stefano, Mike and Emmanueli, Sara the Curvy German, Lara her little friend, Holy Kate the Australian yoga teacher, Joorst the cheerful Dutchman, his 'better half,' and many more.

We sat in the sun with our beers – large ones – and nursed our aching feet. Ali got her massage bar out and she and I offered foot massages to anyone in need. Stefano and Tinker took me up on my offer while Ali tended to the more seriously afflicted. She did some emergency strapping for Joorst's 'better half', who was looking considerably less cheerful than her husband.

Emmanueli, the young Sicilian who Stefano and Mike had befriended, was walking very strangely, trying not to put his weight on his sore foot, and hobbling badly as a consequence. Ali did her best to fix him too while Holy Kate led an impromptu yoga session in the garden. It was the most perfect of afternoons.

Jean, always the rebel, flouted Stefano's golden rule and opted to stay in the municipal with Ingrid. Later, ten of us – new friends and old – gathered in a restaurant in town to say goodbye to Tinker and Lynne.

Jean and Guy hit it off immediately, all barrel chested 6ft 3" of him towering over her. Guy had the telltale nose of an ex-rugby player and bore more than a passing resemblance to Liam Neeson; somehow we just knew everything was going to be OK when he was around.

Everyone was in a party mood. Stefano regaled us with stories of his shrinking waistline and stunned us into silence by breaking into 'Nessun Dorma' in a deep, full tenor voice. We ate potato and squid stew in little metal pots, meat pastries, orange and endive salads, steak, hake and the ubiquitous crème caramel, and washed it down with excellent red wine. At €14 a head it was our most expensive meal of the Camino but it rounded off what had been a truly brilliant day.

Day 21
29th April
Calzadilla de los Hermanillos – Mansilla de las Mulas
Kari, Ali, Tinker, Lynne, Jean, Guy, Saunders
While Ali and Guy were cracking open the champagne and sticking Barry White on the iPhone, the rest of us had a quick confab about the sleeping arrangements. We have two rooms but for Saunders' sake the three of us have given him a room to himself. It only seems right. So Lynne, Tinker and I are sharing a delightful whitewashed bedroom with an en-suite bathroom and all agree that this is the best accommodation we have had so far.

The only hitch in an otherwise perfect day is that I have developed a pretty severe pain in my right shin – it is some sort of tendonitis according to Ali. I have it elevated and have dosed up with ibuprofen. I am hoping for the best for the morning!

CHAPTER 23

We set off late as it took a while for Ali to strap up my leg. I had been so proud of my speediness in the mornings, but now I was the one in need of some patience. She used soft gauze as a base and taped over the top of it with firm zinc oxide strapping which ran down the front of my shin and round my ankle so that my foot was held at a 90-degree angle, unable to flex. As soon as she taped it up my shin felt relieved, as if it was breathing out having held its breath since the pain had become acute yesterday afternoon.

Saunders and Guy joined our band of walkers and there was quite a crowd as we navigated our way through the narrow streets of Mansilla to collect Wee Jean from the municipal. Saunders was sunburnt from the afternoon in the beer garden, and in his short shorts and day-glow fleece he was certainly an injection of colour. Tinker and Lynne had to pick up their hire car in León before 12, so we took the first section at pace.

In Puente Villarente we stopped for breakfast in a café full of familiar peregrinos who greeted us as we stepped inside. I was struck by the notion that we were a travelling village, like an ancient Persian caravan. Old and young, fit and frail, priests and vagabonds, all sections of society were represented and the kindness and confirmation of this mobile community was a daily joy.

The walk of just 18.6km was our shortest in days. I was worried about how I would cope with the pain in my shin but although it took a bit of time to adjust to one flat foot, the ibuprofen and the strapping kept it under control. When we stopped for coffee, Stefano and Mike, who preferred a later start, overtook us and we followed their familiar frames for a couple of miles before we caught up. From this perspective we could see how much weight Stefano had lost but also how stiffly he and Emmanueli were walking.

Emmanueli was a strange one. In his early 20s, the Sicilian was a gentle soul with skin tanned like caramel and intense blue eyes. His gaze was disconcertingly penetrating and he smiled as he looked, as if he could see something in you, and liked what he saw. His tender, affectionate nature was unsettling at first, but it only took a moment to realise his intentions were utterly innocent. He would put his head on your shoulder and look up into your face, as you might expect a small child to do. As he walked ahead of us it was clear that he was in a great deal of pain and we could see that he was turning his knee at an awkward angle and dragging his left foot.

Years of walking with Ali, formerly a consultant gait analyst, had taught me all sorts of things about biomechanics. She was like the six-million-dollar woman and her x-ray vision looked straight through clothing, beyond the flesh, and into the muscle and bone where she made her diagnosis. Stefano, too, had developed some significant pain in his hips and when we caught up with them he was not a happy man.

'I am dead,' he told us. 'I am dead.'

'We can rebuild you. Take off your belt,' instructed Ali.

To my surprise he did as he was told. A risky manoeuvre as his trousers were now hanging off him and without the belt he was in danger of dropping them completely.

Right there, 2km out of León, Ali set up a roadside emergency clinic. She got Mike involved and taught him some impressive moves with the belt that she had looped round Stefano's upper thigh. It must have looked peculiar to anyone passing by, but it gave Stefano instant relief so he was happy to abandon his modesty.

Then she turned her attention to Emmanueli's knee. He was wearing jeans and this proved problematic as she couldn't hoick them up to assess the damage. For an awful moment I thought she was going to tell him to take them off, and I was in no doubt that Emmanueli would comply, but Ali did her best through the thick material.

Saunders seemed completely unfazed by this behaviour. 'Nothing I haven't seen her do before,' he said, 'although usually she's on the side of a rugby pitch.'

Temporary repairs complete, Emmanueli, Stefano and I hobbled into León like the walking wounded and I imagined us with bandages round our heads and crutches under our arms, like extras in a black and white war film.

Guy, who had driven on ahead, parked his hire car in Puente Castro and walked backwards along the Camino to join us for a while. Years of pounding up mountains with a bergen on his back had left him in need of a hip replacement before he was 40; long-distance walking, therefore, was no longer an option. Lynne and Tinker were starting to worry that the car rental place might shut early, and Guy stepped in, their knight in a shining Opel, and drove them into town to collect it. Their instincts were spot on as it was just about to close and all that was left was a large white van.

And so just a few of us staggered into León, our pace now slow. Much to Ali's relief, the last few miles into the city were more agreeable than those that took us into Burgos: it made her wince just thinking about that walk. There was still an industrial zone to negotiate but the *sendas* were good and we were not as close to the busy N-601 as we had anticipated.

From the moment I caught a glimpse of the vast city walls I knew we had arrived somewhere special. Built 100 years before the birth of Christ, León was established as the military encampment for the Sixth Roman Legion. We paused at one of the original gateways to marvel at the thickness of the ancient walls before entering the medieval city within. Stefano and Mike were worried about securing accommodation so they hurried on while we wandered through a flea market that ordinarily would have had me rummaging for bargains.

The narrow streets were full of oddities and the window displays were too good to rush past. We peered into a shop that sold plaster casts of religious scenes; a shop that sold only scythes; a shop with brightly painted papier-mâché figures and a shop full of terrifying dolls; but only the shop with the window full of homemade potato crisps was able to lure us in. And they did not disappoint. The sickly squash, carrot and courgette crisps on the other hand were an aberration. You live and learn.

We met Guy, Lynne and Tinker in the Plaza Regia in the shadow of the cathedral. The 13th Century 'House of Light' dominated the square, its twin towers flanking an enormous rose window. The sky was cloudless and the square full of members of an art class, sketching and painting. I was tempted to join in but the word on the street was that the albergues were full. Stefano and Mike had texted to say that they been turned away from three already. Ali, Guy and Saunders headed off to find a hotel, but Jean and I were bound for the municipal.

This was the first time I had been separated from Ali, and although I had got to know Jean well in the last week, I wondered how I would cope without my 'other half'. Feeling a little anxious, I re-hoisted my rucksack onto my back and we set off.

The medieval city was a maze of narrow streets and although our guidebook had a city map we were not entirely sure which way we were heading. Having taken a few wrong turns, disorientated, we paused for a minute to find our bearings. From out of the crowd a little old lady appeared and walked straight over to us. In Spanish she told us that the Santa Maria Albergue was up the road on our right. This was weirdly wonderful as we hadn't asked, didn't even have our map out, and although we were obviously pilgrims we could have been heading to any number of albergues in the area. Another Camino Angel sent to guide us.

Despite warnings from fellow pilgrims, the Santa Maria

was great: it was clean, it smelled nice and it was warm. There were radiators on for the first time anywhere and we huddled round them enjoying the heat. Located in the Plaza Santa Maria del Camino, its location was ideal, so once we had secured our beds and had a quick shower, we met Tinker, Lynne, Ali and Saunders by the cherub fountain in the square directly outside.

The twin cherubs with their chubby legs and bottoms reminded me of my own twins when they were babies and I sent them a picture to let them know I was thinking of them. Lunch was a leisurely affair and we were surrounded by Spanish families, making the most of the good weather. Black-haired brothers in sunglasses and leather jackets, grandfathers in fedoras and grandmothers in fur coats were taking their time while the children played in the square and small dogs sat patiently under the tables, waiting for scraps.

I breathed a sigh of relief that I had made it, and that tomorrow was a day off, so I could properly unwind. We ordered beer, salads, bread, an enormous platter of cheeses and another of cold meats, including cecina, the cured smoked beef that is a speciality of León. Later we ordered scrambled eggs with garlic and prawns so delicious we ordered another. We had worked up an appetite.

It was a while before Guy joined us. It had been difficult to find a hotel as the following day was Mother's Day, and Monday was a public holiday so the city was full of Spaniards taking weekend mini-breaks. He had finally found rooms at the Marriott and was pleased to inform us that they had sheets and towels and a hairdryer.

'Well we have nuns and a washing line, so who is the real winner here?' Jean asked.

Our late lunch ended at 4.30pm when Tinker and Lynne, having spun out the afternoon as long as they could, headed off to Santander. I knew I would see Tinker when I got home to Edinburgh, but it would be a year or more before I saw Lynne and it was a tearful goodbye.

Jean and I retreated to our accommodation, looking

forward to a bit of down time. I sat on the steps in the sunshine and called home. Connie, like Saunders, had just come back from the Alps. She was going to Tanzania with Raleigh International in June, and inspired by Saunders's visit, I talked to her again about coming to Spain to join us. Her twin brother Joss, who had just finished a foundation course at RADA, had been considering coming out too, but he had just started a new job as a children's entertainer and had decided to stay in London until his lease, or his money, ran out. Alexander, on the run up to his third-year exams, was buried under his books. There was no prospect of him joining us.

It was good to speak to them but seeing Ali with Saunders made me miss them badly: miss their banter and the mess of home, the touch of the skin on their forearms and the smell of their hair. It wasn't that I expected them to stay with me till I was rocking in front of a window like Mrs Bates. I wanted them to be living their own lives and making their own choices, but no one had told me it would be this hard to let them go.

Last Christmas, Connie had been working out in France, and on Christmas Eve, unbeknownst to us, she had lost her phone in a nightclub. On Christmas morning we called to speak to her and a stranger answered. The girl was kind, her boyfriend ran the bar, and she made sure Connie got her phone back as soon as possible. But it was hard to celebrate without her.

Later in the day we had called via Skype, wore silly hats, raised a glass, forced jolly smiles. But when she hung up Joss and I had just sat and sobbed. Three children born in two years meant that all three would be gone in the same space of time. And it was all happening too quickly for me. I was not ready. At home, the boys played the Abba song, *Slipping Through My Fingers*, just to get a reaction, knowing I couldn't hear more than the first two lines without breaking into a sob. 'Schoolbag in hand she leaves home in the early morning, waving goodbye with an absentminded smile,' and then I was off, a dribbling mess. It would be so perfect if

167

Connie did come out for a few days, but whatever the kids decided, David was coming out to Spain in a week's time. He had meticulously planned a tour of the Napoleonic war battlefields, with a few gastro-destinations thrown in for sustenance.

We had arranged to meet up in the square later on in the evening and I went down a little early to write my journal. Over to the right I spotted Emmanueli with a group of young pilgrims who were chilling out in the evening sun. He looked relaxed, as if he fitted in.

The strapping on my leg was beginning to loosen, and my shin was throbbing so I sat down on a bench under a tree and put my foot up. A bride and groom crossed the square to have their photo taken by a propped-up Vespa, and a group of Spaniards were singing and playing the guitar. The yellow trousered, yellow haired hippy that had shared his cookies with us was here and the group of girls that surrounded him seemed keen to make his acquaintance. I sat and watched the soap opera of the young peregrinos unfold a little more until the moment was shattered when a bird pooped on my head. I headed back to the albergue to clean up before the others arrived.

'That's lucky,' I could hear my mum saying.

'It's yucky, not lucky,' I heard the nine-year-old me reply.

Later, we reunited, and Guy ordered drinks while we listened to music in the square. But I was poor company. Worried about my leg, I felt overwhelmed by the bustle of the city which was suddenly overrun with stag parties.

Guy, in his pink shirt and flamboyant scarf, ushered the group out of the square with an emphatic wave of the arm. 'Right, guys, time to find some dinner.' Known in his army days as Big Noisy, there was no missing the order.

For the last three weeks we had been walking towards Santiago, and as we walked the stresses and anxieties of everyday life had gradually, imperceptibly, begun to slough off. Ali and I had established a harmonious equilibrium: we walked, were silent, talked, ate and slept, taking pleasure in the uncomplicated nature of our days, our limited choices and life stripped bare. The arrival of Guy and Saunders had lightly shifted that balance. The meditative state that I had entered seemed somehow under threat.

Tonight, in the restaurant, we slipped into old roles. Guy clapped his hands, hurrying us to order. 'Right, team, what are we having? OK, let's go. Great. Let's get this party started.'

Ali looked overwhelmed. 'No, nothing, I don't want anything. Just you go ahead and order. I'm fine.'

And suddenly I was worried about my friend and anxious about keeping everyone else happy. Would the restaurant be too expensive for some? Would Saunders find something he liked on the menu? Would we be splitting the bill equally when some had chosen the least expensive option? What had been so uncomplicated now had an undercurrent of tension and I found myself riled by the arrival of a man who was used to making decisions and protective of the pilgrim mindset it had taken me three weeks to adopt.

It was a relief to retreat to my top bunk in the convent. There was a quiet buzz in our single-sex dormitory and the conversation was relaxed. Ingrid was there and she brought me an apple and some lip salve for my cold sores. A Kiwi woman with tattoos and a knee brace, leaned on the bedframe and shared some of her story.

'I'm as strong as an ox, me,' she said, her voice deep and gritty. 'I'm a builder and I can give the men on the sites a run for their money. But my bloody knee gave out in week one. The doc told me I either had to call it a day or walk without a pack, so I'm using one of those companies who take your stuff to the next albergue for you.'

She was recently divorced and, like so many of us, was at a junction in her life.

It seemed to me that the Camino offered an opportunity to take a look at life from something of a distance, to float above it, or alongside it for a while. Viewing it from this different perspective might not provide the answers to the questions we came with, but maybe from this altered vantage point we could at least see our choices a little more clearly.

Day 22
30th April
Mansilla de las Mulas – León
Kari, Ali, Jean, Tinker, Lynne, Guy, Saunders
My first night without Ali feels a little odd, but also a little brave. Jean is right below me, of course, but I feel like a solo traveller – and I can imagine what it would have been like if I had been here alone. Tomorrow is a day off and while my mission is to rest my leg, we have to be out of the albergue by 8am. There will be no rest for the wicked.

CHAPTER 24

While Ali was living it up at the Marriott, Jean and I spent a comfortable, if somewhat austere, night in the convent and I awoke feeling full of bonhomie. This lasted a full five minutes, until I found myself brushing my teeth next to a young woman who was clearing her nose into the sink next to mine. I couldn't quite face the communal breakfast after that and had to have a little sit down on my bunk before we were cast out onto the street at 8am.

As I sat, forlorn, a tiny nun swept through the dorm checking the beds. She paused for a moment and put her hand on my head, perhaps sensing my reluctance to join the others in the kitchen. Her benediction touched me and I took a few deep breaths before I continued with the daily rhythm of rolling the dry bags, packing the rucksack.

Emmanueli hobbled by and I smiled up at him and gave him my blister stick. There was something quite extraordinary about him. He spoke absolutely no English and I spoke no Italian so we often ended up having parallel conversations. I might have said, 'We are going to go for a coffee, do you want to come?' and he may have replied by nodding and saying something like, 'Yes, I have five dogs.' He was completely without guile and when I heard that his parents were concerned about him walking alone, I could quite understand why. It seemed unbelievable that he had made it from Saint Jean, but he had.

He took the blister stick, looked at it for a moment, and then sat on the end of my bed. Without saying a word, he took off his sock and presented me with his foot. What could I do but show him how to use it? I rubbed the stick over his heels and toes while he watched me, nodding. Three weeks ago I would have baulked at the prospect of touching a stranger's foot. His skin was young and smooth, his foot clean, his toenails well trimmed. It was a beautiful foot. And as I rubbed in the blister stick I felt strangely honoured to have been given this privilege. To him this seemed like the most natural thing in the world. To me it felt as if he was teaching me something simple and important. How to be compassionate. How to give and receive love.

There were no free beds in the convent for that night and as we left they warned us that there were few free beds in the city as a result of Monday's holiday. But we were not worried as we headed out. Things would work out: Stefano had put in a good word for us with the other nuns. In the cathedral square the giant metal letters that spell out LEON dazzled in the brilliant morning light and we seized the opportunity to take some pictures, since we were the only people around.

We hit the streets before the men with the water hoses, who cleaned up the city on a Sunday morning. They would not appear for another hour and in the meantime, the streets were awash with vomit and the detritus of last night's party. In the doorways, women were taking off their heels and bracing themselves for the barefoot walk home. Despite the sunshine, it was so cold we could see our breath and I did not envy them.

It was barely 8am when we arrived at the second convent of the weekend, and it wasn't yet open. Stefano and Mike were staying there and as it was located just behind the cathedral, it seemed ideal. We decided to wait in a café below a small hotel, and ordered *el gran desayunos*. The big breakfast consisted of coffee, freshly squeezed orange juice, a huge slice of tortilla and a piece of freshly baked yoghurt cake. And we were tucking in when another Camino miracle occurred…

For Ali, our days off had been made by a visit to the

municipal pool and a chance to sit in the bubbles and steam. Sadly, no such pool existed in León. It had taken Ali a few days to get over this disappointment, but she had put it behind her, barely. Over breakfast I noticed an advert on the back of their bocadillo menu.

'This is too good to be true. Look,' I showed Jean, 'it's a spa, right here in this hotel.'

We asked the man on reception if we could take a look and he showed us downstairs to a small private pool with mood lighting, all kinds of jets, bubbles and steamy areas. For €15 apiece we could have the whole place to ourselves from 4-5.30pm. We had found our bliss.

'I can't wait to see the look on Ali's face. She's gonna be so happy,' said Jean.

An hour or so later, we checked into convent number two and a little posse of nuns came to greet us, shaking us warmly by the hand. We were shown to our double room which for €12 had two single beds and a bath and we dropped off our rucksacks and headed to mass at the cathedral.

In the Plaza Regla we ran into Emmanueli who was talking with an older man who pointed out an alcove in the side of the cathedral. He explained that in years gone by, people stood in the recess to see whether their sins were forgiven or unforgiven. I didn't quite follow the story but I think it had something to do with the shadow of the king's rod in the carving above it. All three of us had a go, and stood looking penitent under the arch waiting for the shadow to move. All three, unforgiven.

The morning service was not in the main body of the kirk but in a side chapel where we found ourselves sitting with Stefano, Mike and Maria-Manuela (who we hadn't seen since Hornillos). It was a still, reflective mass, the light slicing in through the stained glass and the music rising up to the high vaulted ceilings.

At the end of the service we were called forward for a pilgrim blessing and I got a better look at the superfluity of priests on the altar. The main celebrant looked like a waiter, with oiled-back hair and hands that were comfortable polishing the chalice. He had an enormous bandage over his nose that gave the unfortunate impression that he had just had a nose job.

While my mind was caught up in an imaginary backstory of gossip and intrigue, Emmanueli had spent the mass reaching out to the old and the infirm. At the sign of peace he walked down the aisle to lay his hands on a lady in a wheelchair who I hadn't even spotted. He knelt in front of her and placed one hand on her shoulder and the other on her head, looking into her eyes. She touched his cheek and he returned to his seat.

When mass was over, Emmanueli and I left together, but when I turned to him a moment later, he was gone. I looked back into the chapel and saw him guiding an elderly blind woman, his hand resting on her elbow, his eyes on her face. He was reuniting her with her son who had been caught up talking to friends.

Emmanueli radiated love in its simplest form and looked at people with an empathy that was disarming. A couple of days ago I had worried that he would be tagging along with us all the way to Santiago and wrestled with the responsibility that this would bring. But that morning, I realised that what he could show me about humanity was worth far more than I could ever offer in return and I wanted him to stay close.

It was Mother's Day in Spain and after mass we sat in the sun in the square and watched the families gather. The little children had baskets of gifts to give to their mothers and were dressed up to the nines for this special day. We watched a brother and sister in knitted outfits chasing each other round the plaza while a lady sang opera outside the cathedral gates.

Foolishly ignoring Ali's strict instructions to rest my leg, Jean and I walked most of the way round the ancient walls of the city. It's not every day that you can follow in the footsteps of the Sixth Roman Legion and it was just too good an opportunity to miss. Inevitably we were overcome with a thirst that only San Miguel could slake and we stopped for some late lunch in San Matteo square. Guy and Ali joined us, Saunders opting for some time on his own. A classical Spanish guitarist played a wee piece by Heitor Villa-Lobos, and we shared some tuna salad. I say we. Not Guy. Guy, like my husband, doesn't do sharing.

After lunch we headed to the cathedral and plugged in headphones for the audio-tour. *El Pulchra Leonina*, The House of Light, is even more breathtaking from the inside. The medieval stained glass is the most magnificent I have ever seen and the scale is awesome. It had the effect of simultaneously humbling me, diminishing my sense of self, and setting my eyes upwards to something wondrous. For me, the light was not just a metaphor for God's greatness, it was an experience of it and this had an effect more profound than any sermon I had ever heard.

From the sublimity of the cathedral, which had nourished our souls, we moved on to the tranquillity of the water that soothed our aching bodies. For an hour and a half Jean, Ali and I bubbled and steamed, putting ourselves back together. The LED mood lighting moved slowly through the colours of the spectrum and its slow, hypnotic progress made us feel sleepy and relaxed. Jean even nodded off on a lounger at the poolside.

Having got over last night's funk I was enjoying Guy's bonhomie and was determined that Saunders, who had been so underfed by tapas, should have a good feed tonight. I Googled 'the best Italian restaurant in León' and found one that appeared, on the map, to be close to the cathedral. We met in the early evening and set off on a search for it. I would be the first to admit that I am no map-reader, but even by my standards I was doing badly. Following Jenny's advice, I orientated my map to the ground, but the streets around the cathedral seemed to bear no relation to my map. I could see the others were getting frustrated so I had one last attempt. And then I realised my mistake. The map I was looking at was of León, Nicaragua. Hmm.

Day 23
1ˢᵗ May
Rest Day – León
Kari, Ali, Jean, Guy, Saunders
Bubbles, churros and, eventually, a fabulous Italian last supper with Saunders and Guy. What a great way to spend our day off.

CHAPTER 25

The nuns had laid out a continental breakfast in the little dining room. Jean and I joined a French couple in their mid-50s and chatted to Stefano and Mike, who were up earlier than usual. Stefano introduced us to 'nun paste' – a sticky quince jelly that the sisters made with fruit from their tree, and tasted delicious spread thickly on crusty bread. It felt like a family breakfast and I particularly loved the fridge magnets that featured Papa Francisco and a blue-eyed Madonna. The sisters insisted we take brioche, madeleines, fruit and biscuits for our journey and sent us on our way with their blessing.

Fully loaded, we headed up to the cathedral to meet Ali and say goodbye to Saunders and Guy. It had been such a beautiful surprise for Ali to see Saunders and she had soaked him up for the last three days. As for me, I was glad to be leaving the noise of the city behind and to be returning to the stillness of the Way. We were a quiet trio as we left León.

The pinnacles of the cathedral stood out against the clear blue sky. It was hard to look down at the yellow arrows and brass cockle shells that were leading us out of the city when there was so much to see when we looked up. We passed through San Matteo square and carried on past Gaudí's masterpiece, *Casa de Botines,* and the statue of the great man sitting on a bench. Just before the Rio Barnesega, we paused at the famous Parador hotel and posed by a statue of a pilgrim with his shoes off. The barefooted pilgrim wore a sou'wester and a giant poncho and Ali looked equally defended against the weather in her woolly hood and red gloves.

While we were taking photographs the boys caught up with us and we walked together for a while. Mike told us that he and Stefano had been playing 'Name that Tune' last night in the convent and he had been driven mad because he couldn't remember the name of a particular song. There was only Wi-Fi in the sitting room so there he was, in his pants, humming the tune and checking his phone, when one of the sisters appeared in the doorway to turn off the lights. I imagine that was awkward for them both.

We hardly noticed the Zona Industrial on the way out of town as we were enjoying round two of 'Name that Tune' too much.

We parted company at La Virgen del Camino. Stefano had given up coffee and alcohol along with his job so he had no need to stop for a caffeine fix. 'Look at my trousers. They are falling down,' he showed us proudly. 'Only the pins are keeping them up. I weighed myself in the pharmacy in León and I have lost 15 kilos. I am a new man!' The weight loss was giving him an extra incentive to carry on walking faster and further every day.

'By the time we get to Santiago, there's going to be nothing left of you,' Ali warned.

For me, Stefano was the heart of the pilgrimage and wherever he went he brought joy. By evening they had walked 31km, and they sent a text to let us know where they were. Our pace was slowing and theirs was speeding up so the gap between us would invariably widen. Perhaps it was inevitable that people would pass in and out of our journey, but they had left an impression and I hoped we would see them again.

In La Virgen del Camino we stocked up on supplies and Ali checked my shin, which showed no sign of recovery. As soon as the strapping loosened I was able to extend my foot, and that was what caused the pain. She strapped it tightly and the relief was immediate. Not for the first time I thought how lucky I was to be travelling with Ali.

As usual we opted for the alternative route and headed

into the open Paramo, leaving León in the distance. At the point at which the routes diverged there was a confusing abundance of signs and we got a bit lost and had to retrace our steps a couple of times. The tunnel under the motorway provided the landmark we needed and soon we were far from the noise of traffic and in the green countryside once again.

The road turned sharply and then, straight ahead, blocking our path, stood an enormous chestnut horse. He was pacing and whinnying, tossing his nose up in the air at us and looking distinctly unhappy. As we got closer we could see he was on a long chain, long enough to reach right across the path.

'There's no way I'm walking past him,' I said, hanging back while the Horse Whisperer assessed the situation. Luckily we had just bought some apples so Ali lured the poor horse, speaking in breathy murmurs and cooing softly, while Jean and I sneaked round the side.

'He seems fit and well cared for,' said Ali. 'I suspect his rider has tethered him while he or she goes for supplies.'

We knew there was an option to do the Camino on horseback, one that Ali had looked into in fact, but this was the first time we had seen any evidence of *el caballo*.

The sun shone and soon fields of yellow rapeseed bordered the path. We couldn't resist stepping into it for a moment and being swallowed up by the colour. As we were larking around in the chest-high crop a lone pilgrim approached. We could tell he was an Englishman by his gait and his attire, dressed as he was in pink corduroys and a Panama hat. We smiled and wished him *Buen Camino*, to which he nodded a grudging acknowledgement.

'It's too yellow,' he said, walking on.

His negativity jarred and we realised how little of it we had come across in the last few weeks.

At Oncino we stopped at 'The pilgrim dome' – a blue octagonal tent run by Manuel. It provided just about anything we could have wished for, from orange juice to freshly brewed coffee, tissues to tampons – all for a donation. A gleaming stainless steel kettle was bubbling away but it was too hot for tea so we asked for three orange juices and sat on little stools in the sun while he squeezed them to order. Refreshed, I pulled the Dora the Explorer skirt out of my bag and flashed my slightly less Scottish-white legs at the Camino once again.

The mountains were now looming large all around us and the open meadows of the Paramo were full of wild flowers – deep purple hyacinths, pink thistles, scarlet-centred daisies and countless others I could not name. We saw fat lizards, a shepherd driving his massive herd of musical sheep, green spiders, tiny yellow butterflies and enormous birds of prey. The path was flat and deserted and we heard our cuckoo, the frogs, crickets and a million bees as we passed through the bean fields. We stopped for lunch in the shade of a cork tree, spreading out Jean's poncho as a makeshift picnic blanket. Cheese, bread and chorizo in the sunshine. Bliss.

With about 5km left to go my shin started playing up, forcing me to walk pretty slowly on that last leg. Ali looked concerned, and although I did my best to ignore the pain, it was a relief to see an enormous mosaic announcing Villar de Mazarife. We stopped to look at the sepia-toned depiction of pilgrims with their tall staffs. The village itself was ancient and stony, baking in the afternoon sun. We headed straight for the *Tio Pepe* albergue, which promised a courtyard, and some shade.

We were delighted they had space for us, and from our shuttered bedroom window, we had a clear view of the bell tower of the church, complete with three enormous stork nests. Each nest had two storks and presumably, from the noise, a clutch of chicks. The hospitalero told us that the parents clicked their beaks in happiness when they welcomed their mate back to the nest and, when nature called, they pushed their bottoms over the edge and squirted with gusto.

We hung up our washing in the sunshine and sat in the courtyard with a cold beer. Soon there was quite a crowd.

Some faces were familiar, like Holy Kate and Sara 'n' Lara. Others were new, like Bill – 'Call me Dollar Bill' – from Texas; Bertie Wooster in his linens and a Panama hat and Maria, a German chain-smoker. We shared stories and Bill touched our knees one too many times, called us all 'baby-doll' and just about stayed on the right side of appropriate. I think his heart was in the right place. I think.

We paid a visit to the church across the way and a volunteer showed us around and explained some of the artworks. Bertie joined us and as we watched the storks he told us about his broken engagement, his decision to quit work and his plans to do voluntary work in Tanzania with Raleigh International in the summer. Today was his first day on the Camino as he, like Maria, had started in León. You could tell they were newcomers. They looked clean and shiny and a little bit unsure. By the time we went in for supper the low sunlight was dazzling and the air full of tiny sparkling particles.

Maria, the solo German woman, joined the three of us for supper. Her face was drawn and anxious, and she worried that, physically, she wasn't up to the challenge.

'My bag is too heavy and my muscles are aching. My legs hurt, and my feet are sore. I'm not sure I can do this.'

'It gets easier,' I told her. 'Three hard days and then your body gets used to it.'

Liar, my leg hissed at me.

We looked at the menu and with great confidence, having recognised the word *garbanzo* from Jenny's tutorials, I ordered what I thought was chickpea soup. The waitress was delighted.

'Good. Good. Only local people order this. It is speciality of the region. I give you big, big plate. I love you.'

'If it's that good I'll have some too,' said Jean, impressed at the response.

I should have smelled a rat. The word I had failed to translate was *callos*. That's tripe. And there was plenty of it. And not a plate of chickpeas with a smattering of tripe, this was a mountain of tripe with a garnish of chickpeas. I pushed it around my plate, remembering the dreadful food at the convent I had attended 38 years ago, where I had tried, unsuccessfully, to hide the liver in my damask dinner napkin (x2 to be clearly named). Seeing my struggle, Jean who hates to see food go to waste, came to my rescue. She, like my father who used to go teary-eyed at the memory of stewed tripe and onion, developed a taste for the revolting stuff and ate her own and some of mine, giving me the empty plate so that the waitress would not be disappointed.

Day 24
2ⁿᵈ May
León – Villar de Mazarife
Kari, Ali, Jean
Jean is in the room next door with Sara 'n' Lara, Holy Kate appears to be sleeping in a broom cupboard at the end of the corridor and Ali and I are in a bedroom with just two other women, both of whom were asleep with the lights off, before 8.30pm. Hopefully there won't be too much snoring tonight. We have worked out a plan and are adjusting tomorrow's schedule to give my dodgy shin a chance to recover. Meanwhile I am following Sara the Curvy German's lead and from now on it's paracetamol all the way.

CHAPTER 26

So much for my hopes of a quiet night. I had the squeakiest of top bunks and every movement set the springs in motion, reverberating for a good minute afterwards. The early-to-bed woman in the bunk below huffed and puffed, letting me know exactly how much I was disturbing her. I tried my very best not to move but the more I thought about keeping still, the more I needed to wriggle. To add insult to injury, my lip salve dropped off the bunk in the middle of the night and landed on her head and I spent the rest of the night afraid that she was going to smother me with my pillow.

Anyhoo – when the beak clattering of the stork family woke us at first light she was already gone. She had never seen my face so at least she wouldn't recognise me if we ran into each other again. In our new morning ritual, Ali strapped me up and I dosed myself with the first of my four-hourly pain meds before we headed down to breakfast.

In the dining room we were entertained by the arrival of a pilgrim with the biggest backpack on the Camino.

'Oh my goodness, it's enormous,' Ali whispered. Giant water canisters were attached to the sides and long hosepipes arched over the shoulders of the wearer.

'If there's a drought, or a fire, he will certainly be well prepared.'

'Forget the fires,' I replied. 'If there's something strange, in the neighbourhood, who we gonna call? Ghostbuster!'

The first section of the walk, through the open Paramo, was

gentle if a little straight but I wasn't looking for a challenge. Thanks to Ali and the drugs, my leg wasn't giving me too much bother but our pace had certainly slowed since Tinker and Lynne had left.

Fields on either side of the rough grey path were fresh with new growth of cereal crops and in the distance, arrows of yellow rapeseed shot through the green. Ali and Jean were in good spirits and it was comfortable to be in a smaller group once again. It felt like we had just hosted a lovely lunch party and now that the guests had left we were sitting down for a drink with just the family. We were completely relaxed and enjoying each other's company. We talked about our favourite books for a while.

In our ordinary lives, like most women our age, time is our enemy. We are pulled in so many directions that even when we do get together we are never fully present. The phones are always ringing and there is always something else we should be doing. Here, on our walk, we had time. We talked about everything, from the most important to the utterly trivial. Strangely, it was through the trivia that we got to know each other best.

David, my husband, can remember the registration numbers of all the family cars of his childhood. Odd, I know. For me, storing this detail about him, along with countless fragments curated over the years, means that when I look at photographs of him as a boy, he is not a stranger to me. He is a Russian doll, and I can see back through the layers to where he started and love the child who shaped him into the man he is.

On our walk, we had time to share this kind of ephemera and there was an intimacy in its ordinariness that made it precious. Although we had only known each other as adults, I felt as though I had grown up with the women I was walking with, slept over in their childhood homes and eaten at their parents' tables.

Our conversation moved on to pets and Ali had a lot to say on the subject. She described the personalities of the animals of her household as if they were human and by the time we arrived at our coffee spot, Jean and I felt we knew them too.

'My first Shetland pony was Tinkerbell, who, despite the name, was a monstrous stallion. I adored him. Even after he bit me.'

Tinkerbell was followed by Spangle, who was followed by Cara, who was followed by Wayne, who was followed by Jamie, formally Abraxis, who was Ali's first love. In parallel to the succession of horses ran a litany of dogs. We recited them like a mantra until we knew them by heart.

'Mac, Mick, Brandy, Shandy, Fella, Struie and Rock. Rock, Rockie, Rockie Dog, Wonder Dog, Dog of Dogs. Border terriers one and all.'

By mid-morning we reached Villavante, and happy to find an outdoor café on a narrow street, we sat down in the sun. We were admiring a cornucopia of artisanal breads, advertising the bakery opposite, when a familiar figure dressed in jeans, a hoodie and a navy tracksuit top, came out of the bakery door. It was Emmanueli and he was as pleased to see us, as we were to see him. He hugged us each in turn and sat down at our table. He had bought himself a big Napolitana for breakfast and offered us each a bite. He seemed uncomfortable eating while others had nothing and held it out, offering some to the pilgrims who passed by, most of whom he seemed to know.

Sara 'n' Lara turned down his pastry, but gave him a packet of cigarettes before they went on their way.

'Are you going to smoke those?' I asked, always the mother. 'They're poisonous. They'll make you ill.' I shook my head and made a sad face, knowing he wouldn't have a clue what I'd just said.

For a long time he sat looking at the health warning on the packet – a grim photo of rotten teeth – until finally he looked up, shook his head and gave the packet to a smoker at another table.

Emmanueli kissed us goodbye and set off again, on his

own. He was in his sandals and it was good to see that the pain in his leg seemed to have abated. As we watched him walk away up the narrow street, I felt a pang of loss and wondered when we would see him next.

The rest of the day's walk was made all the more interesting by the frogs. The noise they made demanded our attention and we stopped to listen and then watch. The waterways that criss-crossed the Paramo were full of them; like squaddies in desert fatigues they were easy to spot in the fluorescent green weed that had coagulated on the surface of the water. They puffed out their necks with hubba bubba bubbles, amplifying the sound of their calls and making themselves look bigger to intimidate their love rivals. We watched as they pursued potential mates, chased off rivals and jumped off the banks like cliff divers – head first into the water. The storks were also in evidence, their huge nests balanced precariously on water towers, pylons and bell gables. We were surprised we hadn't seen any picking off the frogs, as they certainly were not hard to spot.

I fell for the Paramo with its wide-open expanses of green and yellow and its mesh of waterways. According to legend, a local Lord only permitted a suitor to court his daughter when he had proven his worth by diverting a stream to bring water to the area. He succeeded – hence the name – Paramo (for love).

We had planned to walk further than Hospital de Orbigo but my leg was throbbing and we liked the look of this handsome town so decided to stay. A stunning medieval bridge crossed the Rio Orbigo, connecting the towns on opposite banks of the river. This place was proud of its chivalric past and below the bridge there was a large jousting arena.

Here, an information board told us a less happy love story than the legend of the Paramo.

'Tell me what it says,' said Ali, 'I can't be bothered reading all that.'

I paraphrased. 'Once upon a time, a strong, brave,

handsome knight discovered that the girl of his dreams was just not that into him. He couldn't quite believe it, as he was so strong and brave and handsome, so, a bit like the frogs, he decided to show her what she was missing and made a big song and dance on the bridge. Are you with me?'

'Yes,' said Ali. 'It's story time with Mrs Gillespie. My boys will be jealous.'

I continued, 'Like a human troll he declared that anyone who wanted to cross the bridge would have to fight him first. He held the bridge for a month or four (depending on which version you read) and fought with hundreds of men who also wanted to prove how strong and brave and handsome they were. They fought on horseback and hundreds of lances were broken in the process, making the lance makers happy, if no one else. When he had finally broken enough lances to prove to the girl that she was quite mad not to love him, the knight rode off to Santiago. There he thanked God that he was so strong and brave and handsome. The story doesn't tell us what happened to the girl. But I have a sneaking suspicion that she lived happily ever after.'

I toasted her with my water bottle. 'Here's to strong women. May we know them. May we be them. May we raise them.'

Our next stop in Hospital de Orbigo was the pharmacy, well stocked for the footsore peregrino. We cleared it out of tape, bandages and painkillers and the pharmacist also gave me some cream for my cold sores that showed no signs of improvement.

It was still early when we checked in to a parochial hostel that was run by the German Confraternity of Saint James. It was painted blue and there were small dormitories all around the pretty cobbled courtyard. In the large, overgrown garden at the back we spotted old-fashioned stone sinks, a scrubbing board and washing lines and tackled some domestic tasks before heading out for a late lunch.

Guy had brought Ali some walking leggings. They had a

web pattern on the front, like Spiderwoman, and she wore these, with a sarong wrapped around her shoulders. She looked like a superhero. I hobbled slowly behind her, wondering how on earth I was going to make it to Santiago if my leg didn't improve.

We stopped at a café where the menfolk of the town gathered to play cards. The jousting arena may have been empty but they were still engaged in combat – *mano-a-mano*. Every table inside was full but we were happy sitting outside and ordered tuna salad and patatas bravas. The waiter gave us a tea towel of ice for my leg and I kept it elevated on a stool, the coolness taking the heat out of the inflamed muscle.

Holy Kate was staying in the same place as us and she pulled up a stool and joined us for lunch. Over a beer she told us that she had been getting to know a man who she had met on Catholic-Match, an internet dating site with a difference. They had been planning a rendezvous in Santiago and the thought of this was helping her fight off the loneliness. Yesterday, she heard that he had changed his mind and she was sad. What she hoped might have become a relationship, based on a shared faith, was over before it had really begun. But her faith was strong.

'I have always hoped that one day I would have a husband and a family. But I just have to accept that this might not be how things turn out for me. Jesus might have another plan and I just have to say, "Your will be done, Lord."'

She told us that while she walked, she prayed, grappling with the profound loneliness she was experiencing. She had started to consider whether she might have a vocation and we listened as she talked about the religious life. I said nothing but found it hard to imagine a woman with such vitality enclosed in a convent. My limited understanding of religious orders comes largely from my time at school. In that place the pinched, joyless observance of the nuns had none of the rapturous spirit that seemed to burn within Kate.

To cheer her up I invited her to join us for supper. After a leisurely afternoon in the garden I was in the mood for a bit of cooking. I bought some ingredients from the local shops and made pasta and salad in the dark, poky kitchen. While I was cooking I met Andrea from southern Italy. He was in his early thirties with a half-starved look and a mop of black curls. He was clutching a tin of stew that looked so unappetising I asked him to eat with us. I wish I had realised he was a chef before I offered. Making carbonara in a kitchen with no utensils, no salt, no oil and no Parmesan was a bit of a challenge. But no matter – Kate brought wine and the five of us sat in the late sun and had a gentle evening full of easy conversation and warmth.

Andrea told me how he would make a carbonara (using guanciale, cured pig's cheeks) and over the meal he gradually shared some of his story. He told us about his broken heart and his many years working in Switzerland. The punishing hours in a hotel kitchen made it difficult to sustain a relationship, and he spoke movingly of the shame he felt retreating home to his parents' house, and the feelings of failure that he was struggling to overcome.

We were not ready for the evening to end so after dinner, Jean, Andrea and I walked back down to the bridge as he had missed it on the way into town. As we admired the intricate stonework I spotted a heart-shaped stone near the centre of the bridge. Often, when I was struggling, a heart-shaped stone would catch my eye on the path in front of me. I had begun to regard these as symbols of hope, little gifts of encouragement, which helped me to keep going, to keep putting one foot in front of the other.

Andrea had walked 36km that day and since his pace was so fast I doubted we would see him again. I hoped he would find what he was looking for – or at least that he would slow down enough to see it, if it should come his way.

Day 25
3rd May
Villar de Mazarife – Hospital de Orbigo
Kari, Ali, Jean

Tonight my leg is seriously playing up. I took the strapping off this afternoon and realised too late that it was a mistake to walk this evening, unsupported. I now have a swelling down the front of my shin like a chicken fillet and I am grateful that we only have a short walk to Astorga tomorrow – just 17km or so. Our pace has changed and my headspace, like the villages we pass through, has become quiet and inward looking once more. I am not sure I am ready for another big town.

CHAPTER 27

At about midnight, as I stumbled barefoot over the uneven cobbles to reach the only toilet, our quirky albergue lost its charm. It was a noisy night and I was awake, ready to be on my way long before the alarm went off. In the darkness, we sat at an old wooden table, Ali taping me up by the light of her headtorch, in the morning ritual that we conducted in silence. My cold sores were no better, and I tried to ignore the signals that my body was sending me, to let me know it had had enough. Looking for external things to blame, I ditched the water system that I decided must be perpetuating the infection. Stupidly I left it in the donation box and I can only hope that some unsuspecting soul did not pick up more than they bargained for.

It was a flat walk out of Hospital de Orbigo and as the sun came up the world glowed orange. The ochre path was wide and straight and although it was cold, our faces were flushed. We crossed a corroded, red-iron bridge and stopped to look at the birch trees that had just come into leaf on either bank. Rusty ploughs lay abandoned on the verges. I took photographs for Ali's brother and we spoke about her dad who had collected vintage farm machinery. Ali's mum was following our progress with interest and enjoyed our posts. In her mid-80s she had mastered the iPad, just so that she could stay connected.

The sun was still rising as we reached Villares de Orbigo and we stopped to peep through a hole in a pilgrim sculpture in the central square. A large granite rectangle, it had a cross cut out of the centre and doubled as a water fountain. *Aqua potable* was carved into the stone like an ancient motto. Opposite, in keeping with the colour palate of the morning, stood the albergue painted chrome yellow, its side wall a giant mural of a washing line, complete with white socks, stripy T-shirts and vests.

The place was famous for its garlic and there were pictures of it everywhere, but it was a little early to sample it, even for garlic lovers like us. We did, however, find a fabulous café and ate delicious chocolate Napolitanas. The owner brought them fresh from the bakery. With the flakiest pastry and the most melting chocolate they were faultless and we talked about them all day.

In the café we bumped into Dollar Bill who had been so overly familiar a few days ago but who appeared to have completely forgotten us. As he got up to leave he cupped his hand to his ear.

'Can you hear that?' he asked me. 'Come over here.'

I followed his instructions, hoping he wasn't going to touch my knee.

'Listen,' he said.

I listened.

'The Camino is calling,' he said. And with that he did his strange Texan salute and disappeared into the sunrise.

We took our time finishing our coffee. It was only 15km to Astorga, and we were happy to put some distance between ourselves and Dollar Bill. The walk was sublime and as we continued to climb, the peace and tranquillity of the landscape took my breath away. I prayed as I walked and felt a presence alongside me that was companionable and comfortable. Not ecstatic or transcendental, just gentle and reassuring. I had nothing to worry about and everything was going to be fine.

Walking along the path, I glanced at my feet and saw a nail half buried in the dirt track. I picked it out. It was made of iron, ancient looking and about seven inches in length. I put it in my pocket where it joined the nail from Roncesvalles.

Two nails. Two hands. Open and surrendered.

This was rolling agricultural land and every village had more tractors than cars. The locals were proud of their place on the pilgrimage route, and wished us *Buen Camino* wherever we went.

In Santibañez de Valdeiglesia two elderly women who were chatting on a doorstep, stopped us, saying they needed to tell us something important. Fortunately for us, Jean is a fluent Spanish speaker, and she translated. They were wearing their slippers and blue nylon aprons over their floral dresses. They looked like so many of the women we saw as we passed through the villages – the abuelas, whose good wishes were more than platitudes. They told us about a peregrina who had disappeared a couple of years ago on this section of the walk.

'You must not take any risks. Promise us you will not walk alone,' they urged. My thoughts turned to Harriet and her lucky escape.

At home I was scared of the dark and slept with the lights on when David was not home, but nothing seemed to scare me on the Camino. We had each other and the sun was shining.

We walked through a dairy farm and stopped to chat to the cows, which gave Ali a chance to stick her fingers in a calf's mouth. She did this as if it was the most natural thing in the world and the calf seemed to agree, sooking away, quite the thing.

'How about some hand sanitiser?' I asked, offering her the bottle. But she was a country girl and scorned my townie hygiene.

The wild flowers, as usual, brightened our way, the colours hyper-vibrant, new as they were at the start of spring. The edges of the cornfields were dotted with black-eyed, crimson poppies and purple starflowers, campions, asters and vetch. All that purple got me thinking about the girls in the boarding house I had been running, purple being our house colour. There were so many of those girls I carried with me on my pilgrimage. Strong girls who set out sure-footed to take the world by storm and those who needed a hand to steady them before they found their way. I had talked about the Camino with the girls, at that stage when I was planning to walk alone. One evening a group of sixth-formers staged an intervention and sat me down for a talking-to.

'Mrs. G, we don't think you've thought this through,' they said.

'Is it really safe to walk on your own? You could be attacked.'

'What if you get bitten by a snake or contract cholera?' they said.

I had reassured them that there were few poisonous snakes in northern Spain and even fewer cases of cholera. Now I wondered if they'd heard about the poor woman who had been murdered on the road to Astorga.

Up the hill from Santibañez we arrived at a *donativo* where a Spaniard called David and his Australian girlfriend served watermelon, homemade bread and fig jam to weary pilgrims. All around their simple homestead they had built little seating areas and pilgrims were invited, free of charge, to take the weight off their backs and rest a while in the shade, on the big comfy cushions.

Maria, the chain-smoking German was having a cigarette. Just two days into her journey, she already looked like a different person. When we had met her in Mazarife, she was full of self-doubt. Now she was lying back on a beanbag looking completely chilled.

Under an awning Holy Kate was deep in conversation with a pilgrim who looked like GI Joe. Tanned and strong, his head was shaved and he was dressed in army surplus.

We sat in the sun and enjoyed the melon, waiting for David to tell us our 'essence' but there was quite a queue so we made do with the wisdom on the walls. 'Il llave de la Esencia es la Presencia', it said. 'The key to the essence is the presence.' I don't think I had ever felt more present than I had felt in the past few weeks.

Spirits lifted, we set out again but it wasn't long before our serenity was tested as the path we were on was under construction. The trucks ahead of us cast up clouds of ochre dust and in the sticky heat it clung to us, turning us orange on this most orange of days. On the side of the path we laughed at a scarecrow made from many layers of clothes cast off by pilgrims on this sweltering stretch.

Our clothes could have stood up by themselves by the time we approached Astorga. We had the city in our sights for miles before it was under our feet and I concentrated on the rhythm of my steps, forcing my mind away from the pain in my shin. It was a long, hot hike up a never-ending hill and I needed a liquorice toffee by the time I got to the top.

Our first stop was the Plaza San Francisco where most pilgrims seemed to be opting for the accommodation provided by *Siervas de Maria*. Although it looked fine we could not shake the whiff of the municipal and decided to push on. Our chosen albergue was at the other end of town but my legs felt they could go no further so I stopped for a moment in the Church of St Francis of Assisi. It was cool and unlit save for the candles and it felt good to pause. Family flooded into my head.

My sister would have liked it here. She would have loved the simplicity, and the stillness and I wished she could have walked with me. My mum liked to tell people I was a mistake. 'A much-loved accident,' she sometimes added as an afterthought. She was well into her forties when I was born; my sister was nineteen and already in college, far too old to have a baby sister; my brother was fourteen and mortally embarrassed. Growing up, it was my sister, Patsy, who took me to the park, and made paper flowers with me. Who dressed me as a hippie and took me to the zoo.

Later, when I was at boarding school and my parents abroad, she was the one who came to the parents' meetings and school plays. She was the constant in my life, the one who was there when I needed a grown-up. More than once, I jumped out of my bedroom window and ran to her house, when things got bad. Our relationship has always been straightforward – we adore each other. My relationship with my mum was so much more complicated. Though I never doubted her love, I was not my best self when I was with her and I wished it were otherwise.

I needed to get out of my dirty clothes, to wash and to eat. Only then would I become human again. The *San Javier,* our home for the night, was a historic building with washing machines, a comfortable living room and great showers (despite Ali taking a tumble and skinning her foot). Right by the cathedral, it was perfectly located and we were delighted to discover that Mary and Meyrick were staying there too. Holy Kate opted to lodge with the nuns at a convent nearby but she joined Ali, Jean and me for lunch once again. It didn't take Astorga long to win me over with her chocolatey charms.

'My mum and dad have walked the Camino twice, and every day they send me top tips about places to visit,' Kate said. 'When I had a night off albergues in León, they had flowers sent to my hotel room.'

We sat for a couple of hours in a café outside Gaudí's Bishop's House and marvelled at the fact that we had all this architecture and history virtually to ourselves with not a tourist in sight. Ghostbuster, the pilgrim with the enormous water canisters, stopped to chat and told us he had checked into a hotel. Men walked their rabbits and a funeral was taking place alongside us. Dozens of people lined the streets as the hearse, covered in red and white roses, passed by.

After lunch the three of us visited the cathedral: it had a lot to live up to after Burgos and León and it fell rather short of the mark. It was an elaborate structure, ornate from the outside, and inside, home to the world's most ghastly collection of cherubs. Once we had started to giggle at them it was hard to take anything seriously. It looked as though a giant scattergun, packed with cherubs, had been fired at the walls. Their grotesque little faces and super-muscly, infant bodies swathed every pillar and we particularly enjoyed the little guy who was being dangled by the ankle by a maniacal cherub classmate.

Underwhelmed by the cathedral we visited the Gaudi museum that contains the original Cruz de Ferro, the copy of which we hoped to see at Foncebadón, two days later. The highlight of the collection was the Roman head of a man who had clearly stayed at the municipal in Frómista. 'Did someone say bedbugs?' his bulging eyes and raised eyebrows seemed to say. And then, well-soaked with culture, we retreated to the square for a restorative cerveza.

'Gaudy to the left of me, Gaudi to the right, here I am, stuck in the middle with you,' I sang as I chinked bottles with my pals.

That morning, when I had pulled the water system out of my rucksack, I found another postcard from David, damp and a little torn. It had a black and white picture of a forest and the words 'Run Free' on the front. I had slipped it inside my guidebook and while the washing machine did its stuff I sat in the sun and read:

'"Run free" seems fitting. Not changing your knickers very often? No doubt this great adventure will enable you to get in touch with your free spirit and that's a wonderful thing. You feel more than other people and that's what makes you so special. Embrace the wonderfulness that is you... you are the person we love with all our hearts. Best foot forward.'

I missed him; 27 days was a long time to be apart from the people you love.

Ali brought out the washing and while we hung it up we chatted to a couple who had opted to take the bus between Burgos and León.

'We heard that the Meseta was really boring so we just skipped that bit,' one said.

For me the Meseta had been mystical. I wouldn't have missed that section for the world. But I didn't tell them that. Although we were all following the same path, we didn't always walk the same Way, and maybe that is the point.

Before supper Ali and I treated ourselves to massages and Reiki. Although Ali had little truck with woo-woo, she didn't deny that it was good. I think, secretly, she even liked the hug at the end, and the bit when the Reiki lady told her that her energy was powerful. I didn't tell Ali that she'd said the same to me.

The hospitalero, Ramon, warned us when we went out that evening that we must be back by 10pm. We ate supper in the square (sorry, Jenny) so that we could watch the clock strike at nine o'clock, but because we lingered over dessert we had to high tail it back before lights out (how the tables had turned!). As we ran in, the clock striking ten, we bumped into Ramon who joked that he was about to come looking for us.

Day 26
4^{*th*} *May*
Hospital de Orbigo – Astorga
Kari, Ali, Jean
Ramon, true to his word, switched our lights out at 10.10pm and I am in the pitch dark now. Today, Connie called to tell me she has decided to join us, and I am so, so happy. The light from my phone is hard to hide so I had better switch off. We have a big day tomorrow. Those mountains that have loomed large for so long, are now just ahead of us.

CHAPTER 28

If I had had the noisiest bed in the Mazarife on Tuesday, Ali had the noisiest bed in Astorga last night. It sounded as if a donkey was braying in the room every time she moved, and no one got much sleep. Not tempted by the breakfast of bread and water, we wasted no time in saying goodbye to Ramon, the friendly hospitalero, and set off for the Montes de León.

The walk was sliced up into bite-sized portions that morning, and every 4km or so there was a village in which to stop and recharge – usually with the promise of a smackerel of something sustaining. One of the great things about the Camino was that no matter what we ate, we were losing weight by the day. Our clothes were falling off us, and like the teenage boys I used to teach, my trousers were hanging perilously low.

We left behind the wide agricultural landscape of yesterday and were walking through trees and on rocky paths once again. At Valdeviejas we stopped at the medieval hermitage, *Ecce Homo*, and lit candles in tall, red-glass holders. Back in November, David and I had spent a few days in Amsterdam and we had seen a bust of Christ by Louis Royer, in the Rijksmuseum. Pilate's words, 'Behold the man,' had moved me then as they did now.

We caught up with Mary and Meyrick mid-morning and stopped for a drink.

'Two nights ago, in Hospital de Orbigo, we spent a night on a floor in a bell tower,' Mary told us. 'I tell you, I'm getting too old for this. It was filthy. But we got a guided tour of the underground cellars and that was pretty neat. It wasn't as bad as the night they ran out of beds and I had to sleep on the floor in the hospitalero's kitchen.'

There was always room for *this* Mary at the inn, it seemed.

I was on the lookout for Emmanueli, but although many familiar faces passed our way, there was no sign of him. Dollar Bill, without a flicker of recognition, walked by, followed by Maria the chain-smoking German who had found her stride and Andrea the chef from northern Italy who had developed a bad leg and had slowed down considerably as a result. The walk was sometimes brutal in the way it ensured you got what you needed, not necessarily what you wanted, and I was beginning to think that my leg issues were driving home a painful point. Walking through pain was helping me transcend the demands of my needy body, was forcing me to see that there was more to me than flesh and blood.

Later on we ran into Thomas, the pilgrim formerly known as Ghostbuster. He was refreshed after his night in a hotel and we got talking. Inevitably, the conversation turned to his huge rucksack. To my great shame he told us that he was recovering from cancer. The disease had damaged his kidneys and it had taken some persuasion to get his doctors to sanction the walk. They had instructed him that if he were to stay healthy he would need to drink four litres of water per day – hence the massive canisters. How little I understood from that first impression. And how quick I was to judge.

The sky had been heavy all day and storm clouds were building over the Montes de León when I finally staggered into Rabanal del Camino. I was weary, struggling for lack of food and my right shin was burning with a new and somewhat attention-seeking pain. We had walked 650km in the last 27 days, but since our friends had left us in León a few days before, the walking had become more solitary and meditative. As I climbed the hill into the dusty stone village, Ali and Jean were some way ahead of me and I was alone, bringing up the rear. They were still in my sights when I saw the open church door of the *Ermita de San José,* and stepped inside. Candlelight shimmered, like sunshine on water, over the baroque altarpiece and I breathed deep, resting my forehead on the metal screen at the back of the nave, enjoying the ecclesiastical dankness.

It had become my habit to stop at the first church I saw when I reached my destination, and when I stepped out of the hermitage I expected my companions to be waiting outside, pointing the way to the nearest bar, or our albergue for that night. But they were nowhere to be seen, I had lost them. I couldn't remember the name of the place where we were staying and hadn't checked on the map to see where it was. The mountain village was small, just a cluster of ancient buildings around one main street that ran uphill, directly on the Camino. My spirits were sinking as I hauled myself up the long hill looking for a name that seemed familiar.

By the time I reached the far side of the village, still nothing rang a bell. It was three o'clock and I hadn't eaten since breakfast, the pain in my shin was intense and panic set in. I stopped thinking clearly. Ali always pulled the map from my side pocket when I needed it, our movements synchronised now, in a kind of soundless dance. She would hand me her water bottle and I would slip it into her side pocket; I would pass her my poles and she would clip them to my pack. But she was nowhere to be seen and I felt unfeasibly incompetent and alone. It had only been 20km today, but all of it had been uphill and I was bone tired. My shin and my shoulder had been aching for the last 5km and I was fantasising about the lightening that would come when I finally shrugged the weight from my back. The thought of having to put it on again felt like too much to bear.

At the far end of the village, Andrea, the chef from Italy who had shared our supper in Hospital de Orbigo, was sitting on a bench. He was resting his injured leg, and I pulled off my pack and plonked myself down next to him. He saw my sadness, and smiled at me gently, then suddenly, unexpectedly, I began to cry. I had been left behind, and like ice on a bad tooth, the dark fear of abandonment jolted. Tears plopped onto my open guidebook. Andrea shifted awkwardly and put an arm around my shoulder, patting me on the back as if I were an infant. Then, as if he too was remembering something distant and primal, he soothed me with slow words, perhaps the Italian version of 'There, there, there.'

He took the guidebook from me. 'That's where you need to go.' He tapped the page. 'Just go back through the village, it will be on the right. You're tired. You'll feel better after you've rested.' He held up my rucksack and I wriggled myself into the straps once more. As I headed back the way I had come, I saw Ali and Jean standing in the middle of the street, waving. They had been looking for me. From the top of the hill Andrea was waving too. '*Buen Camino!*' he shouted, and I waved back.

Ali took my hand. 'Come with us, we've found heaven.'

She wasn't wrong. Janice and Claire, the welcoming mother-and-daughter hospitalera team at Gaucelmo, an albergue run by the British Confraternity of St James, greeted me with chilled mint water, then showed me the herb garden, the wild meadow and the sitting room with a roaring fire where I sat with an ice-pack while Jean and Ali bought lunch. Much Camino lore is shared amongst pilgrims over communal meals, and one of the phrases most commonly heard is, 'The Camino will provide'. As we sat in the meadow eating chorizo, cheese and crusty bread, the rain held off, and I allowed myself to be restored by this provision.

Later in the afternoon, I got to work making macaroni cheese and ratatouille. An unusual combination, but there were only 15 items for sale in the village shop and I had to improvise in a game I called 'Ready-Steady-Camino-Cook!' There were a few of us in the kitchen but no one could get the cooker to light so the hospitalera sent for Father Javier, a young monk from the Benedictine monastery next door. He appeared in his Barcelona football shirt and got it going.

I enjoy cooking and in the tiny kitchen a Korean family taught me to make rice pancakes, Germans made creamy noodles, two Danish girls ate cold things from tins, Australians did something with tuna fish and a very loud group of American women fried mountains of cheese on toast. Camino communitas.

Just before seven I put the macaroni in the oven and Ali, Jean and I crossed the cobbles to attend Vespers in the *Iglesia de la Asunción*. The interior of the diminutive 12th Century church had once been whitewashed but plaster was long gone from patches of the apse and the pink stone looked warm in the candlelight. None of the gaudiness of the baroque had touched this place and a simple cross was all that adorned the altar. Every pew was filled with pilgrims and as we settled it took me a moment to realise that the monk in the white Cassock leading the Gregorian chant was the same Father Javier who had been on the floor fixing the cooker just an hour before.

Soon the slow resonance of the unaccompanied voices seemed to fill not only the space around me, but the space inside me too, and my heart and chest and fingers began to vibrate with the sound. The words were in Latin, and perhaps it was the ancient mystery of the language, or the timelessness of the sacred song, but whatever it was, the plainsong was leading me. It led me out of myself and into a communion with the pilgrims of the past who had sat in the same place and listened to the same music, who were sitting in the same place, listening to the same music. There was a longing in the plainsong that was my longing, and I wanted to follow where it led.

A note on the order of service said Father Javier was hearing confessions after mass. I hadn't been to confession for 24 years and I wasn't even sure I would remember what to do. When I was about ten or eleven, at my convent boarding school, I had gone to confession regularly. I loved it. I'm not sure what I had to confess at that age, but the sacrament left me feeling unburdened and I would skip away as light as air. I wondered if, as an adult, I would experience the same sense of lightening, of being washed clean. At the end of the service I asked Jean to keep an eye on the macaroni and stayed behind.

There were no confession boxes in the church. Instead Father Javier slipped in and out of the pews, hearing confessions face to face. That meant I would have to look him in the eye while I dredged the darkest recesses of my soul. I considered making a run for it. I could blame the macaroni. About four or five people had stayed behind to receive the sacrament and I reckoned that since I was the furthest back, I would be last. To keep myself from bolting I held onto the pew so tightly that my knuckles went white, then my thoughts turned to my sins. I had a lot to figure out. How was I going to confess all of the sins I had committed in the last 24 years? Should I work through them chronologically? What if I left things out? Did that make the forgiveness null and void, like forgetting to declare things on an insurance policy? What if I ran out of time? No, that method was clearly not going to work. Perhaps I could collate. Create groups of similar sins. That might work. But what could my group headings be? And then, a flash of inspiration – The Seven Deadly Sins – someone had already sorted them for me. I would simply pick the ones I was guilty of committing. Simple. A moment's thought. It wasn't which – it was all. Dear Lord. All. I'd start with Anger. Or Greed. I'd start with Greed. Not Lust – I'd have to build up to that. I barely knew Father Javier, and he looked young enough to be my son. Fortunately, the other penitents had plenty to say so I had time on my side as I prepared.

Finally, it was my turn.

'Forgive me, Father, for I have sinned.' I remembered that much. 'It's been 24 years since my last confession.'

I thought it best to explain my strategy and told him I would start with Greed. A few minutes in, and for the second time that day, tears came from nowhere, followed by deep, wretched sobs, that made it hard to speak. Before I had made it to the end of the first of my seven lists, Father Javier intervened. He was kind, and wise, and told me that tears were powerful, that I shouldn't try to stop them. He told me that being sorry was enough and that he didn't need a complete inventory of my shortcomings.

'A confession of your faith,' he said, his voice tender, his eyes looking straight into mine, 'is every bit as valid as a confession of your sins.'

He gave me absolution and in the peace of the empty church I was returned to faith, reconciled. I felt it as strongly as a laying on of hands, I knew it in the depth of my being.

'Tomorrow, when you lay down your stone at the Cruz de Ferro, you must lay down your guilt and start anew,' he said.

The Cruz de Ferro is the place where pilgrims traditionally part with stones they have brought from home. The significance of this gesture is symbolic. It is an unburdening, but when I had packed two little stones in my rucksack five weeks ago, I had been doing so in a nod to the tradition. I hadn't really considered what this might mean to me.

I sat in the church for a while longer. It was empty now, and the candlelight flickered, but I was not alone. My stone was no bigger than a peach pit. It had slipped into my bag barely noticed but I had been struggling under the weight of it for years. Now I had a thousand years of pilgrims at my back, leading me onward on my journey. And tomorrow I would lay it down.

When I finally returned to the albergue, Ali had rescued the macaroni and we shared it with a young man from Burgos who had only a tomato and a tin of mussels for his supper. Ali is like a sister to me, but I had no words for all that had happened in the church, and she asked for none from me. Jean and I went back for Compline, which finished in darkness, and silence.

Day 27
5th May
Astorga – Rabanal
Kari, Ali, Jean
I am calm and ready for Cruz de Ferro.

CHAPTER 29

The sense of stillness which settled on me the previous night was severely tested by the clamorous farting that rang out in the dormitory. As soon as the lights went off it pealed out over the church bells and shuddered the snorers into submission. After half an hour listening to the rip-roaring trumping, I could contain myself no longer and, in my best 'outraged of Morningside' accent blurted, 'For goodness' sake!' The squeaking of the bedsprings below told me that Ali was trying to hold in her laughter, but my reprimand made not a jot of difference to Thunder Pants.

When morning finally came, the kindness of the hospitaleras went some way to compensate for the noisy night. They gave us bread and jam and a mug of hot coffee before waving goodbye as we continued our ascent of the highest mountain on the Camino. At just over 5,000ft, the summit of Alto Altar would come just after the Cruz de Ferro, perhaps the most iconic cross of the pilgrimage. I was hoping my leg would hold out.

During the night the storm had broken and it was pelting with rain as we set off in wet-weather gear. We rustled along, heads down and silent. Sounds changed in the rain. Instead of the scrunch of dry gravel, boots slapped on wet pathways and poles chimed as they struck stone, setting a beat from the beginning – ting-spank-ting-spank. The mist meant that I was not focusing on distant views but looking more carefully at the things right under my nose. The stony path was slippery, and we had to keep an eye on our feet, especially Ali who, despite her tumble in the shower, refused to take my hand and took off at quite a pace.

The Harris Tweed landscape of low grey skies, vaporous greens and russet bracken reminded me of Scotland and today would be a day where the pull of home was strong. Low stone dykes, covered in lichen, partitioned the modest fields and although the white broom was in flower, the trees were still bare this high up the mountain.

I had been anticipating this day. I had walked 650km, I was two thirds of the way there, and like the centuries of pilgrims who had walked before me, I'd had time to reflect on the purpose of my journey. I knew that I was walking to thank God for my family. But there was more to it than that.

As I walked the words 'let go' beat a steady refrain. When I stopped to pray in hermitages, churches and cathedrals, those were the words that echoed in my head. I thought of Alexander, reaching the end of his time at university and Joss and Connie, on the brink of adult life. I was all too aware that I was struggling to let them go. My sister, Patsy, had told me that mothers are just the bows that fire the arrows, but it wasn't so easy to let them fly. I prayed that I would find a way to convert all that nurturing into a love with some spaces. Spaces where they could discover themselves, distinct from David and me. Spaces where they could flop, miss the mark, choose their own target, or soar. And spaces where I might rediscover who I am, distinct from them.

We stopped for coffee at Foncebadón, about 4km before the Cruz de Ferro. The café was steamy and pilgrims who smelled like wet dogs were huddled in quiet packs hoping, like us, for a break in the weather. A few days previously Jean had shared a short poem with me, and I wrote it out on a scrap of paper so that I could read it at the cross. Then we rifled our rucksacks to find our stones. Ali's came from the farm in Invergordon, mine from our garden at home in Edinburgh. I had dug it up on a wet day in April, a day not unlike today. When I left it under the cross, I would be leaving behind one stage of family life, with love and thanks, and stepping forward into the next with hope. That was the plan.

We were in the clouds as we walked towards the Cruz de Ferro and all of a sudden it emerged before us, high, as if it were floating. The iron cross, no bigger than a sword, was stark against the fog. As we got closer, I could see that it was fixed to the top of a soaring pole staked in a mound of what looked like rubble, the accumulation of stones left by centuries of pilgrims. Saint Francis of Assisi had stopped here.

A bus party of day-trippers had been driven up to the summit and after the silence of our walk we hung back to hold onto some of the stillness. We sheltered from the rain as they left their stones. The simple iron cross was a humble monument, but it rose out of the mist with sovereignty and as we waited for the crowd to disperse, I focused on it, feeling its weight upon me.

I was alone when I approached the cross. I took out my stone and read the words I had written on the scrap of paper:

'To Come Home to Your Self'

May all that is unforgiven in me be released.

May my deepest fears yield their deepest tranquilities.

May all that is unlived in me blossom into a future graced with love.

Unbidden the words of Father Javier came back to me: 'When you lay down your stone, you must lay down your guilt and start anew.'

And then I heard, 'Let go… let go…'

But it was not my children who came to me in that moment, it was my mother, and the whole tangled mess of our relationship. Impossibly, in that split second, fragments of memories came to my mind, ugly and beautiful in equal measure. And then they were gone, the ugliness receded, and all that remained was the surety of the fierceness of her love. It was time to let go. To leave behind the guilt and the anger and move on into the future with love. I had made peace with her at last. I had made peace with myself. In the rain I was washed clean.

Ali followed me, laying down her stone, saying a silent prayer, touching the pole of the cross. And then it was Jean's turn. Ali and I waited at the base of the mound, giving her a moment to herself. She took out her stone and we watched as she kissed it and knelt to lay it down. She had shared something of her sadness and of her loss and we knew that this was a moment she had been imagining for years. And then, as she tried to stand up the weight of her backpack pulled her down. She fell back in a comedy arc and lay stranded like a flipped bedbug, arms and legs flailing, searching for purchase. Ali and I scrambled up to her and took an arm each, pulling her to her feet. We laughed until the tears streamed down our faces and the release was perfect.

A couple of kilometres later we reached Manjarin, a tiny outpost with a resident population of one. The carved wooden head of a bearded king welcomed us, while a mass of signposts pointed out the direction and the distance to capital cities all over the world – home – wherever that might be. It told us that we had 222km to go to Santiago and that seemed like no distance at all. A shack that appeared to have been nailed together out of an assortment of old planks served as the only toilet. We were desperate and joined the queue.

'Well, that is the worst dunny I have ever been to,' an Australian woman called to her friend as she exited the hut.

And just like that, it turned out we were not so desperate after all.

We continued uphill to the top of the mountain, charged with a new energy that made the walking easy. At the summit of Alto Altar we were higher than the clouds. The rain stopped and we could see right across the valley. All around us, like islands in some steamy, primordial landscape, the mountaintops poked above the cloud inversion. I was happy to slow down to let the horde of day-trippers, dropped at the top of the mountain, pass by in a chatty mob. It gave me time to notice the spiders' webs in the purple heather and the gothic lichen draped on the trees.

The steep descent into Acebo was, as predicted,

challenging, especially after all that rain. I was in pain and Ali gave me a lesson in how to walk flat-footed to avoid making the tendonitis worse. While I was well aware that this must look utterly ridiculous, it did help, so for once I did as I was told.

We were cold and soaked to the skin by the time we reached the village but this had been a special walk and our spirits were high. Jean, cloaked in her enormous poncho with a white fleece zipped up at the neck, looked like a little nun and Ali couldn't resist making her pose in front of a large cross in suitably reverent postures.

We were hoping for an albergue that was warm, and which had small dorms with no farting men but all we could see in the village were hotels, well beyond our budget. Jean went into one to enquire about an advert in their window and before we knew what was happening a man with a cigarette in his mouth took our backpacks off our backs and threw them into the boot of his car.

We pointed at our wet clothes and muddy boots and he shrugged. 'Don't worry. Get in. I take you.'

My father always told me I shouldn't get into cars with strange men, but we didn't seem to have much of a say in the matter.

'Is this cheating?' asked Ali, who had been rather derogatory about the day-trippers earlier in the day.

'No, no, no,' we reassured her, sheepishly. Technically we were skipping 300m and it didn't feel quite right. But I didn't say that to Ali who was a stickler for the rules. And did I regret it? Hell, no.

He drove us to a purpose-built albergue, the first of this type that we had come across. It was characterless and modern but as we arrived we bumped into Maria the German chain-smoker, and the wonderful woman on the reception desk put just the four of us in an eight-person dorm. Perhaps she could see from our weary faces that we needed a break from windy men. Yet again, the Camino had not only provided, she had ticked every item on our list.

Our kit was soaked and we had to empty out our rucksacks and dry out the insides as best we could. I waited in line for the washing machines and later ran up and down stairs feeding the dryer with euros. Finally sorted, we spent the afternoon in the sitting room, in front of the fire, eating cake and drinking coffee. All along the corridor the radiators were fenced in by semi-circles of wet boots. By bedtime our clothes and rucksacks were dry and we were well fed and ready for a good night's sleep.

Day 28
6th May
Rabanal – Acebo
Kari, Ali, Jean
As I type in the dark I can't shift the feeling that everything that is happening to me is happening for a purpose. I couldn't have planned for today, all I could do was open myself up to possibilities. Step by step my guard has dropped and my heart has opened.

CHAPTER 30

We woke to thick fog and Ali was worried that the long downhill stretch to Ponferrada might be hard on my shin. Maria the German chain-smoker was not sure that she wanted to walk at all. While we got on with the morning ritual of packing our rucksacks and strapping up my leg, she sat on her bunk, struggling with her sleeping bag.

'No matter how carefully I roll it, I just can't fit it back in the bag. Every day I waste so much time trying and in the end I just have to push it in my rucksack without the bag.'

'Aha. It's a stuff sack. It only works if you stuff it in and keep stuffing.' I said. Ali demonstrated, squashing the air out as she went. Maria was so happy to have found a solution to her problem that her mood lifted and she decided to join us after all.

We were in no rush to get to Ponferrada and planned to take our time. It was not a main stop on the Way, so the demand for beds was not as great. We were taking a day off there the following day, when Connie and David would be joining us mid-afternoon.

Although the first stretch was on road, which made for easy walking, visibility was poor and we had to listen out for cars that came out of the fog with little warning. As soon as we stepped off the road onto country pathways the clouds began to lift, and we caught sight of the valley, the peaks in the distance rising through low clouds.

This was a coarse mountain landscape, far from the rolling agricultural plains of last week. The mountainsides were rocky, covered in shrubby foliage and stippled with white broom that looked, at first, like snow.

At the first café we came to we ran into Thomas, the pilgrim formerly known as Ghostbuster, and it was good to see him looking happy and well rested. Maria joined him as it was time for coffee and a cigarette but being breakfasters of discernment, Ali, Jean and I rejected the desayunos on offer. The coffee was instant and the orange juice from a carton. It was a risky strategy, but we were determined to hold out for better and carried on.

It felt good to be in no hurry and we explored this mountain. The stone was creamy yellow, much wood was in evidence, and the narrow streets seemed maintained. This was a far cry from the villages we had walked through in Navarra where the exodus to the cities had left only the old. Here, in the well-tended gardens, the lilac trees were in full bloom, and toys and washing lines let us know that families lived here.

A few miles later we saw a sign on a lamppost for *Café LaFe* – Faith – a donativo pilgrim rest stop. This sounded perfect and it wasn't long before we heard an enthusiastic welcome. Manuel, the waiter from Barcelona, flagged us down and invited us in for coffee. We sat under an awning in his huge, untamed garden and he told us his story while he made us toast with jam and cheese.

'We are all pilgrims,' he said. 'And I know what a pilgrim needs – good coffee. I serve only the best. Jamaican Blue Mountain.'

It was superb. Manuel had been a hospitalero in Sarria and he had met his Bulgarian wife when she was a pilgrim seven years ago.

'She passed through my albergue and although she only stayed one night, we fell in love. She needed to finish her pilgrimage and went on her way without leaving her phone number. But I knew we would be together again one day. After she had reached Finisterre she walked back to me and we have been together ever since.'

He ran up to his house and spoke to his wife who was

planting vegetables in the garden. She waved at us and he ran back down to show us a grainy scan picture. They were expecting their first baby in January.

'Did anyone ever tell you that you look just like Robert de Niro?' I asked him.

'Every day,' he said.

He turned away and looked back, his chin down and his two index fingers pointing in towards his chest. 'Are you lookin' at me?'

It was his goal in life to provide every pilgrim on the Camino with a good cup of coffee. He existed solely on donations and told us that if people could not afford a coffee it was his privilege to make them one for free. He gave us a recommendation for an albergue in Ponferrada and a little piece of paper that told each of us 'our essence'. Jean's said 'happiness', which made us smile, as her catch phrase is 'I'm so happy', mine said 'friendship' and Ali's, 'life'.

From then on the rock paths were smooth and slippery and the downhill often so steep that I had to take it very slowly. I was pleased to have my poles as they gave at least an illusion of support and I smiled as I thought of the security woman way back in Stansted. I sent her a mental note to say, yes, they came in handy, thanks.

In dark woods, draped with lichen, I pictured Snow White being led by the huntsman, but before it all became too gothic we were once again out in the open where white rockroses edged the path and lavender filled the air. The wild flowers had been a constant source of inspiration and often they came like a gift at the top of a steep hill, or as a reward round a corner when I was starting to flag.

On that day the flower display surpassed anything we had seen before. We had walked from winter back into spring and as we headed downhill again the trees came into leaf. Wild blue lupins, sweet peas, dog roses, wisteria, verbena, apple blossom and countless others added colour and scent to our walk all the way to Ponferrada.

As usual, I lagged behind, stopping to take photographs and smell the lavender, enjoying the solitude. We were mercifully free from the noisy day-packers of yesterday – in fact we were virtually on our own for the whole journey. The path followed the course of several streams and the noise of the water after the heavy rain of last night was exhilarating. I forgot all about the pain in my leg.

Twenty kilometres passed in a flash and it was about noon when we arrived in Molinaseca. We stopped for another orange juice and a chance to watch the locals: mums pushing prams, shopkeepers chatting in their doorways, and old men taking a stroll to collect the bread before lunch. The sun came out as we sat enjoying this prosperous little town. Ali looked relaxed and happy. Her face, all cheekbones, was tanned and her blue eyes sparkled in the sunshine. She looked lean and powerful, and about 15 years younger than when we had started in St Jean. She was relishing these moments, enjoying having time to herself, as I was. At home she was constantly sorting out other people's problems, juggling the needs of those who relied upon her. She had given up a demanding, and highly respected job to care for her mother and her brother, but she seemed to have lost sight of herself in the process. This time was precious and I knew she was savouring it.

Tomorrow Connie and David would be joining us in Ponferrada and I couldn't wait for them to be here. I had missed the feel of them, and the smell of them and longed to breathe them in. Connie would be joining us for a week and David would stay for a night then head off to see some battlefields before joining us again for the final stage of the walk to Santiago. My friend, Marguerite, would also be joining us in a couple of days' time, and I realised with a pang, that this was the last time it would be just the three of us.

The outskirts of Ponferrada began just after Molinaseca but although we usually found suburbs hard going, today the last few kilometres passed quickly.

It was about 2.30pm when we arrived in town and we hit the albergue jackpot with the recommendation from Manuel. It seemed as though we were the only people in a room for just six and we had our own bathroom. Tickety-boo.

The dauntingly powerful Knights Templar castle that sat on top of the hill overshadowed the medieval city. It reminded me of the one my children played with when they were little. Like their toy castle, it had a vast drawbridge, towers topped with crenelations and flags flying from the turrets. In the town, the shops were full of plastic knights, swords and trebuchets and Joss would have been in heaven if we had visited when he was small.

We meandered around the town, getting our bearings and taking it easy, happy that we were having a day off tomorrow and in no hurry to pack in the sights. In the main square Jean taught us a few salsa moves, then treated us to a bodybuilding demonstration beside a billboard of Rosie the Riveter.

'Front Double Bicep. Front Lateral Spread,' she announced as she moved smoothly between poses.

'I'm such a ham. My brother was a ham. My father was a ham. We're all hams,' she said, laughing.

Much to Princess Ali's disappointment there was no opportunity to bubble and soak in Ponferrada but we took things easy back at the albergue and hung out in the communal dining room. Late afternoon, we spotted Dollar Bill at reception and knowing we had a spare bed in our dorm, we kept our fingers crossed that he wouldn't end up beside us. We were in luck.

By dinner time we were so comfortable that we couldn't face heading out so we visited the nearest supermarket and bought a packet of chicken noodle soup, bread, Serrano ham and a bottle of local Bierzo. Ponferrada, the old capital of the El Bierzo region, was famed for its wine, and it went down very nicely. As we were eating, Maria-Manuela from Puerto Rico walked in. Her face lit up when she saw Jean, her Camino mum, and she ran over to hug her. Having spent some time recovering in a hotel and getting buses here there and everywhere she was now very much back on track. She had moved on from the sadness of being ditched by her friend and seemed so much more confident and determined than the girl we had first met. She had lost weight, caught the sun, and glowed with health.

'My momma is surprising me in Santiago,' she said. 'It's meant to be a secret, but she told me to be in Santiago on the 25th May. And why else would she care when I get there?'

Day 29
7th May
Acebo – Ponferrada
Kari, Ali, Jean
We are sad that we have lost track of some of our Camino buddies this week. Stefano keeps in touch via Facebook and we know that they are now three days ahead of us. Emmanueli is no longer with them, but they are walking with Tim, the love-struck Australian, and Ainslie, the right angle of the Camino love triangle. The talk is all about Santiago and we hear that Richard, who walked with Jean in the first week, is there already.

My leg is causing me such a lot of pain, particularly when I stop walking, that now and again the horrible thought that I might not make it has crossed my mind. Ali is doing a brilliant job of keeping me going but her phone calls to her mum, also a physio, suggest she is more worried than she is letting on. I don't indulge the thought for long.

Earlier this evening, the lady in the supermarket told us she had walked three Caminos by three different routes. She said she loved all three but while two challenged her physically, only the Camino Frances was magical.

I can't wait to share it with Connie.

CHAPTER 31

The previous night a Yorkshirewoman who had lived in Sweden for ten years joined us in our dorm. She had walked sections of the Camino over the last five years and she clearly thought of herself as something of an expert. She took stock of the room and identified the only remaining bed.

'I don't do top bunks,' she said.

All three of us suddenly became engrossed in Jean's guidebook, looking down, avoiding eye contact. I had called this rectangle of bunk home for the last six hours, and there was no way I was giving it up without a fight. Jean and Ali evidently felt the same.

'And I snore,' she said, continuing her charm offensive. 'There's nothing I can do about it. It's all just part of the experience. If you don't like snorers you shouldn't be in a dorm.'

We switched the lights off, expecting a noisy night but either we were so tired we didn't notice or the top bunk had cured her problem. She went at first light, without saying goodbye.

I slept well, enjoyed a bit of a lie in and took my time getting ready. David and Connie were arriving later in the afternoon and I felt like I was getting ready for a first date. Jean and Ali helped me pick the right outfit, from my limited choice of three. I borrowed a hairdryer from reception and Jean bought me a small bottle of conditioner to help me get my tiny travel brush through my dried-out hair. Having barely looked in a mirror for a month, it felt strange to consider what I must look like to others.

Dolled up, we headed across the road to have breakfast in an artisan bakery, and made it in just before the rain started. Since Jenny left I had been the keeper of the kitty, and the three of us put €20 into the sandwich bag every couple of days. This bought our breakfasts, coffees and lunches and saved us faffing about trying to figure out whose turn it was. It meant that I was the one who ordered breakfast most of the time and I had become quite fluent, as long as I ordered the same thing every day. Three Napolitanas, three large white coffees, and three glasses of freshly squeezed orange juice.

While we were eating, Sara the Curvy German appeared, for once, not accompanied by Lara, her little friend. She was wet from the rain and breathing hard as she lumbered in, limping badly. She shrugged off her rucksack, clearly despondent. When she saw us waving she seemed relieved and we called her over to join us.

The poor girl was tired, sore and thoroughly fed up.

'I was holding her up so I told Lara to go on ahead,' she explained. 'She didn't want to leave me but my knee is really bad and I just can't keep up.'

I put my arms around her, inadvertently opening the dam that was holding back her tears. She sobbed as if her heart would break and was immediately wrapped up by the three of us in full mummy mode. She had walked from Molinaseca that morning and was heading for the municipal.

'Fuck the municipal,' we said in chorus. 'You're coming with us.'

While Jean and I went to mass to atone for our blasphemy, Ali put Christianity into practice and got Sara settled in.

In the *Basílica de la Encina*, it was Ascension Sunday and a cheery priest and about 30 children preparing for their First Holy Communion led the service. The dark art on the walls and the macabre statuary (which including a waxwork of the dead Christ in a glass coffin) was softened by the children's voices. The girls wore floppy bows in their well-brushed hair and the boys, hand-knitted jumpers that accentuated their round tummies.

At the end of the service we were called up to receive a pilgrim blessing and I was struck with anxiety, as I feared that we might be the only two pilgrims in the very large congregation. There was no way we could get out of it as a lady appeared and ushered us up the aisle. To my relief an Italian, two Koreans, two Germans and a Belgian joined us at the altar where each of us received a blessing in our own language.

As we left the church I told Jean that I'd been thinking about Emmanueli. I had been on the lookout for him for days, but now I felt sure we wouldn't see him again.

'How far do you think he's got?' she said.

'Well it's Ascension Sunday,' I said, only half joking. 'I think he may have gone home.'

We headed back to the albergue to check how Ali was getting on. It was no surprise that she had worked her healing magic and we found Sara tucked up with a hot-water bottle, fast asleep, the pain gone from her face. Ali had sorted out her knee and had helped her formulate a plan. She would rest for a couple of days and when she had recovered she would take a bus to Sarria and walk the last 100km, meeting Lara on the way so that they could be together when they arrived in Santiago.

Ali was confident that Sara would be fine without us, so, in what might be considered an unimaginative choice on a day off from walking, we opted to go for a walk. Up a hill. To Santa Maria de Vizbayo, an 11th Century church. We walked through allotments and pretty countryside and the views from the top more than made up for the fact that the church was locked. As was so often the case.

In a tiny bar filled with locals we sat by a wood burner and enjoyed a long lunch. Serrano ham, cut straight from the bone, and chorizo cooked in wine and oregano could not have been more delicious. Later, we explored the castle and walked the battlements oohing and aahing at the poppies as we went.

I had butterflies in my tummy waiting for David and Connie and I checked my phone every few minutes to see whether they had sent a message. It had been an early start for them, and a long drive from Santander so we were not entirely sure of the timings. We waited in the dining room at the albergue, keeping an eye on the door.

The phone rang.

'I'm lost,' David said. 'Can you come and meet me at the garage on Avenida de Castillo?'

My leg was hurting like hell but I did my best to run down the road to find them. In the distance I picked out Connie's familiar gait and ran towards her. It was so good to be pulled into their familiar arms. Not only did they smell fabulous, they had brought liquorice toffees too.

It felt like a celebration when we walked into the albergue, all of us talking at once, and stories tripping out. They had been reading my posts and were keen to put some faces to the names. They had heard so much about Jean that it didn't seem as if I was introducing them to a stranger. For an hour or more we chatted, reconnecting with home, filling them in on the details.

About six o'clock, David, Connie and I headed to the hotel where we were staying for the night. I understood how Ali had felt when Guy had joined us. Although the thought of my husband, a hotel bed, darkness and towels was undoubtedly appealing, I was unsure that I wanted to step off the Camino for a night. But my guilt dissolved in the tiny bath as my leg muscles relaxed and the pain soaked away. I used the whole bottle of complimentary bubble bath and pocketed the free conditioner for future use.

Later, all five of us met for tapas in a local bar. Our waitress was a feisty woman of reduced stature with a pink Mohican and a pierced nose. Her pugilistic stance bordered on aggression but the trace of smile in the corner of her mouth gave her away.

'Wha you wan?' she said.

'Gambas al ajillo?'

'No,' she said.

'Calamares?'

'No,' she said.

'Botillo?'

'No,' she said.

'OK, bring us what you've got. Enough for five people.'

'Vale,' she said, laughing.

She looked after us well and brought us the best of everything they had left in the kitchen on a quiet Sunday night. Plates of cold meat, salads, a variety of croquetas, tortilla and bread appeared. Plenty of bread. David, keen to take care of us weary travellers, picked up the tab but couldn't quite believe it when the bill was only €25. He had hoped to be more magnanimous.

And when we had eaten our fill, the three Gillespies retreated, slightly shamefaced, to our hotel while Jean and Ali went back to the albergue to tend to the sick and dispirited. Tomorrow, Marguerite would join us in Villafranca.

Day 30
8ᵗʰ May
Rest Day – Ponferrada
Kari, Ali, Jean, Connie, David
David can't quite believe that on our first night together in 30 days, I am lying in bed writing my journal on my phone, but here I am. First things first.

CHAPTER 32

Usually I sat hunched on a bottom bunk, rolling the air out of my dry bags in the cold, dim light of my head torch. But in the hotel, it was a treat to have the lights on and the space to spread out. I was ready to go when Connie knocked on our door. Kitted out in her walking gear, with her scallop shell on her back, she was doing this thing with me and I felt a surge of pride.

'Get going, pilgrims,' said David, kissing us goodbye.

He was heading for Vitoria, the site of Wellington's great victory in the Peninsular War, and would be rejoining us in three days, just in time for his birthday. Connie would walk with us as far as Ribadiso, then take a bus to Santiago to fly home.

For Connie and me it was an inauspicious start as we got lost getting out of the hotel. Fully loaded up with rucksacks and poles we ricocheted off the walls of the narrow corridors like bumper cars until we finally found a staircase to lead us out. Locating the castle was a further challenge and as we consulted the map I realised how much I relied on Ali and Jean when it came to navigation. To our relief, they were waiting by the battlements as we had planned.

'I'm in safe hands at last,' Connie said.

The way out of town took us over the Iron Bridge, the eponymous Pons Ferrada. Walking on asphalt for the first few kilometres played havoc with my shin and by the time we stopped for breakfast I was in dire need of a coffee to wash down the pain meds. In a narrow bar with a counter all along one side and a little kitchen in a room beyond, one young man was struggling to cope. He was frying eggs and bacon, making coffee, squeezing orange juice and taking orders, all with a limited degree of success. The atmosphere was frenzied. Unsure that there was another option, we ordered and waited. And waited. And just as we were beginning to lose hope, his Momia swooped in like a small round superhero and within minutes we had our breakfast.

'And here we see in action, the power of the middle-aged woman, imposing order and bringing calm to the pandemonium that has erupted in her absence,' I said, in my best David Attenborough voice.

Today, there was no shortage of places to stop to adjust packs, drink orange juice and eat toffees. And for once everywhere seemed to be open. At each stop Ali checked my shin and tightened the strapping when necessary. We visited a number of hermitages and chapels and Connie's passport quickly filled up with stamps. Our favourite was a chapel with a fresco of the Last Supper on the ceiling and a gruesome San Sebastián complete with multiple arrows. In the corner we found a statue of San Roque, looking sorry for himself and pointing to a sore bit on his leg.

'Oh look, he's taken a little tumble too,' said Jean, who had fallen over on the way out of mass. And Connie took a picture of her next to the accident-prone saint, pointing at her bruises.

Later, as Connie stopped to photograph the first of many old doorways, Ali groaned, 'Well this apple didn't fall far from the tree.'

At lunchtime I finalised the arrangements with Marguerite. We usually found accommodation when we arrived at our destination, but as we needed to let her know the rendezvous point we decided to book ahead. We were approaching the final section where the walk became busier and we had been warned that it would be hard to find five beds. Pre-booking brought a smile to Ali's face: she would have been booking ahead all the way given half the chance. The two of us had been lucky to travel with Spanish speakers since the beginning and Jean got on the phone to book five spots in a small private albergue.

Back home in Boston someone had told Jean that she would be known as Juanita in Spain and she made the booking in this name. We heard the hospitalero laugh out loud.

'What's so funny?' asked Juanita, in Spanish.

'That's a name you only hear in old movies from the 50s,' he replied.

From then on she was Juanita to us. Complete with cherry red lips, plunging neckline and a big black comb in her hair.

All booked up, we got back on the road, firmly in wine country once again.

Drizzly rain started after lunch and the path through the vineyards quickly became muddy. There were plenty of hills and while the uphill was fine (I had never thought I would say that) the downhill was torture on the tendonitis. My pace was slow but I loved dawdling at the back, finding joy in the little things, and recognising grace in the beauty of the ordinary. *Eucharisteo* – giving thanks.

At the side of the path, someone, probably sitting to take the weight off their feet, had written 'sunshine' in white stones and now that the rain had stopped, it made me smile.

Connie, fit from her ski season, was striding out ahead and I kept her in my sights, following the Boston Red Sox cap on her head. She looked strong and self-contained, lost in her own walk.

In the wheat fields, startling red poppies brought to mind Plath's poem, *Poppies in October*.

A gift, a love gift
Utterly unasked for.

I had come to give thanks, but today my thanks were being repaid with gifts tenfold.

This was a 27.5km day and when we finally stumbled into

Villafranca del Bierzo we found Connie sprawled on a wall. It had been tougher than she had imagined and Ali and Jean grabbed her walking poles and pulled her back onto her feet. Secretly I was pleased. I didn't want her thinking the Camino had been a walk in the park.

Villafranca, or little Compostela, is a town bursting with history – Peninsular War stuff, Roman stuff, St Francis stuff, it was all happening there – but I was pooped and just wanted to take my boots off. Jean pointed out *La puerta del perdon*, the door of pardon, in the 12th Century Church of Santiago. Here pilgrims who were too broken by the journey to make it all the way to Santiago, could receive pardon and complete their pilgrimage. It was tempting.

The hospitalero at our albergue was still laughing when Juanita walked in. Wee Jean, with her cropped hair, walking boots and big green poncho was not quite the smouldering Hollywood starlet he had envisioned but he gave us mint tea and a seat on his sofa and we sat gratefully while the blood slowly returned to our feet.

Our dormitory was a large attic room. The bunk bed Connie and I had been allocated was right next to the deep stairwell and the top bunk had a drop of about 20 feet on one side. Terrified as I am of heights, I am more terrified of other people being next to a drop and struggle to control my urge to hold their hands. At tourist attractions all over the world – Empire State Building, Table Mountain, Eiffel Tower, London Eye – total strangers have been 'saved' by me grabbing onto them. I knew I wouldn't sleep a wink if Connie were on the top bunk so I unrolled my sleeping bag onto it before anyone could object.

Once I had showered and changed, I asked the others if they would like to 'eat in'. They thought that was a good plan so Connie and I decided to head out for groceries. I was dying to have her to myself for a while.

'Would anyone like me to bring them anything?' I asked the others in the dorm. 'Chocolate? Compeed? Wine?'

A German man diagonally opposite us grunted and held

his hand up to say no.

'He was a bit rude,' Connie said, as we left for the shop, and I nodded.

For once the nearby supermarket had everything we needed and Connie and I took our time selecting the ingredients for supper. In the vegetable aisle I put my basket on the floor and took her face in my hands.

'You're really here,' I said and kissed her cheek, pulling her in for a cuddle.

'Yes, I'm really here. And I'm hungry,' she replied.

I cooked chicken fajitas and salad in the tiny kitchen where a wizened old couple sat sharing their dinner of apple and lettuce. They looked like the pair in the painting called 'American Gothic', and without breaking a smile told us they were vegetarians and that they had been in Villafranca for three days as 'His knee was causing him problems.' Their tiny frames spoke of a life of abstemiousness and they advised all those cooking to switch off the gas and turn off the water, pained by the smallest suggestion of waste. There was a joylessness about them that did not invite company and Christina, a woman from Belgium, about our age, tried unsuccessfully to engage them in chat before joining us for dinner.

She had bought a tin of cassoulet and although the beans seemed tasty enough the lumps of unidentified offal looked unspeakably bad. She had begun her journey alone, but for the last four weeks she had been part of a group of women who had teamed up along the Way.

'I enjoyed their company, but I wanted some time to think so I have been going solo for the last few days.'

She worked as a pathologist in an oncology laboratory in Brussels, diagnosing breast cancer. The gravity and responsibility of her role had taken its toll and she was walking to find some peace and perspective. She missed her two children and we shared some stories over supper.

At about 8ish Marguerite arrived, 16 hours after she had left her home in Kent. She had been on planes, trains and buses to reach us and she thoroughly deserved a glass of vino tinto.

Marguerite had been a friend of mine since we were at Oxford together, 29 years before. Then, as now, like Mary Poppins, she seemed practically perfect in every way. Her French heritage gave her an exotic allure that men loved, but she was oblivious to this and her vulnerable charm made women love her just as much. I have never heard her say an unkind word about anyone and to this day she tolerates those who drive the rest of us mad.

Life is sometimes unkind to those who deserve it least and in the years since college Marguerite had been more than tested. She had been living with MS for the last ten years and although she refused to allow the disease to dominate her life, she was fighting a battle with quiet resolve. She wanted to join us to carve out a bit of time for herself but as she was juggling a family and two jobs she had only managed to get away for four days.

Although she was fit and enjoyed walking, our guidebook told us that the following day would be a 'strenuous stage' and I had been worried about how she would cope. We had looked closely at the maps and planned to take things slowly, spending three days walking the next two stages.

Just before I got into bed the German man who had been rude earlier snapped his fingers at Connie and beckoned her over. I was about to get shirty.

'Mum, he wants to speak to you,' she whispered.

I walked over to his bottom bunk where he had been lying since mid-afternoon.

'Yes,' I said. Not smiling.

'I see that your leg is very sore. I have some special ointment that I brought from home. It will help you if you rub it in every morning and every night. Keep it. It's for you,' he said.

Sometimes, people surprised me.

Day 31
9th May
Ponferrada – Villafranca
Kari, Ali, Jean, Connie
I am terrified lying on this bunk. The drop to my right is probably 20ft and although the bed has a small rail, what if I try to stagger to the loo in the middle of the night and get it wrong? Tomorrow we head back up into the mountains. I hope I make it through the night.

CHAPTER 33

The special ointment was rubbed in, my leg was strapped up and we were ready to go long before the new girls made an appearance. Always the slowest in the early days, Ali was quietly pleased about this, and we shared a smile. The albergue offered a simple breakfast of tea and biscuits and although it was nothing to write home about, we were glad of it, as there were no cafés on our route that morning. Instead of following the crowd along the road, we opted for an alternative mountain route towards O Cebreiro.

After just 50m on the road, and still half asleep, we spotted our diversion off the main route. We looked in disbelief at the unbelievably steep path that would lead us straight up to Alto Pradela.

'You're going the wrong way,' said an Irishman, walking with a group of men about our age. We explained that we wanted to avoid walking near the road as much as possible.

'The guidebook promises that it will be quiet and pretty,' said Ali, holding out the map.

He seemed persuaded and we left him trying to convince the rest of his party that the steep hill ahead was a good option.

It really was impossibly sheer. We walked past allotments and smallholdings that might have been pretty had I looked, but I had eyes for nothing but the road beneath my feet. Concentrating on steadying my breathing I blocked out everything around me and counted the steps. Sets of ten works well for me. *Just another ten and then you can stop*, I told myself. I didn't stop, but the option kept me going. Forty minutes and hundreds of steps later, the steep climb showed no signs of flattening out: finally we paused to catch our breath.

The Irishman had succeeded in persuading his group to come this way.

'I'm beginning to wish we had never feckin' met you,' he muttered as he walked past. Six sweaty middle-aged men followed in his wake, none too pleased.

But we didn't regret our choice and once my legs had warmed up and my breathing settled I lifted my eyes up from the ground. We had climbed into the bright morning light, leaving behind the shadow of the mountain that shaded everything below. At 7am we reached the top and the visibility was excellent. We looked back to Villafranca, nestled like a martini glass into the V of the Valcarce Valley and Jean picked out the Monasterio de San Francisco. The peaks behind us rose through the cloud inversion: ahead of us were the mountains still to come.

The sun was strong and we got out the sunscreen. The small tube of Clarins facial sunscreen, which had been my moisturiser for the trip, was nearly finished and I squeezed the last blob onto Connie's palm. Jean produced a huge bottle of sun cream from her magic rucksack and shared it with the rest of us.

'Ocean Potion, smells like summer,' she trilled.

Our senses were wide-awake and the smell of the cream seemed to bring everything into sharper focus. The colours were brighter. The sounds more sharp.

This quiet pathway was remote and once again we had it to ourselves. I needn't have worried about Marguerite who was pounding along with determined energy. She strode out in front chatting to Connie who was enjoying the challenge of spotting the yellow arrows. I liked to keep Connie in view and felt a twinge of panic if I lost her for a moment or two. In my rational mind, I knew she was more than capable of finding her own way, but my maternal instinct had been slow to catch up with this change in status. It saw a warning sign, and rather than giving me a gentle nudge to watch out, it responded with a red alert complete with sirens and flashing lights and it took a while for reason to make its quieter voice heard.

By noticing what was around me rather than in front of me I relaxed and focused on my own experience. The scenery was so familiar we could have been walking in Scotland. The gorse had turned from white to yellow, and the lavender looked for all the world like heather. These mountains were topped with conifers and the bracken was scrubby and tough. Bright yellow lupins joined the blue spring flowers that bloomed all around.

I was thinking about colour as I walked and my mind wandered, wondering if I could make a spectrum with the flowers I had seen on my walk. Poppy red, gorse yellow, lupin blue, calendula orange, lavender purple, apple blossom pink and green everywhere. I was singing the children's song in my head, to make sure I hadn't forgotten any of the colours, and when I looked up I saw a rainbow in the sky ahead. Opposite us three peaks dominated the skyline, weaving a plait at the base of the valley. The rainbow arched behind the crisscrossing mountains: a harbinger of happiness yet to come.

'Ali,' I shouted. 'You'll never guess what just happened.'

I told her.

'You bloody hippy,' she said.

As we climbed the last of the three peaks, we saw a sign for a mountaintop café and followed like the children of Hamelin, drawn by the Pied Piper's music. For far too long we trailed after the fantasy of a freshly squeezed orange juice, the noise of the pipe getting fainter and fainter, until finally we had to admit we were lost.

'I think it's this way,' said Marguerite confidently, jumping over a low wire fence and heading straight down the hillside. Cross-country, off the path, I was completely out of my comfort zone and anxious for a yellow arrow. We hadn't gone off-piste in 32 days and I was reluctant to get behind a new leader. But, she was right. The route was tricky with heavy packs but the arrow, when it came, was a cause for liquorice toffee.

The path continued to descend steeply and the mud and gravel added to the challenge. My tendonitis burned with each footfall. Ali was right, if I could just stop my foot from flexing the pain was much reduced but walking downhill flat-footed was harder than it sounded.

Finally, we could see Trabadelo below us and we walked beneath the massive electricity pylons, the air crackling as raindrops connected with the wires. I could feel the hairs on my arms standing up, my skin prickling with static. It had been a difficult hour and I was ready for a coffee when the opportunity finally came. Not the best coffee of the Camino, but certainly among the most welcome and we sat outside recovering while Ali did Connie's hair in an elaborate French braid.

Ali has two sons, and after a childhood spent plaiting her ponies' manes she had not had much of a chance to put her skills to use. Connie was happy to be her show pony, her own mother being a bit of a let-down in the hairdressing department.

The last 12km of the walk were on the flat and this was something of a relief. We visited a number of little churches, much plainer than the big showy numbers, but more to my simple tastes. We chatted with three or four locals who were keen to wish us well and tell us about their own experiences. People from all over the world do this walk, but the largest group of all is the Spaniards, proud of the Camino and its long history.

Later we bumped into the two Koreans we had met in church in Ponferrada. They had shared the albergue with Jean and Ali on the night I was living it up in the two-star hotel. The Korean man had been struggling with a bad knee and Ali had bandaged him up and got him back on his feet. They greeted her like a superstar and thanked her over and over. We had lost count of the number of people she had helped along the Way and we had christened her 'San Pies' – Saint Feet.

But the number of familiar faces was dwindling and we missed the members of our Camino family who had forged on ahead, dropped behind or headed home. Perhaps this falling away was also integral to the journey. Although I was surrounded by friends, most often I walked alone, lost in my own thoughts. And perhaps on this final stretch, that was as it should be. Now it was just between me and my God.

We had not picked an albergue, or even a town in which to settle for the night, as we didn't know how my leg would hold up. Not booking accommodation in advance might seem like a risky strategy but for me, it was central to the spirit of the pilgrimage. It had given us the freedom to see where the road led and added an element of chance. I continued to have faith that the Camino would provide. And she always did, if not necessarily in the way I might have hoped or expected. Ali found it hard to share this confidence and as things were getting busier I knew she would prefer the certainty of booking ahead.

The rain started in the afternoon and we stopped to consider our options in a café that played heavy metal music. There were four little towns, reasonably close together but now that we were on the flat and my leg was feeling good we decided we should push on to the furthest option at Ruitelán. As the pilgrim menus usually consisted of meat and potatoes, the promise of a vegetarian meal persuaded us that we should head for *Pequeno Portala*. The option of a shiatsu massage nailed it for Ali.

We were dripping wet as we squashed into the doorway of the albergue: it was dark with narrow corridors and rules posted on every door. The grumpy hospitalero told us that we were too late to book the evening meal and that the massage was not available. I looked at Ali, whose head had dropped and, crestfallen, we climbed up a wooden ladder into our bedroom under the low thatched roof. In the dark, windowless attic there were perhaps 20 sets of metal bunk beds. The dark brown bed sheets did nothing to improve the ambiance. Jean was on a bottom bunk in the middle of the room but the rest of us had been allocated two bunk beds in the darkest of corners.

The bunks had been pushed together so while Ali and Marguerite snuggled together down below, Connie and I shared the double bed on top, our heads just inches away from the roof timbers. The heavy rain was pounding and we lay down for a moment on our beds. I looked over at Connie and wondered if she was going to cry. I remembered her at seven years old coming into our bedroom, early one morning, knocking on my forehead to wake me up.

'Mummy! Mummy! I want you to tell me the truth. Don't lie,' she had said with intensity. Her blue eyes bored into mine, huge and beseeching. 'Is that man in the red suit real?'

I thought about how easy it was when she was little, to keep her safe from harm. She looked at me now with the same big, big eyes, willing me to make this better. I didn't like this place, but couldn't let her sense my unease. I pulled her in under my arm and hugged her until her breathing slowed down and her muscles relaxed.

'Toughen up, soldier,' I said.

She laughed and after a few moments we clambered down from our bunks and headed to the tiny shower room to see if the warm water could heat us up.

At about 6pm, dressed in ponchos and waterproof trousers we ventured out in the rain to find supper in a local bar. A husband and wife team looked after us and while James Taylor sang from the CD player we ate a mountain of spaghetti, and drank wonderful red wine. We spoke about music, and films and when the bill finally came it cost less than a fiver each. Who cares about the weather when you have good friends? We couldn't have wanted anything more.

Before bed, Connie asked if she could borrow some oil for

her face. As I rummaged for my tiny washbag I pulled out the final postcard from David. On the front it read, 'Enjoy every day,' and on the back he had written, 'Easier said than done, but when in doubt, or pain, or confusion… Catch Sight of the Beautiful. (And if you can't see it, just take a selfie.)'

I showed Connie and she laughed, 'Typical Dad.' But his mantra had been echoing in my head all day long.

Day 32
10ᵗʰ May
Villafranca – Ruitelán
Kari, Ali, Jean, Connie, Marguerite
There are no windows in this attic and the thatch is so close to my face that I can smell it. I am trying not to think of what might be living in there, or what the brown sheets might be hiding. This place is giving me the creeps. Earlier this afternoon, a dodgy man across the room was staring at Connie and I have not let her out of my sight since. I can't wait for morning to come.

CHAPTER 34

I thought I was still dreaming when I first heard the unmistakable notes of the *Ave Maria* but by the time I opened my eyes the dorm was stirring, and I knew I wasn't imagining it. The music, piped through speakers in the dingy attic dormitory, got louder as the selection became more upbeat. We brushed our teeth to *Good Morning, Good Morning* from 'Singing in the Rain' and everyone was smiling as they stuffed their sleeping bags into their rucksacks. We were singing along to *These Boots Were Made for Walking* as we stepped through the back door, and dancing by the time we set out on the Way.

Overnight, the storm had cleared the air and the morning was fresh and dry. The birds, celebrating the end of the downpour, accompanied us with a dawn chorus and cowbells provided the percussion. Quite by chance we stopped at a café with a Michelin recommendation and a couple of slices of tortilla later we were ready for the big old mountain that waited ahead.

We climbed steadily for the next 12km. At first the land around us was pastoral, gently curvaceous. Apple trees, heavy with blossom dripped over streams that surged with last night's rainfall. Dry stone walls bordered the small fields of caramel-coloured cows. Cats and dogs outnumbered people. And while the others pushed on, I dawdled at the back, taking pictures, enjoying the birdsong.

I stopped beside a wooden doorframe, the wall and the door long gone. Behind it, an abandoned washing machine was now a planter for wildflowers: oxeye daisies grew at the sides, and orange marigolds cascaded from the drum. On the ground, a haiku of sorts had been painted on a roof slate and I stood for a moment, memorising it, feeling its rhythm. I would use it as a meditation, repeating it in my mind as I walked.

With an open heart
And a quiet mind
There are no doors

Soon the gentle landscape became more Alpine. Mountains used to fill me with dread and once would have caused me to stop frequently to catch my breath, but on the way up to O Cebreiro I stopped only to take in the views or fill my lungs with fresh, clean air. Going uphill eased the pain in my leg and I felt strong, on top of the world. For someone like me, who at school was always the last to be chosen when the sporty girls were picking teams, that was a good feeling. Instead of resenting my body for all the things it couldn't do, or hating the bits that didn't look right or work well, I was now grateful for legs that were strong enough to take me 650km and for lungs that could get me to the top of mountains.

As I stopped to look out across the wide valley the light became alchemical, recreating the landscape in colours I'd never seen before. 'Green' seemed somehow insufficient. The intensity of it penetrated my retina and I blinked to check that it was real. The deep blue sky and gathering clouds turned distant mountains indigo and I felt what I saw in my ears and my fingertips, I tasted it on the tip of my tongue. I was surrounded by God's Grace. His benevolence ran through me like a current.

At the first of two little villages we paused for water. A coach of day-trippers must have been dropped off nearby, as the route became suddenly busier. A number of walkers were elderly.

'Right everyone,' said Ali, gathering us around her. 'Is

everyone happy with the CPR procedure? This mountain is steep and there are people on it who look like they are not going to make it to the top.' We ran through a couple of choruses of *Nelly the Elephant* as she reminded us about compressions and breathing. One particularly old man, walking with a stick and unsteady on his feet, set off alone while we filled our bottles. We would keep our eye on him.

By the water fountain a stand-off between a small feisty cat and a wimpy, vocal dog caught our attention. The cat, with every hair standing on end and her back arched into a hairpin bend, looked like a cartoon character. She hissed and spat while the dog edged slowly backwards, barking abuse. He was all mouth and no trousers, and she knew it. They were still locked in verbal combat when we carried on up the mountain. Somewhere, on a harmonica, someone was playing the *1812 Overture*.

As we neared the top I felt, as I so often had, the ghosts of pilgrims from centuries ago walking alongside me, showing me the way. With each hórreo that we passed I stepped a little further back in time and when we arrived in O Cebreiro I had stopped believing in the present. Wedge-shaped dwellings hugged the slope of the mountain, their thatched roofs sitting low, like brows. Bundles of kindling twigs were stacked in the doorways and washing, strung between houses, flapped like faded flags.

We caught our breath in the 9th Century *Iglesia de Santa Maria Real,* the oldest surviving church on the Camino. In the simplicity of the candlelit interior the stillness settled on me like a reward. Up near the altar the old man with the walking stick was kneeling in prayer and I wondered how he'd managed to beat us to it. The walls were lined with Bibles in dozens of languages and looking for the English version in amongst all the others gave me a sense of the pilgrimage's appeal. My place was a small one in a wide, wide picture.

Connie knelt to light a candle and I watched her for a moment before kneeling beside her, praying for mothers and daughters, fathers and sons. All along the side of the church, clusters of candles in red glass jars burned. Hundreds of flames flickered: each one a private prayer, together a signal fire of hope.

On the wall, I read the O Cebreiro pilgrim prayer.

Although I may have made friends with pilgrims from a thousand paths... If I am not capable of forgiving my neighbours tomorrow, I have arrived nowhere.

It was two o'clock by the time we sat down to eat in a tiny bar. We had our first taste of Galician soup, made from stock, potatoes and the leaves of the tall cabbagey plants that were so much in evidence in the fields around us. A plate of fresh white curd cheese, served with crusty bread and an enormous jar of local honey followed, accompanied by chorizo that we sliced ourselves on a thick, wooden chopping board.

And then we set off in search of a bed for the night. Ignoring Stefano's unfailing good advice we joined the long queue at the municipal.

'Oh good,' said Ali, who had long been nursing a sense of injustice. 'The people who haven't carried their own bags have to wait till 4 o'clock to check in.'

Marguerite, Ali and Jean checked in but when Connie tried to do the same she was refused admission. David had Connie's passport.

'She could be a robbery,' said the officious woman on the desk. 'No undocumented peoples staying. Ees the rules.'

She was immovable. Even when David texted a photograph of the passport. The rules were the rules. And so the dangerous desperado and I headed off to find alternative accommodation. On the run from the law. With four middle-aged accomplices.

Although I feigned irritation, secretly I was delighted that we had no choice but to check in to the rustic pensione. Our little bedroom was up a unique herringbone staircase and Connie lay down on the bed, happy that we were on our own for a while. Through a circular stone window I looked down over the town: a man with a wheelbarrow was delivering logs, and bundles of twigs were being stacked against grey stone walls. Connie was asleep by the time I turned around so I tried out the tiny bath that had a built-in seat. My sore feet eased off in the warm, soapy water, but my knees were up around my ears and not much more made contact with the water. Privacy, however, felt like a luxury and I took my time getting dried and dressed.

I was expecting the others to stay in the municipal, but Jean, no coward heart, refused to lie down in the face of mindless bureaucracy and tackled Mrs. Municipal head on. For the first time she was 'Not happy'. After some fierce negotiating all monies were refunded and they appeared at the door of the pensione with a look of triumph on their faces. Jean fought the law, and Jean won. They all loved their warm, comfortable bedrooms but Ali was particularly delighted.

'The municipal smelled of sick and the showers had no doors,' she said.

While they napped, I spent the rest of the afternoon writing in the bar beneath our pensione. The beams in the ceiling were covered in dried flowers and a huge wood-burning stove was throwing out heat. My shin was pulsating, the swelling worsening, so I propped my leg on a stool and ordered a glass of red wine. I wondered when I had last, if ever, sat in a bar on my own. I chatted to an Italian surgeon who was cycling, fast, to Santiago. He was disappointed by the weather and the food.

'Look at those young people over there,' he said. 'On their phones. They are always on their phones.'

People my age seem to do that a lot – complain about young people on their phones. I have spent most of my working life working with teenagers, and I am always on their side. I leapt to their defence.

'We don't know what they're using their phones for,' I said. 'If they were editing photographs on a camera, or writing in a journal, or sending postcards home, you wouldn't mind. They could be doing all of those things on their phones and we would never know.'

He took my point. Over a coffee he went on to say that he

had recently left his wife and that he was on the Camino looking for the answer. I didn't ask, but his question, it turned out, was much the same as my own. The one I had thought was important, earlier on. 'What should I be doing with the rest of my life?' His answer, like my own, had not revealed itself so far and he was beginning to worry that it never would.

I thought about a sign I had read on the way to Villafranca and wondered if he had noticed it as he cycled past at speed. Late in the afternoon we had passed a painted shack. Prayer flags swagged the eaves and bright stars twinkled in the cactuses growing out front. On the spars of the wooden picket fence were the words *Look, Listen, Smile, Dream, Love* and a hand-painted slate sign read:

> *No busques la respuesta en el Camino, el Camino es la respuesta.*
> *Do not look for the answer on the Way, the Way is the answer.*

After he left I sent messages to my sons. Now that Connie was here, and David nearby, I was missing them all the more. Alexander's first exams had gone well and Joss had found his calling. He was working at wilderness parties in wildest Hampstead, making dens with packs of marauding eight-year-olds, and getting paid for it. For a young man who had spent most of his childhood playing in the woods, he was certainly well qualified. They both sent messages most days. They would have loved this walk – the mysticism, and the companionship – and yes, they would have been on their phones.

Before we went into mass, the five of us lay in the evening sun head to toe like fallen dominoes, along a stretch of low wall. The sun was warm on our skin and we bathed in the peace of this mountaintop town, so far from the confusion of urban life.

At mass in the 9th Century church, a large flat-screen TV flashed out the responses in a variety of languages. Individual voices, speaking different words, came together as a congregation in harmony. We sang in Latin, the international language of the church, the *Ubi Caritas* taking me straight back to the chapel at school. Where love is, God is there.

And it was beautiful.

We waved at Holy Kate across the pews and she joined us for dinner. Over a divine meal of fried Serrano ham, eggs and chips she talked to Marguerite and Connie about her interest in Joan of Arc. She was researching the possibility of creating a pilgrimage to Saint Joan's shrine in Rouen, where the poor woman was burned at the stake in 1431. On a more secular note, she and the hunky chap in the camouflage trousers stayed in touch. She continued to walk alone but admitted that they talked every day. So maybe not a nun then.

Day 33
11th May
Ruitelán – O Cebreiro
Kari, Ali, Jean, Connie, Marguerite
It is so lovely to be sharing a room with Connie. We have had hardly any time on our own and tonight it is just the two of us. I had wondered whether having her here would change the dynamics of the group or whether I would be less able to focus on my own experience. But I needn't have worried. She walks alone, engaged in her own pilgrimage, with her own intentions, and has slotted into the group with ease, joining in with the banter as if she'd been here since the beginning. It has given me a sense of how our relationship will be, now that she is grown, and I am filled with joy and hope. I just wish she was staying with us till the end.

CHAPTER 35

Ali, the Camino weathergirl, kept us right with the forecast. As we dressed she usually read to us from her weather app and it generally it went something like this, 'Sunny, sunny, sunnycloudy, cloudy, sunny, cloudy.'

On that morning though, she looked at her phone and shook her head, 'Rainy, rainy, rainywindy, rainy, windy, rainy.'

Bearing that in mind, we left our warm pensione, fully kitted out, ready to take whatever 'Green Spain' had to throw at us. And that turned out to be quite a lot.

The 22km walk ahead of us was up and down all the way, climbing to the highest point in Galicia, Alto do Poio, before the 600m descent to Triacastela where we would be meeting up with David. I was worried about the downhill, and Ali strapped my leg tighter than usual in preparation. It was still dark when we set off and it was some time before we could see the full extent of the gloom. Grey and heavy, the low sky weighed down on us. The tops of the mountains that surrounded O Cebreiro were shrouded in cloud but the vista was not completely obscured. It was hard to believe this was the same place as yesterday as the landscape looked completely different: the edges were blurred and the focus soft. The path kept us well away from the road so at least we were not going to be sprayed by passing vehicles – that was something.

Like O Cebreiro, the little villages we walked through seemed fixed in a bygone age. Linares was the first one we came to, just 3km or so into the walk. As usual we were hoping for breakfast but everything was shut so we pressed on, passing a graveyard on the outskirts of the village. Corridors of family crypts with polished, black marble façades were adorned with arum lilies and stone angels stood like guardians on the roofs.

Just beyond Linares a giant statue of a medieval pilgrim battling the elements made us realise that the weather in these parts must often be challenging. He was bent against the wind and holding onto his sou'wester as his tilted gaze looked out over Galicia and the path ahead of us.

Conditions were poor and before long our group dispersed, conversation being too much of a challenge as we battled uphill in the rain. Hospital de la Condesa provided the rest stop that we were looking for. Here, unusually, there was a toaster on the table and we ordered piles of bread and ate the warm toast with Jean's peanut butter. As we dried out in the small, steamy café, Holy Kate walked in with some men from Minnesota and their Swedish friend.

'You didn't miss anything in the Munie last night,' she said. 'You would have needed more than ear plugs to block out those snorers.'

Warmed up from the inside out, we continued upwards, towards the summit. As we climbed, the weather deteriorated until the heavy rain turned to snow. I had sent my gloves and hat home with Jenny way back in Logroño, and only Ali, ol' blue-fingers herself, had gloves. My fingers froze as I gripped my metal walking poles and I had little option but to stow them. It was nerve-wracking to be without them as the terrain was muddy and slippy and I almost tumbled several times.

Marguerite was finding the going tough. She was walking very quickly indeed, I think in an attempt to stay warm, and I found it hard to keep track of her. The decision to bring a pair of her son's old waterproof trousers with slits down the sides, was not a wise one, but it was just one of the ways in which her wardrobe malfunctioned today. Our mutual friend, Anthony, who we had both known since university, would have thrown up his hands in horror.

Anthony is married to my dear friend, Rachel, and our

three families often spend holidays together in the Lake District. The children have grown up regarding this group as extended family and every one of us knows that Anthony is King Kit. Like the Von Trapp family lining up for their father, Captain Von Anthony, stood them to attention and ensured that every child was properly dressed before we headed out into the hills. He would have checked the adults too if he got the chance and while I usually rolled my eyes at him, on that day I had to concede that he had a point. When Anthony was in charge anyone wearing cotton was sent back to change and there was a full waterproof and additional clothing inspection. But there was Marguerite, in a cotton T-shirt, her son's age 9 waterproofs, and a poncho that looked like she had saved it from the log flume at Alton Towers. She really was struggling to keep warm.

My shin was screaming on the downhill stretches and there was no way I could keep up with Marguerite's pace. Ali was worried that when Marguerite stopped to wait for us her temperature would drop too low, putting her at risk of hypothermia. She walked on ahead to make sure Marguerite didn't stand still for too long and I told them I would see them at the next rest stop, wherever that might be. I hobbled on at the back as fast I could manage.

I could see Connie, her baseball cap pulled down low over her brow and her giant poncho covering her rucksack, keeping her bone dry. She was forging ahead, happy to have a bit of time on her own, and I realised that for the first time since she'd joined me, I wasn't worried about her. Progress. For the remainder of the morning I walked with my head down, digging deep, plugging on. The noise of my boots struck a meditative rhythm that soothed me and took my mind off the pain. I wondered if I would miss that grounding tattoo when I was no longer walking for seven or eight hours every day.

By midday, my fingers had turned into bloodless sausages and when I caught up with the others for a hot drink it was clear that the walk had been tough on us all. Marguerite's lips were quite blue and we rubbed her hands to get her circulation going. Warmed by the coffee, we shared a bag of almonds and a couple of Kit-Kats and waited for a while before setting out again. I was ready for lunch, but since nobody else seemed too hungry I kept my feelings to myself.

As we came down the mountain my fingers gradually came back to life and I gave in to the dampness from which there was no escape. I felt quite intrepid walking in the rain, and I enjoyed the solitude that it demanded. Sounds seem amplified and the wet colours of the landscape were just as rewarding to me as the bright contrasts in the sunshine.

We passed through a series of farming villages, clearly heavily reliant on the dairy industry, as the cows were everywhere. We stood to one side while a woman drove her herd across the Camino, bells jangling all the way.

'Do you remember our walk in the Sma' Glen?' Ali asked. 'And you wouldn't walk past that herd of cows on the path. Look at that brave woman taking on those terrifying beasts all by herself.'

'I'll be braver next time,' I said. And I meant it.

Galicia was suffering from severe unemployment and many of the young people, particularly the men, had migrated to find work. Herds like the one we saw supplied the local cheese industry and the shops were well stocked with delicious produce, like the fresh curd cheese we'd eaten the day before. Less appetising was the ubiquitous hum of manure. That afternoon we walked through the world's smelliest farmyard where Jean and Connie competed to see who could make the most 'disgusted' face. Farmer Ali was not impressed with the cleanliness, or lack thereof, of the barns.

'My dad would never have allowed his yards to get into that state,' she said, holding her nose.

Hórreos were everywhere and these ancient thatched grain stores sat high above ground on mushroom-shaped props. You could tell this was a land accustomed to wet weather, and rats.

Not long before we reached Triacastela, we passed an ancient chestnut tree. A plaque nearby informed us that it was over 800 years old. At some point over the last few centuries, its gnarled branches had grown tired of growing upwards and outwards, and they had turned inwards instead. Driftwood dry and contorted like molten lava, they twisted back around their own immense trunk. I thought about the flow of the Camino, washing pilgrims past this spot and felt the momentum that was carrying me on to Santiago.

It was half past two by the time we arrived at the albergue in Triacastela and I was fading fast. I was not good without food and like others in my family, if I was to keep the monster from rearing her ugly head I needed to feed her regularly. The slice of toast at 7.45am had become a far distant memory and I was past conversation. Poor David arrived as we were checking in and I think he was expecting a warm greeting, but I was so focused on my need for food that I hardly said hello.

'Feed me, David. And then I will be nice,' I said. He knew from experience that he had to act quickly, and took us to a café right next door. Over a steaming plate of *caldo gallego*, the Galician soup, he told us stories of Michelin starred lunches and floodlit walks around the Roman walls at Lupo.

'I'm not sure you've quite got the 'pilgrim' thing yet, Dad,' said Connie.

'There's still time,' Ali countered.

After lunch, the fall and rise in blood sugar had left me exhausted and after a frustrating shower experience that involved flooded bathrooms, buckets and mops, I lay down on my bunk with my leg propped up on pillows. I needed some time on my own and while the others went off to explore the town, I shut my eyes and listened to the silence.

Later, I did a couple of loads of washing and we sat by the log fire in the communal area, feeding the meter in the drier. Cupboards for walking boots had been built into the stone walls around the fire and we stored our wet boots inside.

Domestic duties attended to we headed out, leaving David to sleep for a while.

In the pharmacist we stocked up on tape and across the road in the supermarket bought ingredients for a Serrano ham, eggs and patatas bravas supper. David's birthday was the next day and the girls thought it would be fun to spend a few euros on tiny, lightweight, presents. I had been with David for all but one of his birthdays in the last 29 years, and I was pretty sure that tomorrow would be unlike any birthday he'd ever known.

I cooked dinner in the badly equipped kitchen and worried that I was about to set off the fire alarm when I was frying the Serrano ham. While I cooked a man who had lost a leg and an arm sat down to eat his supper. He had walked from LePuy in France, pulling his belongings in a trailer that he fixed to his waist with a harness. He was quiet and modest about his extraordinary endeavour and once again I felt humbled by the remarkable people I had met on the walk.

Over supper David and Ali started to fret about accommodation at our next stop, Sarria. That was the point at which many pilgrims began their walk to Santiago. To be awarded with a Compostela (the official certificate of completion) you have to give evidence that you have walked a minimum of 100km and walking from Sarria to Santiago takes you the requisite distance. Because of this we had been warned to expect higher numbers on this section of the walk. I argued that we had seen hardly any other pilgrims today, but David was anxious and I knew Ali shared his fears. The following day was his birthday so I relented, feeling that my need to be true to the spirit of the pilgrimage was less important than their need to mitigate risk.

This would be Marguerite's last supper.

'It would have been so lovely if you could have stayed with us all the way to the finish line,' I said. 'I wish Jenny and Tinker and Lynne could have stayed too. It doesn't seem right walking on without them, or you.'

Marguerite had been craving solitude and a time to reflect, but I'm not sure if that was what she got. Perhaps the companionship of the walk was hard to sacrifice for the sake of quietude. I know I felt the same in the early days. Maybe three days was never going to be long enough for a walk to become any more than that.

Day 34
12ᵗʰ May
O Cebreiro – Triacastela
Kari, Ali, Jean, Connie, Marguerite, David
Husband on top bunk, me on the bottom. Another four women sharing the room. This is a bit odd. More rain due but we are up for it – Santiago is just six days away.

CHAPTER 36

It was just the six of us in our dorm last night so when the alarms went off at 6.15am we joined in a very quiet chorus of 'Happy Birthday'. David, unused to waking up in a room full of women, opened his presents (a scallop-shaped pin, some foot cream, a pack of Spanish playing cards, a new buff and a foot massage roller) a little dazed at the attention so early in the morning. After so many years of easy intimacy, it felt strange to be with him, and yet not with him, to be sleeping in separate beds and to see him shuffle awkwardly to the loo, keen for some privacy, when parading in his pants was usually more his style.

When the time came to say goodbye to Marguerite we hugged her and wished her well on her complicated onward journey. It was strange to think that she would be seeing Santiago before us. Part of her, I think, was relishing the challenge of her long trip home, and the chance to taste the solitude she was looking for. We were thinking of her all day as we walked.

Heavy rain was forecast and since there wasn't a possible coffee stop for 10km, we had a birthday breakfast in the café next door. Connie and David cuddled up in the corner of our booth and I felt happy that they had this time together before she headed off to Tanzania, and then to university so soon after that. Fathers and daughters have a special connection and I had often thought of my own dad in the last few weeks. I knew he would have been following our progress, willing me on. A PE teacher for 25 years, my utter lack of sportiness bemused him, but it didn't really matter, he loved me all the same. He often described me as 'physically illiterate', blaming my mum's genes for my poor coordination. I think he would be proud of me now.

The rain stopped within the first few kilometres but with low clouds hovering, we kept on our waterproofs as a precaution. We had the option to go to Samos, the large Benedictine monastery where Holy Kate was planning a two-day silent retreat, but decided to head up to Alto Riocabo instead, in order to avoid the roads as much as possible.

We were happy with our choice, as the natural path was delightful. Slate walls and high hedgerows lined the Way and at times we were walking through tunnels of foliage, green and wet. The moss on the walls glimmered with raindrops and new ivy wound round the trunks of old oaks. Galicia had won me over and I felt at home in this landscape that was so familiar and openhearted.

Ali, Jean and I walked together while David and Connie pushed on at a faster pace. Just before San Xil, we came across David, eyes shut, sitting on a green bench, beside a tiny rectangular building that looked like a dovecote. Ceramic jars filled with wild flowers sat in the nesting boxes and the blue door was open: Connie was inside. The dovecot was now a tiny art gallery and Connie was talking to the artist who had converted it. I pretended to look at the pictures on the walls while I listened in on their conversation.

'When I walked the Camino nine years ago I was at my lowest point,' he told her. 'My marriage had failed, I didn't feel fit to be a father and life had no value. The pilgrimage transformed me. It gave me a sense that my life was worth living and I knew I wanted to be here permanently. I rebuilt this building from a ruin. Brick by brick. And I never want to leave. The Camino gave me my life back.'

He lived beneath the gallery and his daughter, now an adult, was visiting him. He exhibited his paintings here and all over the world and was returning to London for a major exhibition later that year. He had built a haven with his bare hands and we were all struck by a tremendous sense of peace. Music and the smell of lavender filled the air and it was a struggle to move on.

A few kilometres later we passed a tiny stone hermitage where an iron grille stopped our entry. I shone my phone torch through the bars and there was just enough light to see the rough stone floor, the ancient wooden altar and the fading, once painted statuary. Connie and David left us here and strode out ahead, agreeing to meet up at the next coffee stop. We were in hilly, remote territory and it didn't look like that was going to be for some time.

It was still damp and a low fog hung around. Through the mist I caught sight of a dark grey stone circle, evidence of this area's ancient past. The crooked stones were tightly packed like bad teeth, perhaps 50 of them in total. Although I couldn't see far into the distance it was clear that this site had been carefully selected: it looked down through a wide, gentle valley, the mixed woodland in the near distance opening out at this spot. I stood in prayer. Something had drawn people to this place for millennia and there was a holiness in the landscape that connected to some deeply ingrained instinct for worship.

We walked on silently until, unexpectedly, we came across a sign for a donativo. We followed the arrows through the doorway of a tumbledown farm building, unsure whether Connie and her dad would have stopped here or not. It didn't seem like his kind of place. But, in a barn hanging with old ropes and bundles of dried corn, Simon, the man who looked after weary walkers, had already welcomed him with open arms. And my corporate, sharp-suited husband, was chilling out in this hippy paradise. Simon, who knew without words what David needed, had made him coffee 'with love' and was calling him 'brother.' Most surprisingly of all, David seemed quite comfortable – even happy – to be there. Sitting on the stuffed grain sacks, surrounded by 20-somethings, cuddling Simon's cat and eating the breakfast he had provided, he looked every inch the traveller.

'Welcome, pilgrims,' Simon said, opening his arms wide. 'There are fruits and nuts on the table, help yourselves to anything you want. Have a beautiful Camino.' And with that he disappeared into the farmhouse.

We sat for a while, but given that David, 'The Special One', was the only person to be offered a coffee, and that Simon's toilet was a field and a shovel, we were keen to press on. Fortunately, we didn't have to go too far before we found a café where the proprietor made us hot chocolates so thick we could stand our spoons up in them. Yesterday the Camino had provided a birthday candle (I had found it in a drawer in the albergue and stashed it in my pocket) and the proprietor stuck it into our first slice of Tarta de Santiago. He brought it, lit, to David.

For the second time that day, we sang Happy Birthday, and everyone else in the café joined in too. I think we enjoyed that more than David. He certainly didn't touch the cake, his body being a temple.

I felt every step of the 22km walk to Sarria, but Jean and Ali distracted me with chatter and we were on the outskirts of Sarria before we knew it. David had walked fast and he and Connie were sitting on a wall waiting for us when we arrived. We sat down under a plastic awning at a roadside café and took the weight off our backs with a sigh.

'My shoulder is killing me,' David said. 'And I think I have blisters on my right foot.'

I ignored him.

He winced as he sat down and Ali, a much nicer person than me, offered him a massage, unable to see anyone suffering. He groaned as the shoulder therapy began.

'OK, how would you describe your pain?' she said.

'Bad.'

'Hm. OK. Let's rate it out of ten.'

'Seven or eight,' he said, his face contorted.

'Pah,' I snorted. 'It's obvious you've never been through childbirth.'

Suffering in silence was something we had perfected over the last few weeks. There was nothing to be gained by talking about how much everything hurt. Ali's feet were bruised and battered and my shin was getting worse by the day, but I knew better than to complain. She was close to pulling the plug and putting me on a bus to Santiago and there was no way that was happening.

Connie looked at her father. 'Toughen up, soldier,' she said. Birthday or no birthday, he wasn't getting any sympathy from the womenfolk.

The final walk into Sarria took us to the foot of a giant staircase. This seemed like unnecessary punishment at the end of the day and I stood at the bottom and stared up as the others scrambled to the top. If I was a racehorse and this was a fence, it would have been a refusal.

'Come on. You can do it!' they shouted, and willed on by the toffee that Ali was dangling, I made it to the top, smiling.

Sarria was much smaller and prettier than I had imagined and it was good to be there. We were expecting hordes, but in fact the town was quiet and retained a rather sleepy charm.

Our first stop was the church of St Marina where I lit a candle and prayed that I would find the grit to make it all the way. There was a young man at a desk stamping pilgrim passports and he gave us a few tips on what to do when we arrived in Santiago. He told us about the pilgrim office and where to stash our rucksacks, about the times of mass in the cathedral and places to get our washing done. It felt real and not real. For 35 days I had been concentrating on the journey, not the destination, but now we were only five days away. We had walked more than 700km and I tingled with excitement just thinking about our arrival.

We showered and rested before meeting up for a celebratory evening. David and I had opted for a private albergue with a room for two – well, it was his birthday after all – and the girls stayed on the opposite side of the narrow main street in a dorm for three. We found a bar where we played dominoes and at dinner we played Trivial Pursuit without the board. Ali and Connie called for a steward's enquiry when Jean and I won, David having given us a bit of a clue when the answer was Napoleon. He just couldn't help himself. Earlier today he had forced us to play Wellington and Napoleon. Just as well Jenny wasn't here.

Day 35
13th May
Triacastela – Sarria
Kari, Ali, Jean, Connie, David
Over dinner we talked about the best and worst birthdays we could remember, first loves and friendship. Our wide Camino family has shrunk to a little group and we have not run into any familiar faces for days. But we are now on the home stretch. And I can't think of a better group of people to be travelling with.

CHAPTER 37

We were the first people on the streets of Sarria the next morning and the only other living soul was a tethered Shetland pony. We had seen a few peregrinos on horseback but we hoped this fellow would not be carrying any pilgrims to Santiago, or that if he was, it would at least be a very small one.

On the way out of town, Connie found some strange hollow pods, which looked like alien cocoons. She reckoned they were some sort of modern art installation and couldn't resist exploring them. As she leaned back against them, posing for a photograph, her rucksack got stuck in the hollow and it took two of us to pull her out. As she laughed I caught sight of her beautiful make-up free face, tanned and glowing in the early morning light and thought how happy she looked.

'Why don't you just come all the way to Santiago?' I said. 'It seems a shame not to get to the end when you have come this far.'

'Let me think about it,' she replied, never one to be pushed into a decision.

It had been a challenging year for her, making the painful break with the security of childhood and stepping out into the adult world. She had coped with the highs of the A level results, the lows of the UCAS lottery and the pain of exposing the lie she'd been told all her life, that if she just worked hard enough anything was possible. She had dealt with the physical ache of being separated from her twin brother with whom she had shared everything up until then and had learnt to remember who she was while working for people who didn't care. My instinct, like the instinct of all mothers, was to protect her from harm, and shield her from blows, but I knew it was these knocks that would make her resilient. She would grow into a woman who could pick herself up and make her own way. But there had been a disappointment in her eyes that I had not been able to see beyond, and I had been watching and waiting for it to lift. Today she looked happy, happy and strong, and I could breathe out a little bit more.

We began the climb uphill almost straight away and within a quarter of an hour we were taking off layers and feeling pleased that the forecast rain had held off. Galicia continued to charm us and once again we were in gentle farmland with cows every which way. The only downside of this bucolic idyll was the terrible smells that continued to catch us unaware, unleashing a chorus of groans as we pulled our buffs over our noses. More pleasing was the change in the foliage. Suddenly everything was in full leaf and the oaks and chestnuts that were so abundant in this area, unstiffened the hillsides. It was a landscape of soft edges and the curves of the canopy were matched on the mossy walls where a thick blanket of green rounded off the contours. Our cuckoo was with us again.

'I wonder where Mary and Meyrick have got to?' I asked, thinking of them every time I heard that cheeky bird.

'Let's send them a message when we reach Portomarin,' said Ali.

The cafés had begun to stock 'Camino' merchandise, but although the number of pilgrims had increased we didn't feel crowded, and still had the path to ourselves for long stretches of the day. Ali, Jean and I, like the wise old women of the Way, picked out the new pilgrims from the old as we sat with our coffee. The oldguard took their shoes and socks off as soon as they sat down, their clothes were hanging off them and their rucksacks were ingrained with orange dust. The newcomers were still fresh and glossy, they talked more and ate less.

In the corner of the café Jean spotted Lara, Sara the Curvy German's little friend.

'Sara is doing well,' she said. 'She has rested and her knee is much better. It is our wish that we walk into Santiago together so we will meet 5km out of Santiago on Wednesday morning.'

As their 'Camino mummies' we were relieved that it had worked out for them and that they had found a way to keep going, even if it was not how they had imagined it would be.

In Galicia, rather than chalking up the miles covered, the waymarkers had begun a countdown, telling us how far we had to go. We all looked out for them, patting them with some satisfaction as we passed. We were on the lookout for the one that would tell us that there were only 100km left to go. Connie reached the marker first and she and David were waiting for us with a can of cold Kas. We toasted the milestone and celebrated with a happy dance before the rain came on and we decided to make a move. We were on the home stretch.

Our map indicated that the rest of the day's walk was peppered with small hamlets. Usually this meant that there would be no shortage of loo and coffee stops, so we didn't bother to stock up. Big mistake. Unbeknownst to us, this was our last chance of a loo or food till Portomarin and we had rather foolishly squandered it.

The rain did not stay for too long but the Way was very muddy indeed. At times, one side of the path had been raised above the flood plain and we walked on the left while a stream flowed on the right. At one point my boot got well and truly stuck in the mud, the ominous squelch warning me that I had been sucked in. I managed to pull my foot out, leaving my boot behind and some precarious balancing ensued. Much to Ali and Jean's disappointment I stayed upright, no thanks to them.

For the most part, Jean, Ali and I stuck fast together, but I met some characters that day too. They were a motley crew, quite different from those we had met in the early part of the walk, and they took my mind off the pain in my leg. An old Dubliner with a shaggy grey beard, heavy jeans and muddy trainers kept me entertained for a while.

'You've gotta watch out for these feckin' dogs,' he said. 'Big bastards, with great big teeth, keep pouncin' out at me in these little villages. Just about jumped out of me feckin' skin. Just you be careful, pet,' he said. And I walked on, keeping my eyes peeled and my ears open for hidden canine assassins.

Then came a rather dull Austrian accountant with a superb high-tech poncho, who unexpectedly ended up sharing our dinner that night.

Then a young fashionista from Seattle, who was walking with her mother, in cool shades and a long floral skirt that somehow seemed to have missed the mud.

Then Sheila from Perth, an Australian nurse who had the thickest accent I had ever heard. She was wearing a purple turban and was keen for company as she had found herself, unexpectedly, walking alone.

'The woman I was walking with slipped over in the shower and has only gone and broken her bloody ankle. You wouldn't believe it. All the way from Australia and she has spent more of her time in bed than she has on the Camino. I'm walking anyway and I meet up with her in the evening at the hotel. The great thing is she's paying, and it's 5 star all the way!'

Sheila shouted, 'G'day,' to everyone she passed. Her voice was comically loud and I wondered how long it would take me to tire of it. But she was always on the lookout for anyone who needed help, and she had a kind word and a bit of advice for everyone.

'It doesn't matter to me that there are no pee-stops. I'm all sorted,' she said, pointing at her nether regions and sharing more than I felt entirely comfortable receiving. 'Took me a while to get used to the She-wee. I tried it out in me

261

bathroom first and there were a few accidents, I can tell you. But I got it all figured out. It's ripper.'

I was beginning to wish I had put in the effort. It had been a long time since we last spotted a loo and these days the path was a bit busy to duck into the bushes. A sign on the door of the place we had earmarked for lunch informed us they were closed, as they had no water. So no loo, and no sustenance.

It was a long old hike to the outskirts of Portomarin and with about a kilometre to go we were faced with a difficult choice. The quick path was marked 'severe danger' and warned us to take an alternative route but the alternative added another couple of kilometres. I was grumpy, ravenous, and desperate to find a loo so I agreed to 'severe danger' – a warning that for once was fully deserved. More a scramble than a walk, I slip-slided down the rocky gully that could never be described as a path, mostly on my bottom. Didn't they know I was hungry? Didn't they know that I didn't like heights? Didn't they know I was physically illiterate and too mal-coordinated for this malarkey? As the gap widened between the others and me, the critical inner voice that I hadn't heard in a while piped up. 'What in God's name do you think you are playing at?' it hissed.

'What took you so long?' said Connie, when I finally made it to the bottom and it was all I could do not to swear at her.

Portomarin sits on the other side of the Mino River, dammed to create the wide Belesar Reservoir. To reach it we had to walk over an extremely long bridge that crossed the water and took us into the town. Every step felt like a struggle and I spent the crossing looking down at my feet in order to steady my vertigo. This meant I hadn't spotted the giant flight of steps at the far end. It dwarfed the huge flight we had been faced with yesterday.

'Time for a toffee?' said Ali, knowing I was on the verge.

We had only four more nights of albergues and David and Ali had spent the best part of the evening back in Triacastela finding the ideal spot in Portomarin. Ali got out her phone to check the reservation, looking slightly smug at the thought of the nice little place she had booked with just six beds in a room, and clean, white bathrooms.

Her expression changed. 'No,' she said, panic rising in her voice. 'This can't be right... there must be some mistake. This is not the bathroom I ordered.'

She had mistakenly booked us into the one place we wanted to avoid – a massive purpose-built albergue, with 144 beds in one room.

'Ha!' I laughed. 'That'll teach you. The Camino has provided – it may not have been what you wanted but it might be what you needed!'

It was too soon to see the funny side and at 3pm, when we finally checked in, she collapsed on her bed, too exhausted to eat.

'Somewhere out there, my bathroom is waiting for me. Just leave me. I am not fit for company,' she moaned, an arm draped dramatically over her eyes.

David opted for a shower but Jean, Connie and I needed food and headed to the restaurant next door. Bread and an enormous salad instantly improved my mental state. My tension dissipated and as Jean and Connie chatted I sat, contentedly, admiring the view of the reservoir out of the enormous panoramic windows. In the street below I caught sight of a familiar gait. It was Meyrick. Like Dustin Hoffman at the end of *The Graduate* I pressed myself to the glass, banging and calling her name. She caught sight of me and came running up the stairs, followed a few minutes later by Mary, who was muddy and exhausted.

'I can't tell you how happy I am to see you ladies,' she said, close to tears. 'I thought I was finished on that bridge. I just didn't have the strength. I had to call my husband in the States and get him to talk me through it. I can't believe you're here. You are just what I needed.'

They joined us for supper in our albergue, bringing the Austrian accountant with them. We shared cheese, ham and pasta. Mary taught us the names of her ten brothers and sisters – Joey, Jimmy, Bobby, Terry, Carla, Tony, Mark, Paula, Mickey and Dan – and we planned our next walking trip to the White Mountains in Massachusetts.

Day 36
14th May
Sarria – Portomarin
Kari, Ali, Jean, Connie, David
The man in the bunk next to me is snoring so loudly I can feel his breath on my hair, so I have constructed a tent with my towel and I am now in a little cave. Joss, who spent his formative years constructing dens, would most certainly approve. This vast dorm is only a quarter full, but they have squashed us all up at one end. Looking down the rows of beds reminds me of the barracks in a black and white war film but it all smells of bleach and I am strangely comforted by that. And the best news of the day? Connie has decided to walk with us to Santiago. In Jean's now legendary words – 'I'm so happy.'

CHAPTER 38

We knew today's walk would be a long one so, with no prospect of a café for the first 8km, we opted for coffee and toast in the albergue before we left. While we ate, Jean watched in awe as Ali Magic Fingers braided Connie's hair.

'It's like I have three mums,' Connie said.

'And I have a pony again,' said Ali.

Our days now had a gentle rhythm, and our needs were simple: we walked, we ate and we rested. Our tiredness came only from physical exertion and every morning we awoke renewed. I must have been a child the last time I had been this carefree and unwound. I knew I would miss climbing into bed early, exhausted from hours spent in the fresh air. And I would miss typing, one fingered, in the dark, while those around me snored gently. And I never thought I would say that. Conscious that time was running out, I think I savoured every minute of that day.

We picked up the Way at the top of the giant staircase I had crawled up yesterday afternoon. David stood on the edge of the first step like a diver, feet together, poles outstretched, as if he was about to launch himself into the reservoir at the foot.

'And it's Tom Daley, going for gold!' he shouted.

'I should be so lucky,' I said.

For the third time in three days there was a steep uphill as soon as we left town, and we climbed through woodland, to Monte San Antonio. It wasn't long until the sun was slicing through the trees, the dappled light catching the dew on the mossy walls. In the early mornings the beauty of contrasts often struck me, as my eyes struggled to adapt to the brightness and the dark. Not for the first time, I thought of Alexander's favourite poem, *Pied Beauty* by Hopkins. *'Glory be to God for dappled things,'* I said to myself, and gave thanks for *'All things counter, original, spare, strange.'* Perhaps without those shafts of darkness in my life, I wouldn't stop to wonder at the light.

All morning, the sounds of water and birdsong were never far away. Even the trees less quick off the mark were now in leaf and rain made the colours sing.

When I was teaching I used to take a group of children to visit the elderly and one day I overheard Arthur, a resident in his 90s, talking to one of the boys.

'Isn't it grand that the leaves are out?' he said, looking at the tree he could see from the window. 'I call it nascent green, because it is just born.'

David found that day, his third day of walking, hard going. A quick learner, he had not complained since day one, but I could see that everything was hurting, particularly his shoulders. Day three had been difficult for us too, and pilgrims we met often spoke of it as the worst. When the novelty wore off, pain seemed to surface. It was not so much the distance of each walk but the repetitive punishment of walking at length, day after day that made this pilgrimage such a physical challenge.

Things had become easier for us since then, or perhaps we had made our peace with pain. In the past if something hurt I would have quit and waited until the feeling subsided. On this walk I had stopped fearing pain and had noticed that if I kept going, my experience of the hurt altered, and I could tolerate more. A positive mental attitude, that was the secret. But on that day my tendonitis started to grumble at about 8km and thereafter it took more than meditation to keep me going. It was the ibuprofen, paracetamol and a firm restrapping from Ali that got me to Palas de Rei.

While the leg might still have been hurting, my pack at least sat more comfortably on my back, only giving me grief towards the end of the walk. Both Ali and I had tingly shoulder blades (just the one each – mine the left, hers the right) and for a long time I had been imagining that the tingle was a hand on my back, pushing me along. Ali was much too scientific for such fancy but she shared my feeling that we were being willed on by our friends and family.

The messages from home had sustained us and we read them together, every day. They made us laugh and cry, spurring us on and keeping us connected. Their support was matched by the extraordinary kindness of strangers on the pilgrimage. Wherever we went people leaned out of windows and from balconies, shouted from their bicycles and from doorways wishing us '*Buen Camino*'. We really were being carried along on a tide of goodwill and we were now certain that we would reach Santiago as a result.

The sun shone on us all day and my 'Dora the Explorer skirt' made a re-appearance at the first coffee stop, much to everyone's amusement. At least my legs were now less luminously white. In fact we were all tanned and healthy looking and in the sunshine we made a colourful crowd. Connie's pink sunglasses matched her T-shirt and socks, I was in bright blue, David's rucksack was pillar-box red and Jean was all in 'teal'. Ali, was resolutely sticking to grey.

'It matches my hair,' she said.

Connie had now been walking with us for a week and she was blister free and fighting fit. All the skiing had clearly stood her in good stead and she was fast compared to the rest of us. I was happy to take things slow. From my position at the back I felt like a shepherdess, keeping an eye on the flock, making sure they didn't drift off. On that day Jean had her socks dangling down the back of her rucksack, drying them in the sun.

David had his boots off and was rubbing his feet in a café hoaching with day-trippers by the time we caught up with him. The day-trippers were dropped off, usually at the top of a hill, for a short walk down the Camino. They got their passports stamped at a nearby church and were given just enough free time to eat lunch at an authentic pilgrim café before they hopped back on the bus again. There were certainly more of them now, but they didn't stay on the path for long and most of today's walk was peaceful and quiet. They also tended to stay in hotels rather than albergues so we hadn't had any of the expected trouble finding accommodation.

'I think they should devise a system of credits, like air miles,' David said. 'We could call them pilgrim miles – and you could be awarded Bronze, Silver and Gold Compostelas according to how far you have walked, how much you have carried on your back, and what type of accommodation you have stayed in.'

'Oh, yes. I like that,' Ali joined in. 'And obviously, if they have got the bus at any stage they should have points deducted for that.'

'Absolutely.'

'And you, David. You would be getting a bronze. 100km. Call yourself a pilgrim!' she laughed.

But the increase in numbers only added to my excitement and reminded me that Santiago was close. From all over Spain the many Caminos were converging and there was something profoundly moving and strangely atavistic about this gathering. We had met people from Africa, America, Asia and Europe, old and young, of all faiths or none, and we were all moving with a single purpose. To reach Santiago.

David, who was always happy with his own company, slowed down a bit that afternoon and joined us, enjoying the walking banter. He had been quiet for the last few days, I think fearful of intruding.

'It's your thing, yours and Ali's,' he told me when I asked him if he was OK. 'We're just here because we're proud of you. And we want to be there when you make it.'

He and Ali devised a distraction to take my mind off my leg and to get us to our destination quicker. It involved playing an interminable game where you have to think of famous people's names.

'I say Kate Winslet,' Ali said, 'and you have to say a famous person whose name starts with a W. Say Winston Churchill. Then the next person has to start with a C. Say Clare Balding. Got it?'

It wasn't complicated, had very few rules, and apparently could be played for all eternity. After about two and a half hours I was ready to sprint to Santiago – tendonitis or no tendonitis – just to escape the game.

Finally, at about 4pm, we arrived at Palas de Rei. Our albergue was the same place Stefano and Mike had stayed two days earlier. They had sent us a video of the torrential rain hitting the tables outside and we were relieved that the weather was kinder today.

Beer o'clock came not a moment too soon and for once we didn't shower and sort our stuff before we took the first sip: slovenly bliss. We did some washing, found a pharmacist and then left Ali to call her menfolk while we went to mass to celebrate Pentecost.

Afterwards, we headed to a local restaurant for a pilgrim supper. A huge pot of Galician soup was brought to the table for us to ladle out ourselves. It was heaven with big hunks of crusty bread. As a main course Jean ordered *pulpo* (octopus) and great red tentacles, complete with suckers, appeared sliced and piled on her plate, served with boiled potatoes. I tried a little and although it tasted better than it looked I wasn't convinced. Jean however, loved it and said she'd be having it again.

Day 37
15ᵗʰ May
Portomarin – Palas de Rei
Kari, Ali, Jean, Connie, David
Ali and I have walked 823km to date and we have just three more days of walking before we reach our destination. The butterflies are bursting out of their cocoons.

CHAPTER 39

That morning Ali strapped me up good and proper and my leg was the best it had been in three weeks. The walk to Ribadiso was long (28km) but the terrain was gentle and, although there was a steep hill towards the end, for the most part we were meandering through farmland that looked pretty much like Perthshire the whole way. There was something lovely about the familiarity of the landscape at this stage of our journey: we felt as if we were coming home.

The sun shone on us once again and although, as weathergirl Ali had predicted, it was sunny/cloudy in the morning, by about 10am it was just plain sunny. We stopped for coffee in San Xulian and raised a mug to toast our son Joss's godfather, Julian. He and Anthony, Joss's other godfather, were the two who had walked part of the Camino back in the 80s when we were all at Oxford together. They had planted the seed that had taken 30 years to blossom.

Fuelled up, David and Connie zoomed off and Ali, Jean and I stuck together, keen for company, knowing our time together was coming to an end. We crossed six rivers on that day, and the sound of running water accompanied us all the way. At times we walked in the streams, hopping from stone to stone, the malevolent slapstick fan in me hoping that someone would slip, disappointed when nobody did. We walked through a string of little hamlets, clucking at the chickens and stopping to watch a donkey nuzzle his nose in the pocket of a jacket, hanging on a washing line. An abuela in a fishing hat and pink pinnie sat on a stool at the edge of a road, crocheting a baby hat, her feet in black socks and wooden clogs.

'Buen Camino,' she said, smiling a toothless grin as we passed.

Happy for it to be just the three of us, we were in no rush. We crossed a handsome medieval bridge into the tiny village of Lobreiro, the field of hares, and paused to look at the 8th Century church of Santa Maria. Its age astonished me and as we looked up at the Virgin and child, carved into the stone tympanum over the main door, I wondered how many millions of others had done the same over the last 1,300 years. We had stumbled upon so many of these extraordinary medieval buildings, standing quite disregarded in poor rural villages, and I hoped that they would survive for generations to come.

Our group reconvened in Melide, and as the weather was glorious we bought a picnic lunch in town.

'Do you have any salt?' I asked the shopkeeper, miming tearing a strip off the corner of a sachet and sprinkling it on my tomato. The effort I had put into our games of charades had clearly paid off, as he knew exactly what I meant.

'No problem,' he said, taking a large bag of salt off the shelf, opening it and pouring some into a paper bag for us.

Connie bought a pair of shorts and we visited the simple church of Sancti Spiriti before heading out towards the woods.

We didn't have to go far to find the perfect picnic spot in a clearing between the trees. I loved our al fresco lunches and was happy to be eating outdoors once again. An Australian couple that we had met in the morning were lying in the sun, enjoying a break.

'Come and sit down,' they said. 'We're going soon.' They had started their walk in León and were continuing their travels around Europe after they reached Santiago. It was a long and expensive journey from Australia and they wanted to make the most of it. They told us that they had been sceptical about the mysticism of the Camino, but both described feeling spiritually nourished by their walk.

'It's kind of annoying. We're not religious, but God sneaks

up on you on this trail, and makes you feel things whether you like it or not. Even cynics like us.'

They had left Australia bored by the rat-race, unfulfilled by the emptiness of material things. On the Camino the size of a person's car was the last thing anyone cared about and they told us that the connections they made had felt honest and profound.

'There's no bullshit here. You see people for who they are, with all the superficial stuff stripped away. In the dark, all cats are grey, and on the Camino, we are all just travellers.'

When they had gone we laid out the ponchos on the soft mossy ground, in the stippled sunshine, and feasted on pears, ham, cheese and salted tomato, in no rush to move on.

'I just want to take my boots off and dip my feet into ice-cold water,' David said, and we shut our eyes and imagined how that would feel.

Connie and David leaned on each other, back to back, faces up to the sun. *Where love is, God is there,* I thought, and said a silent prayer of thanksgiving in this holy place.

Ali had booked an albergue in Ribadiso and they had warned us that they would only hold our beds till 5pm, so reluctantly we moved on.

It was a long walk through the woods.

'Let's play I Spy,' said Ali, knowing this would torture me. She also knew she had a captive audience and that Connie and David couldn't resist a bit of competition. She may be a Camino Angel but I could see her dark side.

Relief finally came when she was distracted by a large family of day-packers who piled off a minibus at the top of a hill. They were wearing an assortment of flip-flops and sandals but matching yellow T-shirts with 'Fernandez, Camino de Santiago' emblazoned on the back. They were carrying empty water pouches, which worried me a bit as they seemed unprepared for a hike. But I needn't have worried: the bus pulled up to collect them about half an hour later so there was no need for water. One chap, a rotund man in his mid-thirties, had even brought a folding chair with him so that he could rest his weary legs while the others in his party popped into a church to get their passports stamped.

For most of the afternoon, Connie and Jean walked together, enjoying each other's company. There might have been a 35-year age gap, but they had really hit it off, joking and laughing like old friends. Connie was inspired by Jean's work, running a large not-for-profit organisation, and I knew she would like to find a career that could give her as much satisfaction as Jean found in hers. Jean spoke at conferences all over North America and her voice of compassion and tolerance was one that needed to be heard. Perhaps I needed to hear it more when the day-packers got up my nose.

The smell of the sea alerted us to the pulperia long before we caught sight of the chef. A stubbly man with a face like a boxer was boiling octopuses in a vast aluminium pot on the side of the road. As we passed he pulled the huge, pink creature out of the steaming water to tempt us to stop. The thick tentacles curled like a bunch of hideous bananas, covered in suckers and curling to pigs' tails. It was a creature from my nightmares and I imagined it reaching out its arms, pulling me in, sticking to me with its suckers.

'Mmm, isn't he a big one? Unfortunately we have already had our lunch,' Ali said, chasing after me. For once, I was not at the back.

Beautiful as the day had been, the schlep up that last bastard of a hill was a complete killer. I was hot, my backpack was sticking to my T-shirt, and it was a struggle to reach the top. When I finally made it David was buying a Coke from a kiosk and I joined him for a drink. We had certainly been spending more money on refreshments since he had joined us, but nobody was complaining.

The last stretch into the village was the most stunning of all. We walked through streams on huge stepping stones in the dappled shadow of the eucalyptus trees until finally we came to the little medieval bridge over the Rio Iso, leading us into Ribadiso. Down below, a group of young peregrinos was lying on the banks of the stream, enjoying the sunshine.

'Look David, the Camino has provided,' said Jean. And before we went any further, David and I shrugged off our rucksacks, slithered down to the water's edge, took our boots off and splashed into the icy stream. The water washed away the pain and the tiredness and we splashed around, slipping over the mossy rocks, until our energy was restored. Minutes later the water had taken away all feeling, full stop, and numb with cold we teetered out and dripped our way to the albergue with our boots slung over our shoulders.

Yellow stone buildings with orange roofs were clustered around the side of the river and in the late afternoon we had a beer in the café by the water. Our albergue, in contrast, was cold and busy so we were not keen to spend too much time inside. The mixed showers had translucent glass doors that left little to the imagination. By this stage on the pilgrimage, I didn't care who saw my bottom, but there was no way I was going to let Connie expose hers to a stranger. She took the middle cubicle with Jean on one side and me on the other while Ali kept guard by the door.

'You shall not pass,' she cried.

Doped up with painkillers, I was hobbling as we headed back down to the river café for bacon and eggs that night. We shared a bottle of the local red and sat outside in the evening sun. The cows sauntered past ready to hit the hay and by 8pm I was ready to do the same.

Later, back in the dorm, there was much giggling from our bunks at the sight of a middle-aged German man in his vest and very tight pants lolling on his bed not two feet from Ali. Much giggling again when he insisted on swaggering up and down the dorm in the same pants, hands on hips. Less giggling when he started to sing. Relief when the singing turned to humming. Irritation that later, as I lay typing in the dark, the humming had turned to snoring. I took it back: this, I would not miss.

Unfortunately, just before bedtime, when I untaped my leg, the skin on my shin came away with it. Bound for the last three weeks my leg had finally reacted to the tape and I now had a huge wet sore where the strapping had been.

'I've been waiting for this to happen,' Ali said. 'In fact, I'm amazed your skin has tolerated the tape for so long.'

Day 38
16th May
Palas de Rei – Ribadiso
Kari, Ali, Jean, Connie, David
We are hoping for an overnight miracle as Ali won't be able to tape the wound, and I can't walk without the tape. Bugger. Just two days to go and suddenly it seems that crawling to Santiago may be back on the cards.

CHAPTER 40

Ali and I got up before sunrise, sneaking out of the sleeping dorm to find a bit of light in the communal sitting room. We had both spent the night worrying about my leg. The wound had dried in the night and we could see it was formed of tiny blisters that ran all down the front of my shin. Ali had made some phone calls and the physio sorority had put their heads together and come up with a solution. She covered the wound with gauze and strapped tightly over the top of it, right over my foot, using practically a whole roll of tape so that in the end I had a kind of plaster cast to restrict the movement of my foot as much as possible. It felt solid and I could walk with no pain, so my personal physician gave me the green light and I dosed up on painkillers just to make sure. Without Ali, I would not have been able to continue, and with the finishing line almost in my sights, that didn't bear thinking about.

That day, our 39th on the Camino de Santiago, was pretty close to perfect. We left Ribadiso in light morning fog, passing a nun in full black habit, stamping passports at a table outside the church alongside an enterprising Knight Templar who was posing for pictures. But we walked on by. With only a few spaces left on our passports we were getting choosy about our stamps.

The mist had turned the landscape milky: creamy yellow blossom on the hydrangea trees, the chalky green crops and the palest of blue skies looked as if they had been smudged in pastels. There was a steep climb up into Azua and we were ready for coffee when we stopped at what looked an uninspiring café. But, if we had learned anything on this walk it was that you couldn't always go on first impressions, and we were delighted to find table service, mountains of toasted crusty bread and a complimentary batch of fresh 'biscotti' cake, which the waitress wrapped in tinfoil for us to take on our journey. David even got a plate of eggs and that made him very happy.

We followed the natural path through woodland and farmland for most of the journey and although there were another couple of climbs it was pretty gentle. My leg was holding out but I was glad of our relaxed pace. David and Connie slowed down and the five of us were together for most of the day. Whether they, too, were making the most of every step or whether they were worried about me, I'm not sure, but either way, it was good to have their company and we were a cheerful bunch.

We stopped to put our feet up at a wonderful donativo, created in a farmyard just off the side of the road. There were hammocks, bunting and pots of wild flowers, and pilgrims were relaxing in the sunshine at this oasis. David found a wooden sun lounger and stretched out, while we got a coffee and read the quotations that were all over the place.

A thinking wall posed philosophical questions and we took the weight off our backs and pondered for a while, as we sat in the sunshine.

'I'm dreading people asking, "So, what was the Camino like?"' said Jean. 'It will be so difficult to put this experience into words.'

'I think it might take a while to make sense of it. Maybe we never will,' I said. 'But, I'm so glad we came.'

'Me too,' said Ali, not one for emotions. 'I was just keeping you company really, but this has been pretty special.'

David came over and put his headphones in my ears. *One Day More* from 'Les Mis' started playing at full volume and I put one of the buds in Jean's ear so she could hear too. The music filled my head and my heart and I gulped back tears, sad and happy, proud and humble. Grateful to be part of this huge amorphous thing that has held a secret power for hundreds of years and was filling my heart and my soul with joy.

We walked on along natural pathways, passing through plenty of little villages and noticing how the style of the grain stores, the *hórreos*, had changed since O Cebreiro. Here they looked like burial monuments, their ends elaborate tombstones, carved with crosses, monstrances or other religious icons. The sides of these large cuboids were made either from slats of wood or bricks, with air holes that were large enough to let the grain dry out but too small to let the vermin in. The structures were raised on elaborate plinths and every house we passed seemed to have one in their garden. In Edinburgh there is a road where every house has a conservatory, each one a little bigger than the one before, keeping up with the Joneses British style. Here we saw the same thing, each grain store a little fancier than the one before. Keeping up with the Jimenezes, Galician style.

In an attempt to make today last as long as possible, we stopped rather a lot. Stop number three before lunch involved fantastic freshly squeezed orange juice and a monstrously long queue for the one ladies' loo. This was the only toilet for 12km and limited opportunities to pee al fresco explained the popularity of the place. I felt ballsy so joined the much shorter queue for the men's. David raised his eyebrows. 'It's just a loo,' I said. Naïvely. I wouldn't be doing that again.

As we sat, enjoying our juice, Maria the chain-smoking German walked by, not alone. She was tall and long-limbed. In the early days she had seemed etiolated, as if she didn't have the strength to hold her frame. Now she stood solid and strong, suntanned and laughing. She greeted us like old friends.

'If it wasn't for you ladies, I don't know if I would be here,' she said. 'I was really struggling on those first few days and you made me feel like I could do it.'

This took me a little by surprise. As far as I remembered all we had done was show her how to squash a sleeping bag into a stuff sack. She told us she had been walking with Thomas (the pilgrim formerly known as Ghostbuster) for five days, but she had split up from him yesterday as she wanted to take her time and reach Santiago on Friday. So Thomas might be arriving tomorrow too. That was good news.

The Way was peaceful and the warnings about droves of pilgrims joining at Sarria had been wildly exaggerated. For much of it we were alone and all we could hear was the birdsong that had accompanied us every step of the Way from St Jean Pied-de-Port. The birds here started singing at first light, celebrating the new day, and, carried away, they forgot to stop, their chorus ringing out till dusk.

For the first time there was no cuckoo following us but the hedgerows were full of arum lilies and we spotted a few mottled lizards basking in the sun. The butterflies were out too, looping like little yellow kites in and out of sight. I thought of Emily Dickinson: 'Butterflies, off banks of noon, leap, plashless, as they swim.' Butterflies and birds, singing and dancing, just for the joy of it.

Briefly I walked alone, falling behind when I stopped to take photographs. For weeks now I had been talking to God as I walked. The tone had changed since the early days, the beseeching giving way to a gentler discourse. Now I felt as if I was chatting to an old friend. The muddle was sorted, the guilt had gone, the tension had eased and all there was to say was 'thank you.' I looked down at the path, almost expecting it, and saw a third nail, buried in the dust. I picked it up and put it with the others. Redemption. He died so that we might live, and live fully.

By about midday I had caught up with the others and we bumped into Dan the Canadian who seemed delighted that the weather had taken a turn for the better. Maybe it was because, as Scots, we were prepared for the worst when it came to weather, but Ali and I were surprised by how often 'our

279

weather' seemed different from the weather of others we met.

'We've only had one really dreadful day and a couple of days that have been a bit dreich,' said Ali. 'The waterproofs have been on about five or six times wouldn't you say?'

If you spoke to an Australian or an Italian they would tell you it had rained almost every day and that the sun had been hidden the whole time. Maybe some people have their own little cloud that follows them around, like the Englishman we met on the Meseta, who told us that the fields were 'too yellow'.

'Everywhere you go-oh-oh, always take the weather with you, everywhere you go-oh-oh,' I sang, murdering the Crowded House song.

We had lunch outdoors and Ali braided Connie's hair and tucked daisies and buttercups into the plaits. Connie's face was luminous, her bright blue eyes glinting and her cheeks rosy. She didn't stop smiling all day. She had needed the space and the solitude of the early days of her walk, as had David, but today it seemed her hurt had been healed and she had re-emerged, radiant and openhearted. David slept in the sunshine, lying on the grass, still smiling. I couldn't remember the last time I had felt this happy.

After lunch we walked through long tunnels in the woodland where the dappled shade gave a welcome respite from the afternoon sun. For a while Connie walked alongside an old lady in her 80s. She was dressed in the usual black dress and blue checked pinnie, a straw hat in one hand and a wooden staff in the other. I walked behind them watching them smile at each other and communicate without words. Age was no barrier on this walk.

A few miles later, Ali was quite delighted when Connie, who had been too far ahead when we had played the first time round, asked her to teach her the 'name game'. I groaned.

'It has been requested. I am only bowing to popular demand,' Ali said. And Jean joined them for a hotly fought contest while I hung well back and took pictures of doors, or flowers, or anything really.

My leg had held out well, Ali's 'cast' and the drugs keeping the pain at a manageable level. The finishing stretch took us through groves of tall eucalyptus and the smell energised us as we walked. On a day so full of stops it was late afternoon when we arrived in O Pedrouzo. Our last albergue was modern and functional. It lacked the charm and community spirit of some of the places we had been, but that no longer seemed to matter. Our eyes were on the prize.

To our dismay, German Pants Man, the exhibitionist from last night, checked in right after us but we were relieved to see that he was allocated a bed on the other side of the dorm so he could lunge in his underwear to his heart's content.

We did some washing and pegged it on the line before we went off in search of a cold beer. Our patron saint had taken good care of us and he now provided us with a zesty alternative, Cerveza con Limon – my new favourite. Thank you, San Miguel.

Finally, we ate a pilgrim supper with a Frenchman who had walked 1,600 kilometres from LePuy. He had not seen his family for more than two months and he was worried that his young son might not recognise him as he had lost so much weight and grown a bushy beard. He had given up work and wanted to have some time on his own to think about what he would do with the rest of his life. That sounded familiar. Not that I had found the answer to that particularly knotty problem. Yet again, here was someone on this pilgrimage who made me feel humble, who reminded me that the point of the journey was not, in the end, physical.

Over dinner Jean, Ali and I, reluctant to accept that we were nearing the end of our adventure, planned a series of books based on walks. 'The Sturdy Girls' had a catchy ring to it, we thought. 'The Sturdy Girls do the Appalachian Trail'; 'The Sturdy Girls go Munro Bagging'; 'The Sturdy Girls do the Silk Road'… You get the picture. We had a whole range of merchandise devised too, including a little Juanita doll that would fit in a pocket.

Day 39
17th May
Ribadiso – O Pedrouzo
Kari, Ali, Jean, Connie, David

We have returned to the albergue, packed everything up for the last time and have gone to bed in our clothes, using the blankets instead of our sleeping bags so that we can be up and out early tomorrow. As I type in the dark, we have settled down for our last night on the Camino. Soon the final recital of 'night music' will begin, performed as always by our fellow peregrinos. There is something oddly comforting about sharing a sleeping space with others and I wonder if I will miss this when I am home. For the last two years I have been tormented by terrible nightmares, but I have slept like a baby every night since I have been on this journey. At home, I suffer from neck pain and fiddle around with my pillows trying to make myself comfortable. Here, I have no pillow, or make do with the chewed up thin thing that the albergue sometimes provides, and yet I have not given my neck a second thought.

It feels like the night before Christmas and I hope I can get to sleep. Our aim is to be in Santiago for the pilgrim mass at noon. A Santiago!

CHAPTER 41

We shall not cease from exploration
And the end of all our exploring
Will be to arrive where we started
And know the place for the first time.
                    – T.S. Eliot, Little Gidding, The Four Quartets

902.5 kms, 1,274,906 steps, 40 nights on the road, ten packs of
Compeed, nine rolls of tape, eight bags of liquorice toffees, and one bottle
of rucksack-eating bed bug spray later, we are in Santiago.

The alarm vibrated at 4.45am on our last day on the Camino.
Our aim was to arrive in Santiago de Compostela for the
midday pilgrim mass at the cathedral, but there was 20km of
hilly terrain to cover before then and we wanted to beat the
crowds. All of us had spent a fitful night, nobody wanting to
oversleep, so none of us sleeping much at all.

Creeping to the bathrooms while the other pilgrims in the
dormitory slept, adrenalin made my fingers clumsy. 'Sit still,'
Ali whispered, as she strapped up my shin one last time.
'There's no way you should be walking on this. But there's no
point in me telling you that, is there?'

'Not really,' I smiled.

Back in the dormitory we hauled on our rucksacks. As we
crept out, German Pants Man was snoring on his bunk and it
was a struggle to resist the temptation to sing *One Day More*
quite loudly in his ear.

Ali, wiggling her red gloves, head torch shining from a

nest of crazy hair, was part jazz hands, part Mission Impossible, all excited to get going. But the start of our last walk was somewhat inauspicious. Twenty minutes in, we were still in O Pedrouzo, with no familiar yellow arrows in sight. 'Is this the Camino?' I asked.

'Yes. This is Spain. We are on day 40 of the Camino. Your name is Kari. You are amongst friends,' Jean answered, ever the comedian.

Not such a stupid question after all, as it happened. A woman passed us, her head torch glowing. 'You've made the same mistake as me,' she said. 'It's back that way.'

I thanked her and flashed an I-told-you-so smirk. The path, when we found it, took us immediately into a deep, dark wood. It was lucky that we had our head torches or Santiago could have remained a dream. The wood was pitch dark and without their faint light we wouldn't have been able to see a thing: we couldn't even pick out the path. Even with the torches we could see only a couple of metres ahead and unsure of my footing, I was much more scared than I was letting on. We couldn't afford to lose sight of each other and chatted nervously.

Ali, who was normally quite strict about such things, allowed us to sing. In this instance she saw the practical benefits – it would bolster our spirits and help us stick together. She even treated us to her old school song, a rousing number with 17 verses, though thankfully not all committed to memory. We remembered a verse or two of 'To Be a Pilgrim', 'Dear Lord and Father of Mankind', and 'Amazing Grace' and for Jean we had a go at 'The Battle Hymn of the Republic'. That one, I find, always leads to irreverent versions and before we knew it we were onto rugby songs. Songs done, we moved on to the children's books we knew by heart and got quite a long way through *The Gruffalo*, *Hairy Maclary* and *We're Going on a Bear Hunt*. I threw in a few poems for good measure, 'The Listeners', seemed right, as did 'Stopping by Woods on a Snowy Evening'.

The woods are lovely, dark and deep,

But I have promises to keep,
And miles to go before I sleep,
And miles to go before I sleep.

As we walked, we looked behind us, as we often did, to see how far we had come. In the darkness we could see none of the landscape, but we could make out a broken snake of pilgrims, their head torches shining – a field of stars – the Compostela. I imagined a line of lights reaching all the way back to Saint Jean, one for each pilgrim walking the way. And then I saw a light for every peregrino who had ever walked this path: and the lights became the tail of a brilliant comet moving from the East and ending at Santiago. And what would happen when we dispersed, after Santiago? Are there flickers of brightness around the globe fuelled by the Camino, illuminating the dark places? I prayed that the flame that had kindled in me would give me the strength for what was to come.

But there were no stars in the sky that morning and the Milky Way was not visible to us. The birds gave us our first ray of hope and the sun, when it came up, did so gently, with no great fanfare to mark our big day. And perhaps this was perfect as arriving in Santiago would feel like a homecoming. No fireworks, no finish line, just a deep sense of peace.

In the dull dawn we saw that we were walking through a forest of tattered eucalyptus. The smell, like a homey remedy, brought calm. Our chatter stopped and we spread out a little, each of us in our own space, looking inwards, comfortable in the silence.

The last hill before Santiago is the Monte del Gozo and we had been warned to expect bus parties. Unlike other iconic peaks along the way, this one, according to seasoned pilgrims, had been spoiled by day-trippers hoping for an authentic pilgrim experience by walking the last 5km into the city. It was a long, steady climb and I was breathless by the time I reached the top. Uphill was easier on my leg, but I was slow, and as usual, at the back, the coo's tail as my mother would say. Jean was waiting on the flat summit with cold drinks and

I drank thirstily. Our early start meant that we had beaten the crowds and although one busload did hop off with their yellow bags, they dispersed rapidly. By the time we crossed the hilltop we were almost alone.

Santiago de Compostela had seemed an almost mythical destination for so long that when it finally appeared over the brow of the hill, I didn't really believe in it. I stood looking down onto the flat plain expecting to feel something. Some rush of emotion. A sense of accomplishment. But in truth I felt nothing much at all. It wasn't the clearest of days and although the rain stayed off, I couldn't really see the city. I had to just trust that it was there.

Jean and Ali joined me and the three of us stood for a moment, subdued. This simple life had stripped me bare, taken me back to my component parts. And the earth, like a mother, had washed me, nourished me, and put me back together. Was I ready for this to be over? For my journey to come to an end?

I could see the path leading down the side of the hill into the built-up suburbs, the sprawl of the city that was reaching out to meet us, and I set off alone. I would have been poor company. Instead, I breathed through the pain, focusing on keeping my foot from flexing.

'A'right there?' A Liverpudlian man, about my age, joined me on the footpath. 'Mind if I walk with you?' He didn't wait for an answer, but his chat soon took my mind off my shin.

'It was a spur of the moment decision. I phoned into work and told them I wouldn't be in and sent my friends a text that said, going for a walk.' He told me he'd set off the next day and that it had all gone fine until the heel pain set in. A few days ago he'd limped into a monastery looking for a place to stay.

'God's honest truth,' he said. 'This monk met me at the door, in the full monk gear. He took my pack off my shoulders and asked me to follow him. In the kitchen he gave me a chair and knelt on the floor in front of me. He unlaced my boots and took my socks off then he washed my feet in warm soapy water. He massaged them with some oil he'd infused with rosemary then he bowed down and kissed them. It sounds weird, I know, but it was really beautiful. Honest to God, it was. Then he showed me to a room and told me I could stay until I was ready to carry on. I've never experienced anything like it in my life. I just had this overwhelming sense of... well... being loved.'

His story made me think about Emmanueli. I'd been looking out for him for weeks, hoping to see him once more. There was something special about him. I'd felt it. But I couldn't express it before. It was love. Just love. Emmanuel of course, means God is with us, and God's name is love.

The Scouser moved on and up ahead I saw Jean and Ali waiting for me at the bottom of the long slope by a wooden Santiago sign. We were on the final furlong and the suburbs gave way to the ancient stone of the city.

The pavements narrowed and the crowds increased and unable to walk three abreast Jean and I walked ahead, pushing forward into the heart of the city. Suddenly, as if I had breathed in chloroform, my body was overwhelmed by exhaustion. Putting one foot in front of the other felt impossible and for the first time in 40 days I felt close to collapse. Then, from behind, I felt Ali's arms around my waist, and she popped her head between us.

'Look,' she said, pointing. 'We've come a long way to see that.' At the end of the street the spire of the cathedral was just visible. My heart lurched and I gasped. There it was.

We followed the yellow arrows through the maze of narrow streets until they opened out and the cathedral was upon us. The golden square. The Portico of Glory. We had done it. We had arrived. In a giant sweaty knot of arms, walking poles and rucksacks we wept tears of relief and thankfulness and joy.

Tears came, but no words. Even Jean, for once, was silent: Jean, whose wisdom, compassion and unfailing sense of humour had kept us going for the last 400km. It wasn't until we were sitting at lunch, some hours later, that she put the feeling into words. 'I'm so happy,' she said. Of course.

I was bursting with love and pride that Connie and David had shared the moment with me. Their sensitivity and respect had touched me deeply and I felt profoundly blessed to have had them by my side. But the greatest blessing of all was to stand beneath the huge heft of the cathedral with Ali, who'd been with me every step of the way. Her friendship was not effusive or demanding, it was steadfast, unfaltering, sensitive and kind. She was not one for a big show or a loud fanfare, but she deserved the whole heavenly host trumpeting her arrival as far as I was concerned. It may have been my friendship that got her to Spain, but it was hers that got me to Santiago.

And I was not the only one who was there because of Ali. If everyone she had helped had been there to thank her, the line of pilgrims would have reached right across the square. We may be yin and yang, me all arty-farty mysticism and her all science and practicality, but we understood each other without the need for words, and I was filled with love for the unassuming heroine I was lucky enough to call my friend.

'We've done so well,' said Jean.

But Ali swiped away the praise with a red-gloved hand, 'Oh, you know how it is. You get chatting and before you know it you've walked 900km.'

We headed down to the pilgrim office to drop off our bags, hoping to return for the pilgrim mass at noon. I rummaged in my rucksack for the Beatitudes of the Pilgrim, the prayer the nun had given me in the tiny church of San Esteban, way back on Day Three. I pulled out an envelope. 'For Kari,' it said. '(For when you're wet, tired and completely demoralised)'. It was crumpled, and the writing was blotched. I turned it over. One corner had been pulled open a little, but it was still sealed. I returned it unopened to my bag. I had been tired, and wet and sometimes weary, but completely demoralised? Not once.

Seeing the queue for the Compostela we quickly established that there was no way we would get our certificates that morning so we stored our rucksacks and headed back up the hill. The cathedral was completely full, crammed with pilgrims and tourists. Inside I hardly noticed the magnificent space, looking only at the altar ahead of me, ornate and golden. We were lucky enough to find seats in the benches reserved for pilgrims and as soon as I sat down my feet felt unbearably sore.

'Undo your laces,' whispered Ali, who had experienced the same sudden pain.

'Look, it's Thomas,' said Jean, pointing out the pilgrim formerly known as Ghostbuster. He was tanned, healthy and at least two stone lighter than when we had first seen him. He had clearly been shopping as his clean, smart clothes fitted him perfectly. Unlike ours. I looked at my dusty clothes and filthy boots – everything was loose and saggy. There was no mistaking that we were pilgrims.

I had The Beatitudes of the Pilgrim folded in my pocket and I read it now as I waited for mass to begin.

Blessed are you pilgrim, when you contemplate the 'Camino' and you discover it is full of names and dawns...

Blessed are you pilgrim, if on the way you meet yourself and gift yourself with time, without rushing, so as not to disregard the image in your heart.

Blessed are you pilgrim, if you discover that the 'Camino' holds a lot of silence; and the silence of prayer, and the prayer of meeting with God who is waiting for you.

As I read, tears rolled down my cheeks. My journey had been about 'letting go' and as I walked, I had become lighter and lighter, unshackled almost. My 'knapsack was emptying.' Despite the sweat and the dirt, I felt washed clean. I had 'met myself on the way' and found myself looking in the wrong direction. The answer did not lie in a search for what I should *do* with the rest of my life, but in who I wanted to *be*.

At the end of mass, much to our surprise, six robed men lit the famous Botafumeiro. This giant, silver thurible is essentially an incense burner and has been used in the pilgrim blessing for centuries, for spiritual and practical purposes – to get rid of the smell of the pilgrims. The giant burner swung, accompanied by music, in a 65m arc across the transept. We were right below it and it was spectacular, and a little frightening, to behold.

'You Catholics certainly do these smells and bells in some style,' Ali whispered.

We spent the afternoon, after a bit of lunch, queuing to get our Compostelas. That meant another interminable round of the Name Game, which everyone but me seemed to love.

'We've already had Bambi,' said Connie.

'OK, right back at you, Buffalo Bill,' Ali replied, pleased with the new twist that double letters reverse the order.

While we were queuing, an Irish woman with soft brown eyes and a gentle voice spoke to us.

'It's a long time for you to queue. If you want a little sit down you could always pop into the chapel for a while. It's cool and quiet in there.'

Connie and Jean took her up on her offer as I went to find out about trips to Finisterre, leaving Ali and David to hold our place. About half an hour later Jean rejoined us and I went to find Connie. She was bent over with her head on her hands, leaning on the pew in front of her. I put my hand gently on her back and realised she was fast asleep. I sat with her for a while, giving thanks and praying for my boys, wishing they were here, and for my mum. I knew from speaking to her that things were not good and that there was something she was not telling me. I felt, not for the first time, that the Camino was fortifying me for a more difficult road ahead.

As I prayed the woman who had spoken to us in the queue came to see if everything was OK.

'She's asleep,' I whispered. 'She was up before five.'

'Oh the poor soul,' she said and Connie stirred. 'Would you like a little cup of tea?' To my surprise, Connie jumped at the chance and the pair of them headed off to a sitting room off the side of the chapel. When Connie returned to the queue she was fully animated once more. The woman, Sister Katherine, was an FCJ sister. When we had lived in Jersey in the Channel Islands, all three children had gone to FCJ Primary School, and they remembered those days with much fondness. Connie had adored Sister Cecilia, the headmistress, and as the order was small, Sister Katherine knew Sister Cecilia well. They chatted about FCJ and Jersey and it turned out that Sister Cecilia was coming to Santiago to work in the pilgrim office, in just a few weeks' time.

By that stage we were nearly at the front of the queue. When my turn came I presented my pilgrim passport to the lady at the desk and she checked it over. It was tatty. The corners dog-eared, the writing on the front smudged by the rain. Front and back it was covered with stamps, some intricate and elaborate, others just a name of the albergue or bar, a record of every day of my journey. Just two boxes were empty.

'What was the purpose of your journey?' she asked.

'Spiritual,' I replied.

Then she stamped my passport and wrote out my certificate in ecclesiastical Latin. Rolled in a cardboard tube the illuminated documents made us feel as if we had graduated and we posed with our Compostelas outside in the sun.

Finally we made it to our hotel. Not an albergue, not a hostel, not a pensione but a hotel. It was odd. Quiet. Private. And odd. A few hours and a bottle of Cava later, clean, fragrant and refreshed we headed to the famous Café Manolo, which did not disappoint. The pilgrim menu – € 9.5 – consisted of squid chowder and the best sole I have ever eaten.

It would take months for me to make sense of the Camino and to realise its significance. Perhaps it would always be a feeling and not something I could intellectualise. All I can say is that something wonderful had happened to me and I was overwhelmed with gratitude, and peace.

Deep peace.

Day 40
18th May
O Pedrouzo – Santiago de Compostela
Kari, Ali, Jean, Connie, David

CHAPTER 42

'The Camino' has entered our parlance; books have been written; films have been made. But The Camino de Santiago remains a secret and to get 'in on it' you must first become a pilgrim and walk the Way yourself. The people I met all walked with a purpose but there was an unspoken rule: you don't ask and you don't tell. Although they shared some of their stories the significance of their pilgrimage remained theirs and theirs alone. There was a tacit understanding that, in the end, although we walked together our transformation was unique, and one that would only be reduced with words.

We stayed in Santiago for three days and, suddenly conscious of our worn-to-death clothes, visited *El Corte Ingles* on the first morning. To our delight Ali and I both fitted into size 12 jeans, and Connie picked out a pretty dress for my nephew's wedding, which was just a week after we got home.

Over the next few days, it felt as if the cast of characters we had met on the Camino was gathering for the post-show party. Coming back from our shopping expedition, we walked through the Praza do Obradoiro, just at the moment when Mary and Meyrick completed their Camino. We joined in their sweaty knot of celebration and took them for churros to toast the moment.

Later, as we were sitting in the café, I asked Jean if she had heard from Luis Pilgrim, the little Spaniard with the twinkly eyes, and she shook her head. I sent him a text and immediately the reply came, 'I am walking into Santiago right now!' and we ran up to the square to greet him too. Soon afterwards, we spotted Christina, the Belgian pathologist, as she arrived in the square. She collapsed onto the cobbles and on her hands and knees, she wept. Later, we took her for a cup of tea but the tears kept coming, and at 6 o'clock mass, she was crying still.

'I'm not sad,' she said. 'I just can't explain everything I am feeling. I am so full. I am overflowing.'

Later in the afternoon we met up with Holy Kate, and spent much of the day with her. She was, as we had come to expect, glowing with light and life, ecstatic to have reached Santiago.

'I queued up with everybody else to go behind the altar and touch Saint James. But when it was my turn a touch just didn't seem enough. I threw my arms around his huge gold neck and just hugged him.'

Later in the evening, as we walked through the narrow streets, we bumped into Sara 'n' Lara who had fulfilled their dream and walked into Santiago together. Sara had made it on cigarettes and paracetamol after all.

'We wouldn't be here without you,' they said.

We had coffee with Maria-Manuela from Puerto Rico, hugged Eurista, who had walked from Croatia, still underplaying his achievement and laughed with Andrea from northern Italy who was finally relaxed and happy. Everywhere we looked, there were people we recognised and who celebrated with us.

On our second day we took a bus trip to Finisterre and I burned my pyjamas in the ceremonial fire. As we sat in a seafood restaurant, in the little harbour, watching the boats, I heard a familiar voice behind me, and hands covered my eyes.

'My angels! My Camino angels!' It was Stefano. He looked incredible, tanned and smiling: Super Mario had morphed into Bruce Willis. He joined us for lunch and we caught up on news of Mike, who had gone to London for a job interview. He and Stefano had been walking with Tim, the love-struck Australian, for the last week. The love triangle had lost a corner when Alex the Brazilian went on ahead and Tim and Ainslie had settled for friendship after all.

I marvelled at friendship. At how strengthening and sustaining it could be. At the strength of the women I had walked with, and the women who had supported me throughout my life. At friendship and the resilience of middle-aged women. Women who kept going when those around them buckled; who bandaged the broken, made them dinner and got them back on their feet. Unfettered women, who no longer cared how the world regarded them, powerful and free.

And then I stood at the end of the earth, where the sun sinks into the sea, and threw the final stone from my pocket into the water. This part of my journey was over.

Blessed are you pilgrim, because you have discovered that the authentic 'Camino' begins when it is completed.

POSTSCRIPT

The Camino fortified me, prepared me for what was to come. Back in April, I hadn't known it, but I had been fractured, held together by the armour I had spent a lifetime putting on. And the walking strengthened me. As my skeleton firmed up, piece by piece and step by step my carapace was shed. And without all that weight, my heart bloomed, ready to give and to receive.

My mother made it to Greg and Charlotte's beautiful wedding. Although she left before the meal, she still managed to make it a two-outfit day, and did a high kick for the family photographs, showing off the legs of which she was so proud.

On the Monday after the wedding she told me that the tumour in her neck had grown. We made an appointment at the hospital and they saw us within the week. The cancer had spread and there was nothing that they could do so she was discharged to palliative care and wanted to be at home. She died on the 18th August, three months to the day after I finished the Camino.

A week before she died we asked her if she wanted to see a priest, who could hear her confession.

'What would I want that for? I have nothing to confess. My conscience is clear,' she said.

There would be no putting to bed, no tying up of ends, no Desmond Tutu moment of truth and reconciliation, but I felt none of the old resentment or anger. 'Without forgiveness there is no future.' I had let it go.

The week she died, the word 'fierce' echoed in my head. She was fierce in her determination that she should stay at home, and equally fierce in her determination that she should be admitted to a hospice when she felt the burden of care was too heavy for Patsy and me. One of the doctors told us that it said on Mum's notes that she was a fiercely independent woman, and he was under no illusion that this was the case.

I found it easy to remember good things – Coke floats on the patio in the sunshine, sand pits and buckets of soapy water. Endless supplies of chocolate biscuits and my children being told, 'Don't worry, you're at your granny's now.'

When we were clearing out her house I found a note in one of her books. It looked almost like a little poem and it read simply: 'Social justice, democracy, peace, Tony Benn.' That just about summed up her values.

She didn't always get it right, but she never grumbled. I never once heard her say she was tired or that she was feeling unwell. 'I'm trachling on,' was as close as she got to a complaint. She was small but she was made of iron and her will was indomitable.

Three weeks before she died she told us that she wasn't quite ready to go because she still had things to teach us. She loved to buy plants that were dying and nurse them back to life, as was the case with one particularly beautiful orchid that sat on her windowsill. Six or seven large blooms clung to an arching stem, and three buds remained unopened at the end. Anyway, she was looking at the orchid when she told us she wasn't quite ready to go.

'When the last bud opens, then it will be time,' she said.

The Camino taught me to receive. To receive the joy that is so abundantly given by the birds and the flowers and the trees and the skies and the light and the people. It opened my heart and brought me back to my mother and to all she had given me.

In her last days she taught me about stoicism, and bravery and although she could not speak she showed me how it should be done. At the hour of her death, the last bud opened.

THE END

ACKNOWLEDGEMENTS

I begin by acknowledging the enormous debt I owe to my sister, Patsy, who may not have been with me on my Camino but who has always been with me. Tribute too, must be paid to Mother, Pat, who taught me all I know about courage.

This book would not have been possible without the love and support of so many people and I begin by thanking Lindsey Fraser from Fraser Ross Associates who believed in *Pilgrim* and helped me turn it from a diary into a memoir. Thank you to my sons, Alexander and Joss, who were my first readers and to Helen Weavers, Rachel Parsons, Jenny Davey, Laura Macdonald, Sharon Riva, Lindsay Linnell, Jenny Wright and Claire Askew who were perceptive and constructive second readers. I am grateful to Brian Gill (whose proofreading skills are superhuman), to Julie Evans for her patience in the later stages of the process and to Greg McAlinden and Lily Larsimont for their invaluable help with the design of the book. Thanks to my teacher Melanie Whipman, and all of the brilliant 'Thursday Group' for their constant encouragement. At the University of Surrey, I was lucky enough to find the best workshopping buddies a fledgling writer could hope for – Julie, Emma, Jane, Celina, Hannah, Flo, Trevor, Seth, Manuel, Alan and Evan – and to them, and my wonderful tutors, Carl Thomson and Liz Bahs, I extend my gratitude.

I joked with my husband, David, that the only dedication I would ever give him would be one that said, 'despite him' (his fervour with the red pen being legendary in this household), but joking apart, none of this would have been possible without him, he's the best, and I love him with my whole heart.

The biggest thank you, however, is reserved for the extraordinary pilgrims I walked with on the way to Santiago: to Stefano and Mike, Kate, Harriet, Sara, Lara, Sandra, Emmanueli (wherever you are) and of course, our team, the

Sturdy Girls. It is my privilege to have shared this experience with Jenny, Tinker, Lynne, Marguerite, Connie, Jean and the one and only Ali Richardson, to whom this story is dedicated.

ABOUT THE AUTHOR

Originally from Scotland, Carolyn Gillespie now lives in the South of England. She has a first degree in English from Oxford University and an MFA in Creative Writing. A short career in publishing was followed by a longer career as an English teacher. Recently, inspired by the words 'Noli Timere' which were displayed in her classroom, Carolyn gave up teaching in order to pursue her dream to become a writer.

Carolyn has written a collection of poems for children called *Wonder Child* and recently finished her first novel, *Visitation*. Her work has appeared in *Molecule Tiny Lit Mag*, *The Crank*, *Oddity* magazine, Coin Operated Press's Poetry zine and *Scotland Outdoors*. She has been shortlisted for the Soutar, Wells and Fish prizes. Carolyn was a panellist at the Guildford new Writers Festival, 2020, where she read an extract from *Pilgrim*. She has spoken on BBC Radio Surrey about the benefits of reading during lockdown and runs creative writing workshops in schools.

Carolyn in married with three grown-up children. She is currently fighting a losing battle to gain control over her unruly garden and Bernard, her rumbunctious pup.

Twitter: Kari Gillespie @kari_storybox
Instagram: karigillespiewrites
Facebook: Kari Gillespie
Photographs and the Camino Playlist are available on the author's website: www.carolyngillespie.co.uk

Printed in Great Britain
by Amazon

10398361R00173